Mistehay Sakahegan

The Great Lake

by Frances Russell

The Beauty and the Treachery of Lake Winnipeg

Mistehay Sakahegan

The Great Lake

by Frances Russell

The Beauty and the Treachery of Lake Winnipeg

Heartland

Heartland Associates, Inc.
Winnipeg, Canada

Printed in Manitoba, Canada

Ancient granite rises from Lake Winnipeg's east shore DENNIS FAST

Library and Archives Canada Cataloguing in Publication

Russell, Frances, 1941-

Mistehay Sakahegan, the Great Lake: the beauty
and the treachery of Lake Winnipeg / by Frances Russell. -- 2nd ed.

Includes bibliographical references and index.
ISBN 1-896150-08-X

1. Winnipeg, Lake (Man.)—History. 2. Winnipeg,
Lake (Man.)—Description and travel.   I. Title.
II. Title: Great lake.

FC3395. W5R88 2004   971.27'2   C2004-904071-5

Heartland Associates Inc.
PO Box 103 RPO Corydon
Winnipeg, MB R3M 3S3
hrtland@mts.net   www.hrtlandbooks.com

Credits

Editor
Barbara Huck

Editorial assistance
The Manitoba Archaeological Society, Harry St. C. Hilchey, Phil Manaigre, Jerry Zaste,
Erik Nielsen, Clifford Stevens, Gerald Friesen, David Arnason, Peter St. John, Doug Whiteway,
Jens and Barbara Nielsen, Dennis Peristy, Donna Parisien Guiboche

Research assistance
Catherine Macdonald

Design and maps
Dawn Huck

Prepress
Image Color, Winnipeg, Canada

Printing
Printcrafters, Winnipeg, Canada

Cover photographs
Main image: Sunrise on the west shore of Lake Winnipeg: Ian Ward
Inset image: Storm spray at Victoria Beach: Ian Ward

Back cover painting
Legends of the Lakes and Rivers, by Jackson Beardy, by permission of Paula Beardy
Courtesy of the Government of Manitoba art collection

Shrubby cinquefoil   GEORGE BACK /
NATIONAL ARCHIVES OF CANADA / C–93027

Acknowledgements

Large bodies of water have lives of their own. The lifeblood of human existence, they are fundamentally uncontrollable and indifferent to human society. Our master as well as our servant, they inspire fear and admiration in us. Herman Melville wrote of the tiger heart that pants beneath the surface of the sea. Lake Winnipeg, too, has the heart of a tiger. Yet the story of this fascinating and historically pivotal body of water has never before been told.

It is this that prompted me to write about Lake Winnipeg, a lake that is intertwined with three generations of my family. My grandfather tented on the lakeshore at what is now Matlock in the 1890s. He and his brother, a Winnipeg architect, constructed a Russell family compound at Matlock. After their marriage, my parents summered first at Victoria Beach and later at Whytewold. Some of my earliest memories are of building sandcastles at the foot of the Patricia Beach stairs. I feel fortunate that my husband and I were able to give our son Geoffrey the opportunity to build his own Lake Winnipeg memories. So it is with families who have fallen under Lake Winnipeg's spell.

The Great Lake is the product of many willing and eager hands, Manitobans who almost unanimously agreed that a biography of the lake is long overdue. Their assistance and encouragement turned my longstanding dream into a reality.

My deepest thanks and appreciation goes to Heartland Associates, who believed that a political columnist could make the leap to book writing, from the Manitoba Legislature and Parliament Hill to Lake Winnipeg's shores. Their commitment, advice, support and inspiration were invaluable, as was their determination to find superb photography and art to help tell the lake's story and their ability to provide some of the best book design in Manitoba.

Historical research consultant Catherine Macdonald was indispensable for her analysis and insights, her ability to penetrate the maze of the National Archives Online, to separate the wheat from the chaff in the sheafs of newspaper clippings and, above all, for her good humour and cheerful willingness to take on any task despite other commitments.

Leo Pettipas and Gerald Friesen provided invaluable assistance, charting trails for me, supplying names and sources and generously assisting my application for a grant from the Historic Resources Branch of Manitoba Culture, Heritage and Tourism, an application kindly sponsored by the Manitoba Historical Society under the presidency of John Lehr.

The staff of the Historic Resources Branch – Bruce Donaldson, Ed Ledohowski, Peter Walker and Henry Trachtenberg – helped track down books, articles, art and sources. Their library and even their own personal research were at my disposal. Lorraine Crierie and Pauline Bélanger were patient and generous towards a beginner at grant applications. Particular thanks goes to Minister Diane McGifford and Jeff Harwood and the board members of the Heritage Grants Program for believing in this project.

Equally vital was the assistance of the *Winnipeg Free Press*: editor Nicholas Hirst who generously gave open access to the paper's library and, especially, to librarian Lynn Crothers, who sacrificed coffee breaks and lunch hours over many months to chase down clippings and photographs.

The staff of the Provincial Archives and the Provincial Library were unfailing in their assistance; I am especially grateful to Janina Skawinska and Louise Sloane. Michael Moosberger and Cheryle Martineau of the Department of Archives and Special Collections, University of Manitoba Libraries, willingly responded to calls for copies of *Winnipeg Tribune* stories and photographs.

Special recognition goes to the talented photographers whose work enhances the manuscript: Dennis Fast, Mike Grandmaison, Ian Ward, Roger Turenne, Jerry Zaste and Dr. Scott Norquay, as well as Barbara Endres, whose lovely drawings infused archival photographs with life and colour. Paula Beardy and W. John H. Phillips and the Phillips family generously allowed the wonderful work of Jackson Beardy and Walter J. Phillips to be displayed in the pages of this book. Equal gratitude goes to those who facilitated the translation of the artworks into book form: Doreen Millin of Culture Heritage and Tourism's arts branch; Ernest Mayer of the Winnipeg Art Gallery and last but by no means least, Gary Essar, curator of The Pavilion Gallery. Government Services Minister Steve Ashton helped clear the way for the Beardy paintings in the province's collection to be brought to Winnipeg to be photographed for reproduction.

Many other Manitoba public servants donated time and expertise to wend a neophyte through eons of geology, geography and climatic conditions. Erik Nielsen of the Manitoba Geological Survey was my very first interview, imparting more knowledge about the lake than I had gathered in a lifetime. Subsequently, he patiently read and commented upon the manuscript. Gaywood Matile, also of the Geological Survey, willingly answered questions about and provided maps of Lake Agassiz and ancestral Lake Winnipeg. Sherman Fraser of Manitoba Conservation's fisheries branch took numerous calls and contributed the photographs of Lake Winnipeg's famous finned inhabitants. Gerald Holm of the Manitoba Geographical Names Program endured a seemingly endless stream of queries about origins of place names with unfailing good humour. The staff of the Maps and Surveys Branch always had time for my visits as did Glenn Schneider of Manitoba Hydro.

Then there are those whose lives and memories shape the book. Most are mentioned by name in the text. Without them, the book would have been bare of what makes history live: the personal experiences of those who were there.

I extend special thanks to the Manitoba Archaeological Society for its unfailing help and support and to Donna Parisien Guiboche and Dennis Peristy of the Treaty and Aboriginal Rights Research Centre. Particular appreciation goes to Captain Clifford Stevens and his wife Beverley, and to Jim and Nancy Brennan, who opened their homes and family memories to me; to Jerry Zaste, Phil Manaigre, Roger Turenne and Jens and Barbara Nielsen, who helped me feel the heartbeat of the lake; and to Eric Robinson and Margo Thomas, who shared their childhood reminiscences with me.

In conclusion, there are two special people I wish to recognize: Val Werier, whose many articles about the lake over the years inspired and influenced the writing of this book, and my husband, Ken Murdoch. He lived every moment of this book with me, was my unfailing and ever-supportive partner, friend, literary critic and computer saviour. You have him to thank for the book's index.

To all of you, and to those I may unwittingly have forgotten, thank you for helping to bring a major part of Manitoban and Canadian history to life.

Union Jacks and wicker rockers decorate a cottage at Winnipeg Beach in the summer of 1914.

Table of Contents

Sand and water – for kids the lure is timeless.
PETER McADAM COLLECTION / PROVINCIAL ARCHIVES OF MANITOBA

Preface

Does one ever, fundamentally,
get over a great lake?

– *Gabrielle Roy,* The Road Past Altamont

Few bodies of water have had as many names as Lake Winnipeg. To the Cree, it was *Mistehay Sakahegan*, "Great Lake". To the Ojibwe, it was *Gitchi gumee*, also "Great Lake". To the Assiniboine, it was *Men-ne-wakan* or "Mysterious Water".

When the Europeans came, many took the name of the lake from the word or words the residents used to describe the colour of its water: *Win ni pak, Wi nipi* or Winnepe is Cree for "turbid or muddy water". An Ojibwe legend

Even during autumn, the season of its greatest treachery, Lake Winnipeg beguiles with its beauty

MIKE GRANDMAISON

recounting how it became muddy calls the lake *Weenipeeegosheeng*.

Nicolas Jéremie, a Quebecois who served in the French fur trade on Hudson Bay from 1694 to 1714, gave two different names for the lake: *Anisquaoui-gamou*, meaning junction of the two seas, "for the shores almost meet at the middle of the lake"; and *Michinipi*, or "Big Water".

At the end of the 17th and the beginning of the 18th centuries, the north basin was known as the "Lake of the Crees" – *Lac des Christineaux, Cristinaux, Kristineaux, Kinistinoes, Killistinaux, Killistinoes, Killistonons, Knistineaux*. All these were French translations of the Ojibwe name for their Cree northern neighbours.

The whole lake's name, according to Alexander Henry the Elder, was *Lac des Assinipoualacs, Assinebouels, Assenepolis, Assinipoils, Asiliboils*. But he sometimes referred to it as Lake Winipigon.

Pierre Gaultier de Varennes, Sieur de La Vérendrye, called the south basin *Lac Ouinipique* and the north basin, *Lac Bourbon*. The variants appearing in early French journals, maps and other accounts range from *Ouinipique, Quinipique, Alepimigon, Ouinipigue, Ouinipigon* and *Vnipignon* to *Winepic* and *Winnipeggon-e-sepe*.

Alexander Mackenzie and Alexander Henry the Younger called it Lake Winipic. Valentine McKay, a fur trader acquainted with the Cree language, supplied another version. "Winnipeg is a Cree name. When properly pronounced it sounds like *Wee-ni-pake* and the word means sea or something beyond an ordinary lake. In Cree, ocean is *kitchi-wee-ni-pake* meaning the 'great sea'".

The 19th-century painter Peter Rindisbacher called it Lake Winipesi and fishermen along the west side of the lake have been known to call it "the Gray Lady".

Dedication

To my parents, G. Leslie and Evelyn Russell, and to my family, Ken, Geoffrey and Tammy Fleming Murdoch, with deepest love and appreciation.

Sunrise on Hecla Island   MIKE GRANDMAISON

Introduction

by Val Werier

I like to walk to the harbour at Winnipeg Beach to talk to the fishermen, returning from the lake with their catch. What they will find in their nets is always a surprise and I share their wonder with them.

Recently I met Robert Olson, from a family of Icelandic fishermen who have cast their nets in the lake for 110 years. Like other fishermen, he had tried different jobs, one of them running a rock band. Now the lake is the love of his life. There is joy in his voice and light in his eyes as he talks of his happiness as a fisherman. Others may not share his exuberance for the work is demanding and the lake is treacherous.

But from my many talks with fishermen I know most share a feeling of expectation and awe and trepidation too, seeking their livelihood on the lake. Alone in their skiffs, they become part of nature and the serenity of the sea.

Fishermen don't underrate the lake as many Manitobans do. Do they recognize the glamour and eminence of our Lake Winnipeg? It is a giant among lakes of the world.

It is four and a half times the size of the province of Prince Edward Island. Because of its relatively shallow

Challenging winds and waves draw sailors and windsurfers.
DENNIS FAST

nature, it is more productive, more easily absorbing the beneficent rays of the sun.

We think of Manitoba as a prairie province. From my cottage by the shore, Lake Winnipeg looks like an ocean and indeed the Cree called it a sea or ocean lake. Along with neighbouring bodies of water, it constitutes the biggest lake district on the plains of North America. It is the dominant feature in Manitoba and sometimes I think of its form shaped by the ice age as an exclamation mark. I am not given to hyperbole, but isn't it marvelous that we have a sea on the prairie?

We do not know what we have. On the basis of a map four miles to the inch, at least 638 islands show up in the lake, 399 of them unnamed, all with vegetation. Not counting the big islands, many of these are up to a mile in length. These hundreds of islands contribute to providing one of the best habitats for birds on the continent.

More transcending, it tells us how the world behaves. It illustrates vividly how nature and humanity are interconnected and that we are influenced by development thousands of kilometres distant.

Lake Winnipeg drains a vast watershed, stretching from the Rockies to within 80 kilometres of Lake Superior, as well as part of the U.S. The rivers that drain this huge area reveal the behaviour of people and industry in their impact on the lake. Fertilizers, chemicals, pesticides and other pollutants may show in the lake and ultimately in Hudson Bay.

We are of this world and in the heart of the continent. I don't think there is an appreciation of the splendour and magnificence of the lake elsewhere. We can walk on water which comes as a surprise to visitors from Texas, that the lake freezes to a depth of three or more feet in winter.

I am fortunate to have a cottage on the shore of Lake Winnipeg and from my talks with cottagers and readers of my column, I know there is a deep attachment to the lake. I detect a kinship among people who have lived by the lake. The binding force is nature and summer associations. And they aver there is no finer delicacy than fresh pickerel pulled that day from the lake.

The lake is generous in its compositions of cloud, sun, lighting, cast in so many colours. Sometimes it is clearly a prairie sea, the water and the sky becoming one on the horizon. The composition of the people is even more dramatic, the Aboriginals, descendents of early homesteaders, immigrants from many lands who chose to live by the lake.

All these matters and much more has Frances Russell addressed in this informative book. I've written about the lake over a period of 50 years but I have a lot to learn from this authoritative work. Ms. Russell, an accomplished and recognized journalist, has done extensive research to bring the lake to life, enhanced by a lavish display of pictures.

This book fills a big gap in Manitoba history. I prophesy it will become a staple in cottages and homes around the lake.

For those who prefer calmer waters, the lagoon at Grand Beach beckons.

the ANCESTRAL LAKE

Upper right: The complex craft of birchbark canoe building likely arrived in Manitoba millennia ago, with early Algonquian people.

Below: Woolly mammoths, creatures of a cooler world, disappeared soon after the great glaciers receded, their demise undoubtedly hastened by intrepid human hunters.

Lower right: Manitoba's ice age bison survived the changing climate and human predations for much longer. As the south basin of Lake Winnipeg, shown here about 6,500 years ago, slowly filled, among the last bison occidentalis met their end along the Winnipeg River.

Rugged limestone cliffs above the north basin, by Roger Turenne

Illustrations courtesy of Manitoba Historic Resources

The Making of a Great Lake

Oh Agnes, Mabel and Becky. You got to watch when they come, boy. Sometimes Becky, she's the last one, and when she comes, boy, you have to watch out for that one. Cause them three sisters, boy, they are the ones you have to watch out for if you're out in a storm.

—The Icelanders

The Making of a Great Lake

HUMPHREY OLSON'S TALE of the legendary Three Big Sisters is every Lake Winnipeg sailor's worst nightmare. The Sisters are three huge waves that pile one on top of another; the last is the greatest and most dangerous. These three sudden, stealthy, lethal waves, rising out of nowhere, can swamp an unwary boat, regardless of size. They capture the essence of Lake Winnipeg – its inscrutable capriciousness and awesome power.

Roger Turenne, a veteran wilderness canoeist, never ceases to be amazed at the quicksilver changeability of the lake's many moods. "I've never seen any other body of water like that. It happens so incredibly quickly. Lake Superior gives you 15 minutes from calm to dangerous waves. But with Lake Winnipeg, you get five."

Jerry Zaste, who circumnavigated the lake in 1995 in a kayak, admits to a life-long love affair with the lake based on "the sheer power of it ... The bigger the storm, the happier I am."

Arriving at The Forks at the end of the 1,500-kilometre odyssey, Zaste's companion adventurer Phil Manaigre said, "I've never been so scared. It's definitely the roughest, meanest lake in Canada. One minute it charms you and 15 minutes later it tries to kill you."

Lake Winnipeg is Manitoba's most prominent geographic feature. It stands out on satellite images, an inverted teardrop resting on the vast, unwrinkled face of North America's central plains. It accounts for one-quarter of the province's freshwater area and almost four per cent of its landmass.[1]

Tyndall stone fossil rubbing   DAWN HUCK

It is one of Canada's three all-Canadian great lakes. The receptor of a vast watershed of nearly a million square kilometres, it was the crossroads of the northern half of North America for more than two centuries.

Manitobans normally associate their province's role in forging Canadian nationhood with political events. Manitoba was the first "in" province in 1870, the first to join after the original four of Confederation in 1867. It was the place where Louis Riel first took up arms against Canada on behalf of the Metis in 1869-70. Manitoba was the first Canadian polity to give women the vote in 1916 and it was the site of North America's only truly general strike, in 1919 in Winnipeg.

But in a very real sense, Manitoba's contribution to Canada is Lake Winnipeg. The Great Lakes watershed brought Europeans to today's northwestern Ontario. The watershed of another great lake was required to take them west to the plains and the Rocky Mountains beyond, and north to Hudson Bay. That great lake was Lake Winnipeg; in time the waterways it linked created Canada.

Lake Winnipeg was the centre of the fur trade's three "hub" lakes, the others being Lake Superior to the east and Lake Athabasca to the northwest. Lake Winnipeg was the link between – and crossroads of – the nascent nation's east and west, north and south.

It was, therefore, at the epicentre of an historic chain of events that forged two nations and two contrasting societies in North America. Eric W. Morse, prominent Canadian naturalist and wilderness traveller, believed the fur trade was responsible for determining Canada's boundaries and for the acendancy of east-west thinking over the natural north-south pull of geography and economic synergy.

"Canada's extension from sea to sea, in the face of American 'Manifest Destiny', is attributable largely to the fur trade," Morse wrote. "In Harold Innis's words, 'It is no mere accident that the present Dominion coincides roughly with the fur trading areas of northern North America.'" [2]

Lake Winnipeg is a creature of geography, climate and time. It straddles a major mid-continent fault line, where the ancient granite rocks of the Precambrian Shield give way to the Paleozoic limestone and dolomite sedimentary rocks of the plains. That fault line, or place where two differing and sometimes conflicting rock plates meet, the lake's north-south orientation and, above all, its unusual shallowness for its size (an average depth of 12 meters in the south basin and 16 to 17 meters in the north) create its wild and treacherous personality. In the ocean and other deep bodies of water the waves are farther apart and rolling. But in shallow waters like Lake Winnipeg, the waves rise, steep-fronted, from the bottom and hit close together.

The lake's violent and intractable qualities were remarked upon by all who experienced them: aboriginal fishers and trappers, Canada's celebrated voyageurs, Icelandic fishermen and steamboat captains, cartographers, adventurers, wilderness kayakers, canoeists, windsurfers, sailors, swimmers and cottagers.

Virtually every mention of the lake in books, journals and articles is accompanied by a reference to the awe-inspiring nature of its instant and terrifying storms. Their power seems magnified by the immense prairie sky, so vast it often displays multiple weather conditions at once, like a movie theatre with several features screening simultaneously: a black thunder cloud flashing and rumbling to the east, blue sky and calm sailing to the west, gray sky and a

soaking downpour to the north and scattered cloud over the south. "The Big Weather", Balsam Bay cottagers Ken and Susan Skinner call it.

Little wonder, perhaps, that when roads of water gave way first to those of steel and then, of asphalt, the lake quickly receded in importance and public consciousness. The glory days of its steamboat era are now long gone, the remnants resting in the Marine Museum of Manitoba in Selkirk if they were lucky, or in the lakebottom mud if they were not.

Now the lake splits its value to the people of Manitoba among three major industries. It is Canada's largest inland fishery. In 1999 it provided livelihoods for close to 1,000 fishers, producing about 4.2 million kilograms of fish and contributing $14.1 million to the provincial economy. Fishing, however, stands threatened as never before as a result of environmental pollution from inside and outside the province.

The lake's role as a summer playground for thousands of Manitobans continues to grow as cottage lots open farther and farther north on both the eastern and western shorelines of its south basin. And Lake Winnipeg is at the epicentre of the province's vast resources of electric power. The Jenpeg control structure has turned the lake into a giant reservoir for Manitoba Hydro's massive generating network along the Nelson River, embroiling the Crown utility and the lake itself in controversy.

While the lake's role in the province's economy and society is ever-changing, its unpredictable and dangerous character – a character forged by the geographic and climatic forces that gave it birth – remains as always to challenge those who seek to use or enjoy it.

The Hudson's Bay Company's Colvile, *shown here in a drawing from* Picturesque Canada, *was among the first steamers to test the waters of Lake Winnipeg. For nearly 20 years, from 1875 to 1894, the little oaken ship battled storms to carry freight, passengers and even soldiers during a period of sweeping change on the lake.*

NATIONAL ARCHIVES OF CANADA / C-83178

Lake Winnipeg is the third-largest lake entirely within Canada and seventh-largest in North America. It covers 24,514 square kilometres and is 425 kilometres long. Its north basin reaches a width of 100 kilometres, the south basin, 40 kilometres. In Canada, only the Northwest Territories' Great Bear Lake (31,792 square kilometres) and Great Slave Lake (28,930 square kilometres) are bigger. [3]

Lake Winnipeg is 25 per cent larger than Lake Ontario (19,550 square kilometres) and only marginally smaller than Lake Erie (25,670 square kilometres), though it is dwarfed by the three Upper Great Lakes. The largest freshwater lake in the world, Lake Superior, covers 82,100 square kilometres,

A line of glacial erratics on a limestone beach provides a snapshot of the lake's dual personality.

IAN WARD

while Lake Huron envelops 59,830 square kilometres and Lake Michigan, 57,750 square kilometres. [4]

Where Lake Winnipeg stands in the world is a source of continuing confusion. That's because there are two variables. The noun, "lake", can refer to all landlocked bodies of water, salt as well as fresh. In this group, Lake Winnipeg is twelfth-largest. But the list includes the Caspian and Aral Seas, both salty. Should the list be restricted to fresh water alone, Lake Winnipeg moves up to tenth. [5]

Rick Bowering, manager of surface water management for Manitoba Conservation, says the world ranking also depends on when lakes are measured. Lakes are living things and as their water level rises and falls, so does their size. A higher lake level floods more shoreline.

There is another reason Lake Winnipeg is on the move. The north basin is gradually tipping into the south basin as the northern part of the province slowly rises due to a process called isostatic rebound. During the last glaciation, the Laurentian ice sheet, which covered all of what is now Manitoba, was as much as four kilometres thick in places. So heavy was the weight of the ice that the rock surface of the land was depressed by at least 700 metres and perhaps as much as one kilometre. As the ice retreated, the land began to lift, first in the south and later, but faster, in the north. Scientists estimate that the rebounding process is causing the south basin to rise by about 20 centimetres a century, while the north basin is rising at a much great rate.

Lake Winnipeg's 990,660 square kilometre drainage area is among the largest in North America, second only to the Mackenzie River Delta in Canada. Via the Saskatchewan, Winnipeg and Red Rivers and their tributaries, respectively, it extends west to the Canadian Rockies, east to the height of land in Quetico Park just west of Lake

Superior and south into North and South Dakota, Minnesota and Montana.

Based on long-term flow, about 43 per cent of Lake Winnipeg's water comes from the Winnipeg River, another 32 per cent from the Saskatchewan and the remainder from a number of rivers including the Red, Dauphin and Berens and their tributaries. [6]

Because of the lake's shallowness, its water is emptied and replenished every three to four and a half years. By comparison, it takes between 21 to 185 years to replace the water in the Great Lakes. This speedy replacement and regeneration makes Lake Winnipeg one of the most fertile lakes in the world.

Lake Winnipeg's origins are lost in the mists of time. As mentioned earlier, the lake straddles two ancient rock formations. Along its eastern edge is rock resulting from one of geology's greatest dramas, an orogeny or period of mountain building. Between 2.6 and 1.7 billion years ago, during the Precambrian era, a series of enormous granite ranges were thrust skyward in what is now eastern Manitoba. This ancient rock comprises three-fifths of Manitoba's bedrock surface, but today the towering mountains, which once rivalled the Himalayas, are gone, worn by time and ice to a relatively flat plain that we know as the Precambrian or Canadian Shield. Because only primitive forms of plant life existed at that time, the primeval rock is almost devoid of fossils. It has often been called "the bones of the earth".

Then, about 570 million years ago, another spectacular geologic event enveloped Manitoba. At the time, the province sat close to the equator part of a great supercontinent known as Pangaea. During the Paleozoic and Mesozoic eras 570 million to 65 million years ago, this enormous land

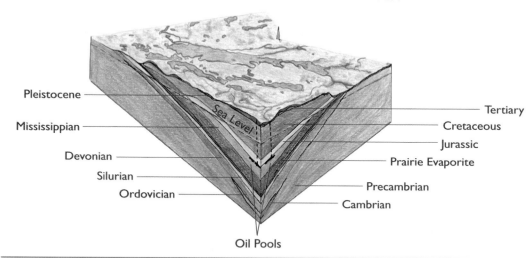

A SECTIONAL MAP OF SOUTHWESTERN MANITOBA

Pleistocene
Mississippian
Devonian
Silurian
Ordovician
Sea Level
Tertiary
Cretaceous
Jurassic
Prairie Evaporite
Precambrian
Cambrian
Oil Pools

mass began to split apart; its remnants divided, migrated and gradually regrouped in their current form.

During this period, much of Manitoba, indeed the entire central plains of North America, was submerged under tropical seas. These warm waters deposited thousands of metres of sediment. The further west one goes in Manitoba, the deeper this sediment is.

If you could take a knife and cut through Manitoba like a layer cake and then turn the slice on its side, you would see a wedge that widens dramatically from east to west, acquiring more layers as it goes. The Precambrian Shield, which is at the surface on the east side of the province and the east shore of Lake Winnipeg, gradually slides under the sediments of these prehistoric seas until, at the westernmost edge of the province, it is almost 4,600 metres below ground level. [7]

The molten past of the Canadian Shield is clear in the rock off Drumming Point at Black Island's east end, below.

COURTESY OF THE NIELSEN FAMILY

The Paleozoic limestones, dolomites and shale are the first to cover the Precambrian granites. That this first layering begins under Lake Winnipeg is perhaps most obvious on Punk Island in the lake's south basin just north of Hecla Island. The island's towering cliffs and rock overhangs are composed of the sandstone and shale of the Winnipeg Formation, topped by thick beds of the dolomitic limestone of the Red River Formation.

Proceeding westward, the limestones and dolomites are, in turn, covered by the red shale, anhydrite, gypsum and sandstone of Mezosoic times. Finally, at the height of the Manitoba Escarpment, the Mezosoic sediments are buried under the shales and lignites of the Cenozoic period. A layer of glacial drift, up to 250 metres deep in places, acts as a kind of icing on top.

A Mixed Blessing

Lake Winnipeg's fertility is a mixed blessing. Every summer, lake residents are literally swarmed by fishflies, elsewhere called mayflies. The lake produces up to 87,000 metric tonnes, literally billions of these little insects annually. In early July, they hatch from the water, fly to the land to mate and then return to the lake to spawn and die. They are unique in that they have no mouth parts and cannot eat. Each tiny sail-winged creature has a normal life span of between two hours and three days. But many come to an untimely uglier end, trapped in spider webs or mesmerized by any bright light on the shore. These unfortunates litter the beaches, paths and roadways while their more successful relatives who make it back to the water to reproduce provide needed nutrients to the lake's population of whitefish, pickerel, sauger, northern pike, perch, mullet and goldeye.

During the Paleozoic Era, life evolved into many complex forms. Invertebrates like lampshell brachiopods, three-lobed trilobites and corals were most abundant. These creatures not only produced the calcium carbonate of which limestone is composed, but etched their myriad shapes and sizes for all eternity in Manitoba's beautifully varied and highly-prized Tyndall limestone. [8]

The Jurassic and Cretaceous periods of the Mesozoic era witnessed the climax and extinction of dinosaurs. No land-based dinosaur has ever been found here because Manitoba was still underwater. Nevertheless, the province harboured interesting aquatic life forms. *Portheous*, a four-metre fish with a bulldog face and a mouth full of sharp teeth, and *Dolichorhynchops*, a five-metre fish-eating reptile, swam about in the warm waters. These creatures probably shared the province with other reptiles and the first birds. [9]

The Cenozoic or mammalian era, which began 65 million years ago and continues today, saw the final retreat of the warm seas and the formation of the continent as we know it. No one is certain about the extent of life in Manitoba for much of this time because most of the palaeontological clues have been removed by erosion and glacial scouring.

On the basis of finds in adjacent states and provinces, however, scientists speculate that exotic species normally associated with other continents roamed the province. Crocodiles, alligators, primitive primates and marsupials, hyena-like carnivores, forest-dwelling horses, sabre-toothed cats, aquatic and fast-running rhinoceros, chevrotain deer, tapirs, swine and two types of antelope all called Manitoba home. [10]

Then, about two million years ago, the Pleistocene epoch, the period many call the "Ice Age" began. Since then, scientists believe the planet has gone through as many as 20 warming and cooling periods. The most recent deep freeze, the Late Wisconsinan glaciation, began about 25,000 years ago. At its peak, some 18,000 years BP (before present), Canada's central plains were entombed beneath a massive ice sheet that reached as far south as Des Moines, Iowa.

So much water was locked up in the continental glaciers that ocean levels dropped dramatically, perhaps by as much as 140 metres, exposing continental shelves. The resulting shorter distances between relatively close continents stimulated mass migrations of plant and animal species.

At least two actual land bridges joined North America to continents. One, Beringia, the Alaska-Siberia link, was 1,280 kilometres wide, more a continent than a corridor. The other, connecting North and South America, was 192 kilometres wide. [11]

While these land bridges allowed for the intercontinental movement of many species, including humans, scientists now believe that North America's first people probably arrived during an earlier interglacial period, perhaps the one that began about 65,000 years ago. Certainly, there is evidence that North America's first inhabitants lived right up to the edges of the giant glaciers.

Since each glaciation partially or completely erased the evidence of its predecessors, the best scientific information arises from the most recent. From its centre just west of Hudson Bay, the Laurentian ice sheet advanced southward, eroding the landscape and carrying the accumulated soil and stones within it. This debris was deposited in many glacial forms when the ice stalled or retreated. Long ridges called terminal moraines marked the point of maximum advance.

The retreat was characterized by a northward recession of the ice. As the climate improved, the southern edge began

melting at a rate faster than new ice was being forced towards it. Deglaciation was not a continuous event, however.

About 11,500 BP, the extreme southwest became the first part of Manitoba to throw off the icy shroud. Over the next few centuries, glacial Lakes Souris and Agassiz were formed from meltwater which, for a time, drained southward into the Mississippi watershed. Lake Souris, largely in North Dakota, was short-lived. But Lake Agassiz, initially restricted to the Red River Valley of North Dakota, began its expansion to the north in concert with the glacier's retreat.

Ten thousand years ago, Lake Agassiz's north and northeastern shores washed against a continuous cliff of ice, but its southern and western shores formed what geologists call the Campbell Beach. Manitobans are familiar with the Campbell Beach, though they may not recognize the name. It runs in a northwesterly directon along the foot of the Pembina, Riding, Duck and Porcupine uplands of southern and western Manitoba. Archaeologist Anthony P. Buchner says this extensive sand and gravel ridge, most evident in southwestern Manitoba, "is possibly the most eloquent testimony to the existence of this once-great lake." [12]

Shortly thereafter, a new outlet opened to the Lake Superior Basin, allowing Lake Agassiz to drain eastward. This outlet was subsequently blocked by a glacial re-advance and again the lake rose to the Campbell Beach.

Then, about 9,500 BP, a cataclysmic event occurred. The eastern outlet re-opened and Agassiz emptied in a raging torrent. As much as 3,000 cubic kilometres of water (seven times the volume of Lake Erie) coursed into the Superior Basin in just a few weeks. Evidence of this spectacular deluge is visible today in a series of huge canyons north of Thunder Bay and west of Lake Nipigon.

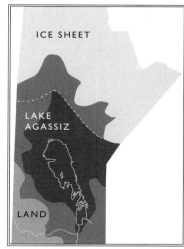

DAWN HUCK / FROM THE MANITOBA ARCHAEOLOGICAL SOCIETY

As the continental ice sheet melted, Lake Agassiz's size and shape changed constantly. The shorelines it formed at its largest extent in Manitoba collectively constitute the Campbell Beach.

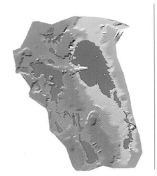

G. MATILE, C. F. M. LEWIS, E. NIELSEN, L. H. THORLIEFSON, B. J. TODD/ HOLCENE EVOLUTION OF THE MANITOBA LAKES REGION / COURTESY OF MANITOBA ENERGY & MINES / OF 96–8

Isostatic rebound is mainly responsible for the changing shape of Manitoba's great lakes, shown here as they may have appeared 7,700 years ago, left, and 4000 years ago, with their present configuration at right for comparison.

Geologist James Teller, who charted the canyons, says they provide evidence of a tremendous erosive flood. Lake Agassiz resided west of the continental divide "and once the glacier retreated to the point that waters could escape over that continental divide, it overflowed catastrophically. It eroded those canyons." [13]

The flows gouged wide, deep channels in bedrock and left behind boulders ranging from one to three metres in diameter. The largest of these canyons is 150 metres deep and several kilometres wide.

Teller has located 17 different groupings of these canyons. The one most familiar to Canadians, and most dramatic of all, is Ouimet Canyon, between Lake Nipigon and Lake Superior. Teller believes it was formed when Lake Nipigon, swollen with water from Lake Agassiz, finally burst, releasing a torrent that bored its way through bedrock into Lake Superior.

Once the eastward flow abated, Lake Agassiz commenced its final drainage to the north. By 7,700 BP, only the ancestors of Lakes Winnipeg, Winnipegosis, Manitoba and the province's other smaller "great" lakes remained, progenies dwarfed by their gigantic parent.

At its peak, Lake Agassiz was larger than any other glacial or modern lake in North America and was rivalled only by other prehistoric lakes in Asia and Africa. Its basin covered more than 500,000 square kilometres. But because of its constantly changing shorelines, no more than 200,000 square kilometres were inundated at any one time. And, unlike its present-day offspring, Lake Agassiz was deep. The site of present-day Winnipeg was at times under 213 metres of water.

Lake Agassiz's disappearance did not, as might be supposed, leave Manitoba's three great lakes as they are today. The largest of these, Lake Winnipeg, went through multiple transformations in both size and shape before attaining its modern form.

According to geologists, Lake Winnipeg actually began as a series of small lakes along the ancestral – and much longer – Red River. At that time, the Red emptied almost directly into a far bigger Hudson Bay, the shoreline of which was much farther south than it is today. Geologists have named this widening of Hudson Bay the Tyrrell Sea in honour of the Canadian geologist, Joseph Burr Tyrrell.

About 7,700 BP, when the elevation of what is now the lake's south basin was 40 metres higher than that of the north basin, Lake Winnipeg was actually a small, oval pool nestled in the most northern part of today's north basin. Over the next several centuries, as the land rebounded from the weight of the ice, the lake expanded along its north-south axis and extended southward, first filling the north basin and then engulfing the ancestral Red River's chain of small lakes down through The Narrows into today's south basin.

Evidence of the lake's southward migration was further confirmed by seismic profiling and coring by scientists from

Jack Pine, *a woodcut executed by Walter J. Phillips in 1940, perfectly evokes the ancient landscape of Lake Winnipeg's east shore.*

A relic of an earlier age of global warming, a clump of tiny cactus sits on a south-facing rock above the Rice River on Lake Winnipeg's east shore.

Manitoba Energy and Mines (now Manitoba Industry, Trade and Mines) and the Geological Survey of Canada. They chartered the Canadian Coast Guard ship, *Namao*, in the summers of 1994 and 1996. Their work uncovered submerged 4,000-year-old shoreline features south of Hecla Island.

Manitoba's climate went through more changes while the lake was expanding southward. Between 8,000 and 5,000 BP, Manitoba was much warmer and drier than it is today, a lot like present-day southern Saskatchewan and Alberta. Climatologists call this period of global warming the Hypsithermal.

Botanist James Ritchie believes that open grassland extended over all of southwestern Manitoba, including the Turtle, Riding and possibly Duck Mountains, as well as throughout the southern half of the Interlake and as far east as the Winnipeg River. This ecological reconstruction is based upon some rather startling recent discoveries. For example, prickly pear cactus, which is a grasslands-adapted species, has been found growing in the Canadian Shield east of Lake Winnipeg. A further confirmation of the widespread dispersion of grasslands in Manitoba was the discovery of the bones of grazing animals in what are now heavily forested areas. A bison cranium recovered from a site on the Winnipeg River was radiocarbon-dated at circa 6,400 BP. Also, the inclusion of a bison in rock paintings at Artery Lake northeast of The Narrows suggested knowledge and presence of bison in an area that is now entirely boreal forest. [14] The province's north was warmer as well, pushing the treeline several hundred kilometres north of where it is now.

Then, about 3,000 BP, the climate cooled again and became wetter. Water levels in Lake Winnipeg rose, and forests returned to the lake's eastern shore and across the Parklands into Riding Mountain, creating habitats similar to today's.

About 2,000 BP, the lake assumed more or less its current shape and size. But, like the living things on, around and in it, Lake Winnipeg, too, is ever-moving, ever-fluctuating over time.

Today's cottagers can attest to those changes. The shoreline is eroding in places all around the south basin. Many residents blame their disappearing beaches on the hydro dam and control structure at the north end of the lake. But Harvey Thorleifson of the Geological Survey of Canada believes the lake level rise is largely driven by the glacial uplift process, not the man-made Jenpeg station. [15]

Scientists know that the Lake Winnipeg region tilted after the retreat of Lake Agassiz because the shorelines of Lake Agassiz, horizontal at the time of their formation, now rise in elevation towards the northeast. These shorelines have left vestigial "beaches" of sand and gravel in many places.

Northern Manitoba is elevating by about a metre a century relative to southern Manitoba and is expected to continue to rebound at that rate for at least the next 1,000 years. The northern end of Lake Winnipeg has risen about 100 metres in the last 10,000 years and the southern end, about 37 metres. Farther north, Baker Lake and Chesterfield Inlet have rebounded by about 262 metres, Churchill, by 200 metres. Brown's Valley, Minnesota, the most southerly end of the Red River, may be the area of zero rebound.

All lake levels fluctuate as water is gained and lost and this fluctuation is dictated chiefly by climate. In recent millennia, Lake Winnipeg has been an outflowing lake with a positive water budget. In other words, more water goes into it through river inflow, direct precipitation and groundwater discharge from lake bottom springs, than leaves it through river outflow, evaporation and seepage into the lake bottom.

Moreover, says Thorleifson, "because the outlet of Lake Winnipeg is in the north, uplift of the north end of the lake progressing at a rate more rapid than the basin to the south has meant lake level rise over the entire basin, with the rate increasing southward." [16]

Geologist Erik Nielsen, who participated in the *Namao* cruises, says Manitobans need not worry about an earthquake occurring under Lake Winnipeg along the junction between the Precambrian granite and the Paleozoic limestone and dolomite. The differing types of rock get on very well. They don't grind against each other, nor does their meeting create the kind of instability that leads to tectonic plate movement, the cause of earthquakes. "This area forms sort of a soft spot … [with] the lake in a trough between the two rock types," Nielsen says. [17]

The most dramatic evidence of Lake Winnipeg's split geologic personality is on vivid display in the 500-metre channel between the eastern point of Black Island and the mainland, particularly in a northwest gale. This is the lake's real "narrows", its narrowest point, not The Narrows, the 2.5-kilometre-wide channel between East Doghead and West Doghead Points at the junction of the north and south basins. Nielsen describes the Black Island narrows as "a very strange place. We can see some faults. It is a bit of a unique place in that the water is very deep. I think it reaches a depth of about 60 metres and there are some very strong currents that run through it. When you get a big storm from the north, the water just goes firing through that gut at a tremendous rate and scours out the bottom of the lake."

The Black Island narrows also fascinates Jens and Barbara Nielsen, who visit the area a few times each summer on their boat *Fylgja*, old Norse for a benevolent little spirit that accompanies families on their journeys. "It's the deepest spot in the lake, up to 200 feet deep," says Jens Nielsen. "The eagles gather there because the current is often so strong

that there are eddies and turbulence and the fishing is better. The east side is very deep, but on the west side, there are all sorts of reefs underwater … you can see the water rising up. That's the fault line. This is where the Precambrian rocks are, where one plate has separated and the limestone comes on top. It's also the axis of the lake." [18]

Lake Winnipeg is defined by dramatic changes in water level, all due to the strong prairie winds. The north-south orientation of the lake can aid a strong north wind in piling up water at the south end and it's not unusual to get a metre of water level rise. Scientists have a name for this wind and wave elevation; they call it "set-up".

A casual glance at a map of the lake reveals its most prominent visual feature aside from The Narrows. Long Point (*Kitchi-nashi* in Ojibwe, *Missineo* in Swampy Cree and *Le Grand Détour* to the voyageurs) is an apt, though prosaic, name for a 40-kilometre finger of land that extends eastward almost to the middle of the north basin about two-thirds of the way between The Narrows and Warren Landing.

GEORGE BACK / NATIONAL ARCHIVES OF CANADA / C–28258

In Limestone Rocks – Lake Winnipeg, *George Back caught the towering cliffs and pounding surf that confounded so many who sailed the lake's western shore.*

25

Long Point is part of The Pas Moraine, an enormous, elongated C-shaped deposit of rocks, gravel and sand left behind by the retreating glaciers. Five of the lake's 25 major islands – the north basin's Little Sandy, Big Sandy, Cannibal, George and Little George – are also part of the same moraine, which begins just north of The Pas, sweeps in a large curve southeast across the top of both the Interlake and the lake itself, onto the east shore and up into the Canadian Shield, where it finally disappears.

Another interesting feature of the north basin is Limestone Point, a 20-kilometre long sandspit separating the lake's north shore from Limestone Bay. Roger Turenne says it is the longest sandspit in Canada and so narrow (150 metres) at one point "it won't be long before it becomes an island. A couple of big Lake Winnipeg storms with strong southerly winds could cut through. It's one continuous beach with nothing on it but sand." Storms keep adding sand to the point's two-kilometre wide end, giving it the appearance, Turenne says, of "a pendant with a giant brooch at the end". [19]

The lake's other attractions include the fine silica or quartz sands of the east shore, the massive dolomite limestone cliffs on Punk Island and Grindstone Point and the Kasakeemeemisekak Islands just north of Deer Island in The Narrows. These islands demonstrate most dramatically Lake Winnipeg's bipolar nature. Here, travellers have no sense of the immensity of the prairie sea. Here, they are transported into the rocks, pines and deep waters of the Canadian Shield. Canoeists say that as they paddle through the hundreds of islands and smaller rock outcrops, they can only think of the Muskoka District in Ontario.

With its many faces and myriad moods, Lake Winnipeg can mimic the Muskokas, the North Atlantic or, as the cliffs and water of Hecla Island do here, the Mediterranean.

MIKE GRANDMAISON

Long Point, Limestone Point and Bay, and Black and Deer Islands are being considered for a new national park. It will be a strange park, Turenne admits, because it is situated on Lake Winnipeg "but there won't be a drop of water in large parts of it because only the islands are being designated. As well, it's 200 kilometres as the crow flies between the south islands and the north end of the lake." The idea of the park is to include all the ecosystems and natural features of the Manitoba Lowlands.

To this day, the most picturesque descriptions of Lake Winnipeg are those found in the journals of Henry Youle Hind, the University of Toronto geologist commissioned by the Canadian government in 1857-58 to survey the basins of the Red, Assiniboine and Saskatchewan Rivers. Hind's tasks were to assess the prospects of these areas for settlement and to find an appropriate route from Canada to the Red River Colony and thence westward to the Pacific.

John Fleming, a member of Hind's party, wrote this account of their arrival at the Saskatchewan River:

We entered Lake Winnipeg at sunset, and camped not far from the mouth of the Saskatchewan, upon a narrow spit of gravel, separated from the wooded shores by a marsh. The night was clear and beautiful, and the lake wonderfully calm. From our bivouac, where we lay with cramped limbs outstretched on the shingle beach, could be seen the great headland, Kitchi-nashi, vanishing away to the southeast in the far distant horizon. A view very extensive and beautiful, but which betokened many hours of paddling and tracking out of the direct course to the Red River. To the east and north the only limit to our gaze was the dim horizon of the great lake which lay tranquilly outspread before us like an unruffled sea. [20]

Goldeye: A Prince of Fish

Some call it the prince of fish. It is the reason most non-Manitobans have heard of Lake Winnipeg. But fishermen once scorned the monarch of the gourmet's table.

Goldeye, like the lake sturgeon, is a mysterious fish and, like the sturgeon, only infrequently interested in propagating its species. This leaves both goldeye and sturgeon vulnerable to extinction through overfishing. Even today, experts haven't fathomed the goldeye's love life, except to note that it prefers turbid to clear water. Males mature in their third year, females in their fourth or fifth. A mature female may contain from 5,000 to 25,000 eggs, an average being 14,000. Goldeye spawn in the very early spring, at night. The eggs do not sink to the bottom because each one contains a globule of oil which makes it float a few inches under the surface of the water. There, the relatively high temperature causes early hatching.

Within the first year, a young goldeye may attain a length of 15 centimetres. At spawning size, the fish averages about 31 centimetres. Goldeyes rarely grow large. A one-kilogram fish is considered exceptional. The oldest goldeye on record attained 16 years. Despite its age, its size was not remarkable.

Cree fishermen knew the value of smoking these fish over fires of local oak and willow. Initially, white fishermen spurned the goldeye, throwing them back or selling them for a mere cent or two a pound, but they finally learned from the Cree. At the beginning of the First World War, a chef at Winnipeg's Royal Alexandra Hotel popularized "Lake Winnipeg goldeye". The taste soon spread to hotels, restaurants and railway dining cars across North America.

At the time the Royal Alex's chef made his find, the lake was producing about one million pounds of goldeye a year. But ensuing intensive fishing, combined with the fish's restricted reproductive cycle, almost wiped it out. Making matters worse, goldeyes cannot be farmed or hatched through artificial stripping of eggs and milt.

Today, the fish is back in the lake, but its numbers remain so small, the Freshwater Fish Marketing Corporation includes it under "other" in its annual production reports.

Goldeye COURTESY OF MANITOBA FISHERIES BRANCH

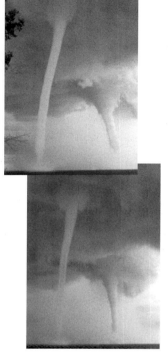

In a rare meteorological ballet, waterspouts dance across Lake Winnipeg's south basin, above and right.

The next day the arduous paddle to the mouth of the Red commenced.

> *Being favoured with a light breeze for a few hours we reached the neck of the great promontory, Cape Kitchinashi, about noon. From the mouth of the Saskatchewan to this point the coast trends to the southeast and is indented in a remarkable manner by a series of deep bays of every shape and size. As it would require unlimited time and resources to penetrate into every sinuosity of the coast, we generally steered straight from point to point, although in doing so, some long traverses had to be made ...* [21]

Hind's journals are peppered with references to nine- and 10-metre limestone and sandstone cliffs along the western shorelines of The Narrows and the lake's north basin. One site, on the northeast side of Punk Island, provided ochre.

> *On rising slabs there is seen between each stratum a soft and very pure ochre of a beautiful yellow colour; it is found filling small depressions in the limestone ... The ochre, when moist and fresh, is easily worked by the fingers, quite destitute of gritty or hard particles, of a uniform pale yellow colour and when burned, of a beautiful cinnabar red. It is used by the Indians in both states as a pigment; the limestone in which it occurs is extremely porous and often honeycombed ...*
>
> *We made the traverse of Great Washow Bay, 13 miles across, and breakfasted at a point halfway between Bull's Head and Dog's Head. The limestone cliffs here were about 30 feet high ... Ascending the cliff, I found large portions detached from the main body, forming deep clefts or cracks. Some of these fissures were 12 feet wide and 20 feet deep, others three feet wide and of greater depth. Sometimes the fissures were roofed with masses which had slipped forward, forming long narrow caves lined with moss. One cave was more than 60 feet long and with the exception of a small aperture, closed at one end and roofed throughout.* [22]

The 1994-96 *Namao* geological expedition's core samples were taken on a north-south transect. They demonstrate the layer-cake quality of the lake bed, with the lake's own sediment forming the icing. This lake sediment is soupy, "almost like a custard", says Nielsen. Beneath it, 100 metres deep in places, is the sediment left by Lake Agassiz. This layered and laminated mud is compacted and very hard. Beneath these sediments are two "basement" structures: glacial till and bedrock. Bare rock forms the bottom in spots on the east shore just north of Black Island, reflecting the abrasive action of the lake at this, its narrowest place.

The lake's shallowness, coupled with its soft sediment, leads to annual ice scouring. The lake ice forms pressure ridges with deep keels. When the wind blows, they plough the bottom. "The lake bottom is just covered with these little furrows," Nielsen says.

Core samples have also supported the isostatic rebound theory, demonstrating that the north end of the lake is some 6,000 years older than Netley Marsh. Despite its relative youth, Nielsen calls Netley Marsh "an interesting feature. When you go through there, you think you're in the Mississippi Delta."

Manitoba lies at the northern boundary of the Great Plains' "tornado alley", where hot, moist air sweeping up from the Gulf of Mexico encounters cool, dry air flowing eastward from the Rocky Mountains. Because they are large and shallow, prime breeding conditions for updrafts of hot and humid air, both Lake Winnipeg and its smaller sister, Lake Manitoba, are vulnerable to waterspouts and their much more ferocious cousins, tornados. Usually, these terrible winds are buried in thunderstorms.

On August 8, 1984, a remarkable weather event occurred on Lake Winnipeg that witnesses will never forget. It brought together all the unique elements that make up the lake's fascination: its propensity for storms, its size and the singularity of its geographic location. At least six and perhaps eight 600-metre tall waterspouts made a stately, 25-kilometre procession southeastward from the middle of the lake east of Gimli to Balsam Bay. Some were thin, black threads while others were thick, gray or gleaming white pillars. They dangled from a flat-topped, ragged-bottomed black cloud and marched soundlessly across the water. Around the foot of each was a circular fountain composed of a wall of water and spray about a metre high. Two of the spouts embraced each other as they travelled.

The entire spectacle lasted almost 45 minutes and was observed as far away as the airport tower in Winnipeg. What witnesses most recalled at the time was the utter silence. There was no wind, no thunder and hardly any lightning. When the spouts hit land, they disappeared up into the cloud, but their expiry was accompanied by a terrific gust of wind and a sudden downpour of rain, "like a bucket of water being dumped," according to one observer.

Balsam Bay cottager Scott Norquay recalls the event vividly. His pictures have been reproduced in Environment Canada's dangerous winds warning pamphlet and in *National Geographic*. He remembers that the afternoon was very humid and partly cloudy. He was painting his cottage when his youngest daughter spotted the spouts. He continues:

I saw two cylinders out in the lake, and that was the end of the painting. I ran for my camera and got so excited taking pictures of these things as they got closer that I forgot all my photographic knowledge and technique.

He stood on his lawn at the edge of the beach, clicking his camera continuously for about 20 minutes. He saw six spouts in total. Some formed and then, just as swiftly, expired.

You could see a disturbance on the water and above it, coming down from the cloud, the beginnning of a twister. Then the condensation started to whirl around ... There was a pair that marched directly towards me. One went off to my left as I was facing the lake and I lost sight of it beyond the trees. But the other one on the north kept coming closer and closer ... The one that marched right towards me was about 100 feet across at its base on the water ... There were wind sounds in the trees and thunder-clouds behind [the spouts] but toward the end, the sun was out.

Finally, responding to his wife's entreaties, Dr. Norquay joined his family and their neighbours in the basement of his cottage. "I had no idea whether this thing was going to come up on shore and take the house with it," he says. [23]

An Environment Canada climatologist subsequently described the Lake Winnipeg waterspout event of 1984 as a "most remarkable display of unusual weather".

the SACRED LAKE

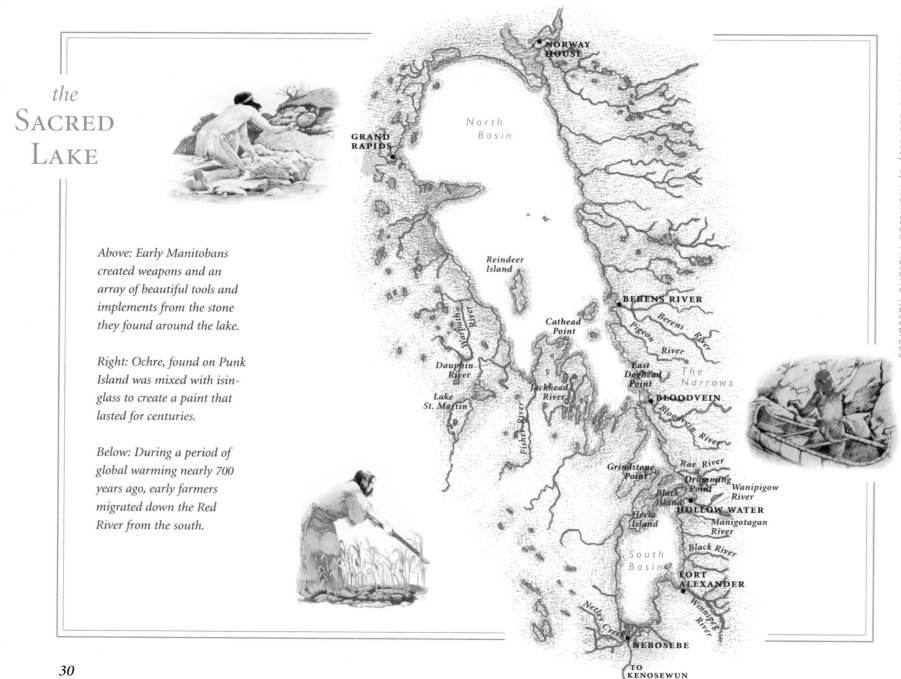

Above: Early Manitobans created weapons and an array of beautiful tools and implements from the stone they found around the lake.

Right: Ochre, found on Punk Island was mixed with isinglass to create a paint that lasted for centuries.

Below: During a period of global warming nearly 700 years ago, early farmers migrated down the Red River from the south.

NORWAY HOUSE

North Basin

GRAND RAPIDS

Reindeer Island

BERENS RIVER

Berens River

Pigeon River

Cathead Point

Warpath River

The Narrows

Dauphin River

East Doghead Point

BLOODVEIN

Jackhead River

Bloodvein River

Lake St. Martin

Fisher River

Rae River

Grindstone Point

Drumming Point

Wanipigow River

Black Island

HOLLOW WATER

Hecla Island

Manigotagan River

South Basin

Black River

FORT ALEXANDER

Netley Creek

Winnipeg River

NEBOSEBE

TO KENOSEWUN

Anishinabe campsite on Black Island by Dennis Fast

Illustrations courtesy of Manitoba Historic Resources

Spirits of the Lake

*B*efore people set out
on their journeys, they
would offer something, usually
tobacco, to the spirits of the
water, for a safe travel, that
no lives be lost. That was how
sacred that lake was regarded
in days gone by

— Eric Robinson

Spirits of the Lake

THE SON OF a Norway House Cree fisherman, Eric Robinson became a member of the Manitoba Legislature and then one of the first cabinet ministers of aboriginal ancestry in Manitoba and Canada. He recalls almost losing his brother to Lake Winnipeg.

My older brother, who is now 60 years old, was fishing on Lake Winnipeg and his boat overturned in a storm ... He tied himself to the bottom of the boat, which had capsized. It was about a day before he was finally rescued by some other fishers.

There was gratitude on my mother's and father's side that his life was spared by this water ... My father and my uncles told us that this lake not only held our sustenance in the form of fish, but also it held much more spiritual significance ... We were always told, if we were fishing or going on a trip or using the lake for whatever purpose, that the lake is in command and it should always be respected. We were advised by the old people that extra care must be taken because of the power of the lake. [1]

People have been living in and around the Lake Winnipeg basin for at least 8,000 years. Long before Europeans first set foot in Manitoba, native North Americans were as familiar with the land around the great lake as the Angles and Saxons were with England, the Celts with Ireland and Scotland and the ancient Franks with France. Like those cultures, they had beliefs, customs and practices arising from their life experiences that had been passed on through many generations. How did they come to be here? How did they manage to survive in this often hostile environment? What happened once they encountered Europeans?

It's little wonder that these first Manitobans, dwelling in what was truly "the great, lone land", regarded themselves as part of the natural world, rather than as its master. Living in small, scattered family groups, they were dwarfed by the sheer magnitude of the space they inhabited.

They traversed prairie where grasses would, in places, grow to the height of a tall man. They dealt with bodies of water so large and threatening that they chose to circumnavigate rather than traverse them. They encountered bison numbering in the tens of thousands, herds that engulfed the land and shook the earth when they moved. They witnessed flocks of passenger pigeons so vast they blotted out the sun. They walked through deep, dark forests that harboured cold, seemingly bottomless lakes, fragrant stands of spruce and pine and unusual outcrops of ancient rock. They observed the four seasons and the four winds, experienced the biting cold of winter and the shimmering heat of summer, the return of the birds in the green spring and their departure in the brightly coloured fall. They watched the sun rise and set, the moon revolve through its phases, and heard and saw the eerie hum and dancing shapes and colours of the aurora borealis.

They developed seasonal rounds to survive the rigours of the mid-continent climate, using the rivers and the lakes as their highways. Evidence of this ancient lifestyle is still visible today. All the reserves around Lake Winnipeg are found at the mouths of rivers. These sites were chosen because, for the most part, they were the places people gathered. In the spring and summer, the river mouths offered excellent fishing and berries in abundance as well as the opportunity to

Spirit Rock near Grand Beach DAWN HUCK AFTER SIGNAGE BY MANITOBA PARKS & NATURAL REGIONS

congregate in large groups to celebrate feasts and spiritual healing ceremonies like the Midewiwin. In the fall and winter, the rivers provided access to the ripened wild rice and ultimately, to the forest interior with its relative protection from the fierce, elemental cold. There, dispersed into their immediate families, the people gathered firewood, hunted caribou, moose and elk and trapped beaver and other fur-bearers. [2]

Nature's omnipresent power informed all the circumstances of their lives and, inevitably, found its expression in every aspect of their culture: its teachings, its legends, its spirituality. In aboriginal eyes, the earth and everything on it is sacred and mystical. Each animal, bird, fish and plant has a specific characteristic or personality, a role in the natural order of things. All beings, humans included, are interdependent, of equal value and worthy of equal respect. Aboriginal societies resolved the dichotomy between the concept of human-animal-plant equality and their need to hunt, fish, trap and gather in several ways.

Unnecessary pain was never to be inflicted on an animal. Nothing was to be killed wantonly. An animal's remains had to be treated with respect and even returned to or buried where the animal was caught. The unused parts of plants were similarly put back in the earth. Each species was seen as having a spirit, which served as the mediator. Humans were given success in the hunt, but unless they meted out just and kind treatment, they would never hunt successfully again.

One cultural difference above all separated the North American and European worlds. Over centuries of contact, this divergence turned the relationship from one of equals into one of exploited and exploiter.

The people of Lake Winnipeg had an egalitarian world view. The obligation to share what one had with others was central to their social organization and economic life and arose from the rigours of their environment, according to ethnologists like Irving Hallowell. It was based on the principle of reciprocity: if I have more than I need today, I share it with you, because I know that you, in turn, will share what you have with me if I am in need tomorrow.

There also were no incentives for individuals to surpass their fellows in the accumulation of material goods. On the contrary, no one was expected to have much more than anyone else. Amassing possessions was considered to be evidence of personal greed, which was abhorred. Similarly, the covetous acquisition of power was also discountenanced. [3]

Aboriginal societies had unique political and cultural systems. Decisions affecting the entire community were normally taken after discussion in a council composed of most male adults. Still, bands did have leaders. They were chosen by ability as well as heredity and exerted their leadership by persuasion and example rather than by decree or force.

Humour and public ridicule were the primary means of social control. However, retributive justice, whereby a wronged family was permitted, even required, to take revenge, was also part of the norm.

But among small, isolated groups of people like those dwelling on Lake Winnipeg's shores, no external sanctions were deemed necessary. Proper behaviour was

The forests of the Canadian Shield on Lake Winnipeg's northern and eastern shores provided all the necessities of life, from birchbark for canoes and lodges, left, to plants and animals the people harvested for food.

enforced through psychological mechanisms. Individuals were expected to use inner control. Illness was thought to be the punishment for misdeeds. [4]

Marriage was arranged by parents and was made formal by public pronouncement. Divorce was effected in a similar fashion. Polygamy was fairly common. Child-rearing was gentle and affectionate.

Aboriginal culture is rich in legend and spirituality, yet the creation stories of Lake Winnipeg's peoples also bear a strong resemblance to the Biblical account of humanity's fall from grace, its ejection from the Garden of Eden and the Great Flood.

According to Cree tradition, creation was overseen by Weese-ke-jak, a supernatural being who is also a trickster. However, no sooner were all the animals and mankind on the earth than the animals rebelled against man. Weese-ke-jak built an immense canoe into which he herded a pair of every kind of creature. The rest were destroyed by a giant flood. The Earth was reborn when Beaver (Amik) brought up a quantity of mud and gave it to Weese-ke-jak.

This was not the first time Beaver had risked his life. Weese-ke-jak had to lasso the Sun (Ane-ne-ke) to put order in its relation to Earth. Amik offered to gnaw the ropes to release the Sun, but as he did, he was badly burned. For his courage, Weese-ke-jak clothed him in a beautiful soft fur coat and gave him a new set of long, sharp teeth, coloured brown to commemorate the scorching. After Beaver brought back Earth, Weese-ke-jak rewarded him again, this time with a broad, flat tail like a trowel with which he could plaster his house. [5]

At the end of the last glaciation, big game hunters entered Manitoba from the south, likely in search of mammoth herds. They travelled lightly, but carried with them a wealth of information about the land and its animals. Around campfires these legends and stories were passed from one generation to another.

In Ojibwe belief, when Ah-ki' (the Earth) was young, it was said to have a family. Nee-ba-gee' sis (the Moon) was called Grandmother and Gee' sis (the Sun) Grandfather. The creator of this family was called Gitchie Manitou (Great Mystery or Creator).

The Earth is Mother, for from her come all living things. Water is her lifeblood. It flows through her, nourishes her and purifies her. The Four Directions are sacred, because each has special physical and spiritual powers and contributes to the Earth's wholeness. When the Earth was young, it was filled with beauty. The Creator sent his singers in the form of birds to the Earth to carry the seeds of life to East, West, North and South. The Creator also gave life to the plant and insect world and placed the animals on the land. All lived in harmony. Gitchie Manitou then took four parts of Mother Earth and blew into them using a Sacred Shell. From the union of the Four Sacred Elements and his breath, man was created. Gitchie Manitou then lowered man to the Earth. This is the origin of the Algonquian name Anishinabe: *ani*, "from whence"; *nishina*, "lowered", and *abe*, the "male of the species". [6]

Man and nature lived in harmony for a long time. But then quarrels, fighting and finally killing arose. Gitchie Manitou sent a great flood to purify the Earth, but man and some of the animals escaped on a large log. The Earth was reborn from a tiny pat of land brought to the surface and given to the last man by Muskrat. Muskrat's exertions cost him his life.

The Assiniboine creation story centres on Lake Winnipeg. To the Assiniboine, or Nakota, the Creator is Inktomi, a human being in form, who made all things in four stages over millions of years. When he had finished, he realized he had no one to rule over his creation. He took clay and formed man and woman. The first people multiplied and became numerous, but as time passed, cruelty and savagery stalked the land. Inktomi selected one man he could trust and told him to build a raft. When it was finished, water came and covered everything, destroying all human and most animal life.

Inktomi visited the man again, gave him a great power and told him to float to a specific area which he called Men-ne-wakan or "Mysterious Water". The legend says Men-ne-wakan is Lake Winnipeg. When the man reached Lake Winnipeg on his raft, Inktomi summoned all the water birds. Selecting seven, he instructed them to dive to the bottom and not return until they had retrieved mud but the birds perished without finding land. Next, Inktomi selected a muskrat, a mink, a beaver and a fisher and instructed them to dive into the lake and not return until they had found mud. They were gone for four days and four nights, and then, like the birds, they floated to the surface dead. But unlike the birds, the animals all had tiny specks of mud on their feet. Inktomi took the mud from the animals' paws and created first, the land, then a partner for the man on the raft and, finally, six more men and six more women. [7]

Archaeological evidence indicates that people entered the province from the south or west sometime between 12,000 and 11,500 years ago. In all probability, their forebears had long been adapted to the tundras and forests that fringed the glacial margin. [8] Much older finds to the northwest and southeast may indicate a human presence in Manitoba during a much earlier period, prior to the last glaciation of 25,000 years ago, but to date no trace of earlier habitation has been found here.

The early Manitobans who ventured into the province following the diminishing ice fields were hunters; their food likely included such species as mammoths, mastodons, caribou, big-horned bison, musk-oxen and American camels and horses, most of which are now extinct. Manitoba's geological deposits have yielded remains of these ancient species, but few have been radiocarbon dated, so their age is uncertain. Still, their locations give some clue. For example, the discovery of caribou skulls on Turtle Mountain imply they were there shortly after the last glaciation.

Lake Agassiz also contained a variety of fish, but no evidence of fishing in those ancient times has yet been found.

The earliest cultural markers of human habitation in Manitoba are finely crafted fluted spear points often called "Clovis", for the town in northeastern New Mexico near where they were first found in association with mammoth bones. Evidence of the 12,000-year-old Clovis culture is extremely rare in Manitoba. Only three or four isolated points have been found, all in western Manitoba, between today's Swan River Valley and the U.S. border. The rest of Manitoba was uninhabitable 11,000 years ago; the entire north lay under an active glacier and all of the area south and east of the Manitoba Escarpment was covered by Lake Agassiz.

Leo Pettipas of the Manitoba Archaeological Society and author of the book *Aboriginal Migrations: A History of Movements in Southern Manitoba*, says that these fluted points and the bones of animals identified with the last glaciation indicate early big game hunting occurred on the uplands west of Lake Agassiz as early as 11,500 years ago. As

MUSEUM OF MAN AND NATURE

This exquisite spear point, crafted of Knife River flint from southern North Dakota and belonging to a mammoth hunter more than 11,000 years ago, was found on the Manitoba Escarpment.

These leaf-shaped-points, right, were used to hunt large mammals between 10,000 and 8,000 years ago. Similar points, often called Agate Basin, have been found from Wyoming east to Lake Superior. In Manitoba, many have been found along the Winnipeg River and north to Manigotagan.

Plains and prairie side-notch points, far right upper and lower, are much more recent innovations. Small and finely-crafted, these tiny points speak of the widespread use of the bow and arrow beginning about 1,500 years ago.

MELANIE FROESE

the land emerged from beneath the melting glacier, the people moved in. The populating of Manitoba would have been a slow, gradual process spanning several millennia and involving many generations.

The warming climate pushed back the boreal forest. About 10,000 years ago, prairie grasses began to cover the lands southwest of Lake Agassiz. The grasslands beckoned bison, already ranging over much of the North American midcontinent, into Manitoba, making it part of what archaeologists call the Great Bison Belt. The animals attracted small groups of hunters. The earliest brought other fluted spear points, known as Folsom and Midland, found throughout the grasslands of Western Canada and the U.S. This culture is called Lindenmeier after the landowner of a famous site in Colorado.

Then, around 9,500 years ago, lanceolate spear points were introduced during what archaeologists call the Plano period. While the earlier fluted point finds are confined to the province's southwest, these lance points have been discovered throughout southern Manitoba, as far east as what is now the Ontario border. Shaped like a slender leaf, the Manitoba varieties include types known as Hell Gap and Agate Basin. The early hunters of Manitoba's southeastern boreal forest used them, often in combination with an atlatl, or spear-thrower, to fell their favoured food sources, woodland caribou and a now-extinct species of moose called *Cervalces*. The atlatl multiplied the throwing power of the human arm 15 times.

By 7,500 years ago, Lake Agassiz had drained, leaving behind only the early, much smaller, versions of

Manitoba's Great Lakes – Winnipeg, Manitoba, Winnipegosis and Dauphin – as its legacy. The rest of its giant basin became a sea of another sort, a sea of grass. This grassland stretched across a seemingly limitless horizon east to the western shore of ancestral Lake Winnipeg and north to the Saskatchewan River. Covering an enormous area compared to today because the lakes were only beginning to form, it offered considerably larger living space for the early bison hunters and their prey. Boreal forest prevailed on the Canadian Shield country east and north of Lake Winnipeg. By 7,000 years ago, says Pettipas, all of Manitoba's major ecological regions were very likely populated.

The Hypsithermal, the warm, dry period between 8,000 and 5,000 years ago, saw the introduction of the side-notched Logan Creek and Oxbow spear points, associated with peoples moving into Manitoba from the south and the east. Manitoba's more northerly lakes and river valleys, with their denser vegetation and higher rainfall, provided respite for animals and humans alike from the hot and arid plains. Just how hot and arid the Hypsithermal was is evidenced by recent geological studies, which indicate that the south basin of Lake Manitoba dried up completely and remained that way for several hundred years. The Hypsithermal also allowed the grasslands to encroach well into the boreal forest.

People who hunted and gathered were present on what is now the east side of Lake Winnipeg as early as 8,000 years ago. Based on the styles of their tools, the first people most likely came from the high plains of central North America soon after the local landscape was habitable. Stone spear points and adzes, as well as ancient implements for heavy wood-chopping and woodworking, demonstrate the forest adaptation of these ancient people. [9]

Five thousand years ago, the Old Copper culture came to the lake's shores, probably through the development of trade routes utilizing the far-flung network of the lake's many rivers. Copper nuggets from as far away as northern Lake Superior provided the raw material for well-made copper tools for hunting, wood and hide working and fishing. The presence of bone and antler implements and ornamental objects suggest that this culture was quite diversified. At Manigotagan Lake near Bissett, an ancient workshop has been excavated containing finished tools and "trim bits", scraps of waste material. These ancient artisans also practised an early form of blacksmithing, occasionally heating the metal in a fire to prevent it from becoming brittle during the manufacturing process.

Then, about 2,500 years ago, the climate became cooler and wetter. These changes as well as the effects of isostatic rebound described in Chapter One changed the land around the great lake. Lake Winnipeg, along with its eastern forests and western grasslands, gradually assumed their present shapes and conditions.

Though there is no question these early peoples were the ancestors of today's native North Americans, it is all but impossible to directly relate them to modern-day First Nations. But movements in the past 2,000 years are easier to track. During that period, Manitoba has been home to at least five indigenous language groups. About 2,000 BP, the first people to whom a known language can be ascribed arrived in the Lake Winnipeg area. They came from the east and gradually extended their lands to cover the entire Lake Winnipeg region north to Hudson Bay. It has been suggested that they spoke an early form of Cree, an Algonquian language that is related to many others across Canada.

MELANIE FROESE

The early Cree culture had a range of artifacts that included toggle-headed harpoons, stemmed and notched spear and arrow points, awls, barbs, chisels and beads made of hammered copper, and hafted beaver incisor gouges. These tools indicate that the people were at home in a range of environments from the inland seas of Hudson Bay to the myriad rivers and lakes of the Canadian Shield.

The knives or gouges made from beaver incisors make it likely that the Cree were adept at building birchbark canoes and this technology, along with their fired earthenware pottery, equipped them to expand throughout the eastern half of Manitoba.

Cree pottery, tempered before firing with bits of granite and shell, changed in form and shape through the centuries. Archaeologists have identified three variants, named after the present-day communities where they were first located – Laurel and Blackduck (from Minnesota), and Selkirk (from Manitoba). All had unique designs made by pressing variously shaped objects into the soft clay before firing. Found from the Red River north to Grand Rapids and beyond, the distinctive pottery allowed the people to process and store food such as wild rice, a major vegetable source in the forests west of Lake Superior.

Cree language and customs were apparently adopted by the resident populations the Cree encountered as they occupied the lands around Lake

MANIGOTAGAN RIVER

Manigotagan is Cree for "bad throat". In 1915, geologist Joseph Burr Tyrrell noted the river's full Cree name was Manigotagan Sipi, meaning "Bad-Throat River". The 1957 edition of *Manitoba Pageant* listed the name as Manigottgan, a name that apparently came from the call of a moose that had a peculiar sound in its throat. The Canadian Permanent Committee on Geographic Names (1975) added to the origin stating that at Wood Falls, upstream, the river makes a peculiar gurgling sound like a person clearing one's throat. [10]

Winnipeg. When Europeans began arriving in the early 18th century, the Cree were still the predominant nation occupying the lake region.

Alexander Henry the Elder gave this description of the dress and appearance of the Cree he encountered at what today is Fort Alexander, near the mouth of the Winnipeg River in 1776:

> *Every man and boy had his bow strung and in his hand, and his arrow ready, to attack in case of need. Their heads were shaved, or the hair plucked out, all over, except a spot on the crown ... The women wear their hair of a great length ... collecting the hair of each side into a roll, which is fashioned above the ear ... Their clothing is of leather or dressed skins of the wild ox [bison] and the elk ... Girls of an early age wear their dresses shorter than those more advanced ... The stockings are of leather, made in the fashion of leggings ... The wrists are adorned with bracelets of copper or brass ...* [11]

A Cree legend explains the presence of gold in the Rice Lake area near Lake Winnipeg's eastern shore.

> *Long ago, a fair-skinned blond young man visited the Cree on the east side of Lake Winnipeg. The Cree believed him to be a messenger of Manitou. He brought with him good hunting and the Cree adopted him and named him Pigowi Manitou. A beautiful young woman called Etomami lived in the village and had many suitors, including Manigotagan, but she was in love with Pigowi Manitou. After a time, Etomami and Pigowi Manitou were married and travelled to the interior to gather wild rice. Manigotagan was jealous and followed the couple to Rice Lake. Here he struck Pigowi Manitou down. The*

spot where the blond head fell was marked by threads of yellow running through the rock. [12]

Between 600 and 700 years ago, another group of people whom archaeologists call the Oneota established what may have been Manitoba's first agricultural community on the east bank of the Red River at the Kenosewun site in present-day Lockport, about 15 kilometres north of Winnipeg. These early farmers were probably Siouan-speakers from the south. They cultivated corn and had a unique pottery tradition whose predominant motifs were chevrons or stylized representations of the peregrine falcon, especially its wings and tail. The peregrine motifs appear on numerous Oneota artifacts, including pots. The bird of prey symbol denotes aggression and was designed, perhaps, to intimidate competitors. However, all indications are Manitoba's early farming people lived peacefully with their neighbours. [13]

Archaeological excavations at the Kenosewun site between 1984 and 1988 recovered tools such as wooden-

The Oneota, early farmers from the south, were tilling the alluvial soil along the Red River at Kenosewun, just above the Lockport rapids, nearly 700 years ago.

COURTESY OF MANITOBA HISTORIC RESOURCES

The land the Oneota cultivated lies lush and green in the sunshine above the Lockport dam.   DENNIS FAST

handled hoes made from the scapulae or shoulder-blades of bison, bell-shaped storage pits, grinding mortars and charred corn kernels.

Kenosewun's location was no accident. People had been gathering at the Red River's rapids for millennia to spear fish during the spring spawning season. For the Oneota farmers, the river's propensity to spring flooding added another inducement – an annual infusion of nutrient-rich soil for their crops.

The gardens were probably organized and controlled by family groups and tended by the women of the community. The land was cleared with axes, and wooden digging sticks were likely used to break up the soil. Although no evidence has been found, it is also believed that beans, squash and perhaps even sunflowers were grown, as well as corn, for these were the crops that thrived to the south, along the Mississippi and Missouri Rivers.

The pottery found at the Kenosewun site is decorated with chevrons and stylized depictions of the peregrine falcon.

Harvesting involved the entire community. Whole ears were cut, husked in the field and carried to the main camp for processing. There, the ears, alone or braided together in strings, were placed on drying racks. Once dry, the cobs were stored directly or were shucked and the kernels winnowed and then stored. After the next year's supply of seed was secured, the surplus kernels were boiled alone or with other vegetables or, more commonly, were ground into meal and then boiled. The dried vegetables were kept in underground pits lined with dried grasses, bark or tanned hides to keep the corn from spoiling. [14]

This agricultural period lasted about a century. Then, about 600 years ago, most of North America entered what

has been called the Little Ice Age. Manitoba summers became much shorter and cooler, agriculture was abandoned and the farming people moved on.

Farming did not reappear in Manitoba for another 400 years, when the Odawa (or "Ottawa", as Europeans called them), an Algonquian people related to the Ojibwe, moved into the Lake Winnipeg region around 1808, accompanying fur traders from the Great Lakes. They brought their farming customs with them and established an agricultural community at Netley Creek. The thermal effects of the lake and its surrounding marshes ensured a longer frost-free period than in the Red River Valley to the south. Also, the soils of the Red River delta were quick producers of corn. However, the Odawa abandoned the site by 1812; their crops were being pilfered and pillaged by their neighbours, allegedly at the instigation of the North West Company, which wanted to keep people dependent on the fur trade.

The Odawa were preceded in the Lake Winnipeg region by the Nakota, a Siouan-speaking people. They moved north from the headwaters of the Mississippi River in north-central Minnesota about 500 years ago. Known as *Assiniboin* in the Algonquian language, they had broken away from their parent population of Yanktonai Dakota due to a social dispute or feud. A thousand lodges detached themselves and relocated to Lake of the Woods. However, hostilities persisted with the Yanktonai Dakota, and the Nakota moved deeper into Cree territory. At Nebosebe (Netley Creek), the Cree and the Nakota established a confederacy.

Part of the Nakota territory included the lower Lake Winnipeg area. When Pierre Gaultier de Varennes, Sieur de La Vérendrye, arrived on the lower Winnipeg River in the mid-1730s with his crews of Ojibwe and French voyageurs, he observed that *Cris ou Christinaux* (Cree) inhabited the right bank of the Winnipeg River and *Assiniboils et les Cioux* (Assiniboine and Sioux) its left.

"Sioux" is the contraction of *Nadowessioux*, a French corruption of the Algonquian word *Nadowesiw*, meaning "snake" or "adder", and by metaphor, "enemy". Assiniboine, actually *Assini poet* or *Ussini pwat*, is Algonquian for "Stone Sioux", which has been shortened in Western Canada to "Stoney".

According to La Vérendrye, the Winnipeg River marked the boundary between the Nakota on the south and the Cree to the north, but ethnologist A. Irving Hallowell has noted some Nakota may, at one point, have lived along the east side of Lake Winnipeg as far north as The Narrows.

The Nakota's time in southeastern Manitoba came to an abrupt end with the smallpox epidemic of 1781-82, when the local population was decimated and the nation became concentrated in territories farther to the west.

The last major cultural group to arrive in the Lake Winnipeg region was the Ojibwe, also an Algonquian people. According to the old stories, a large group of Ojibwe departed their homeland around Michilimackinac to seek the Land of Abundance, eventually arriving on the shores of the Atlantic Ocean. About 700 BP, with guidance from visions and dreams, the Ojibwe began a homeward trek, referred to as the Chibimoodaywin. [15]

They gradually moved up the St. Lawrence River and through the Lower Great Lakes into their original homeland in the Sault Ste Marie-Mackinac Straits area. The French, who found them living there in the 17th century, called them *Saulteurs* (people of the sault or rapids), which the English converted into *Saulteaux*.

Charles A. Bishop, in his book, *The Northern Ojibwa and the Fur Trade*, says that the Ojibwe originally lived in a confined region near the upper Great Lakes. Competition with the HBC and depletion of the fur resource around Lake Superior drew them west in concert with the French traders.

By the 1770s, all the northern First Nations were being supplied with quantities of goods at the expense of the competing traders. The well-equipped Ojibwe, who traded mainly with the French and later with the North West Company, were able to penetrate deep into territory formerly inhabited by the Cree. Although skirmishes with the Cree were frequent in newly disputed fur regions, intermarriages and friendships developed, resulting in a fusion of the two cultures. The Cree name for Ojibwe is *Nahkawiyiniw*, which the Europeans turned into "Nakawewuk". The Ojibwe call the Cree *Mushkego*.

Ojibwe society was organized into clans named after and reflecting the personalities and characteristics of many animals. Aj-ji-jawk and Mahng (crane and loon) were given the power of chieftainship. Between them stood the Gi-goon (fish) clan, the intellectuals or star gazers. The Mu-kwa (bear) were the guardians and healers. The Wa-bi-zha-shi (marten) were the warriors. The Wa-wa-shesh-she (deer) were the pacifists and finally, the Be-nays (birds) were the spiritual leaders. Be-nays were said to have the characteristics of Mi-gi-zi, the eagle, the symbol of their clan, in that they pursued the higher elevations of the mind just as the eagle pursued the higher elevations of the sky. Intermarriage between persons of the same clan was strictly forbidden.

COURTESY OF THE NIELSEN FAMILY

This fine collection of artifacts, all found at the mouth of the Bradbury River, bears witness to the intensive use of the east shore of Lake Winnipeg.

The clan system was an important part of the Midewiwin, practised on Black Island and several other sites around Lake Winnipeg to this day. The Midewiwin, the Grand Medicine Society or "feast of long life", is the most important ceremony of Ojibwe culture. Midewiwin members practise a code of ethics promoting a long and healthy life through commitment to the values of wisdom, love, respect, courage, honesty, humility and truth. The membership provide spiritual, physical and emotional healing to all who come to seek their help. Increased knowledge of natural medicines and the power to heal are recognized by the member's passage through four to eight stages or "degrees". Advancement from one degree to another involves intensive instruction, quests for spiritual knowledge and initiation rites. The details of these rituals were often recorded in picture form on birchbark scrolls. [16]

Black Island is named after a Mide priest called Kagi'webit (or Kakeivepit), whose English name was David Black. The island's Ojibwe name is Kapipikwewi'k, after the peculiar reverberations or thumping sounds heard near Drumming Point on its eastern extremity caused by the action of the waves on the rocks. The island is just one of numerous Midewiwin sites on the lake. Others are at East Doghead Point at The Narrows and the Pigeon, Berens and Hollow Water Rivers, also on the east side, and at Jackhead River on the west side. Oral tradition speaks of several famous Midewiwin priests or headmen who performed miraculous acts. One, Yellow Legs, an early 19th-century priest, was once seen walking on the water over to Jackhead Island. He was brought back to the mainland by Memengweci'wak, semi-human creatures who live in the rocks and travel in stone canoes. Another legend told of Yellow Legs killing a golden eagle simply by holding a spear point in his hand. [17]

A jack pine stands sentinel north of Black Island. DENNIS FAST

According to one account, the Black Island Midewiwin was held annually in the early summer months and lasted eight days, from sunrise to sunset. The lodge, covered with birchbark, was 25 metres long and four metres wide. Close by was a smaller roofless enclosure containing a big square pillar and a large boulder. This was the place of honour where the head medicine man, dressed in buckskin, sat. On the top of the square pillar was a carved kingfisher. The bird carving revolved, following the sun's path from east to west.

A wide variety of herbs as well as animal pelts and a row of stones placed from smallest to largest were used as medicines and healing tools. At the time appointed to begin, the servants of the medicine men would stand in a circle around the head man. One by one, the sick were brought in to select his or her preferred medicine man and give him an offering. One of the servants had a special drum. The head medicine man would sing a drum song, and every time he changed from one song to another, the servant would strike the drum four times. This ritual was repeated each time a new patient arrived. When the ceremonies were over, the medicine men and the cured would begin a dance in the enclosure, moving to the birchbark lodge. The dance would last all night. [18]

Jens and Barbara Nielsen have never forgotten their accidental discovery of the Midewiwin site on Black Island several years ago. They had anchored their boat in one of the coves of the island and come ashore in their dinghy near Drumming Point. They found a grass clearing with mounds and hollows. Jens Nielsen picks up the story: "There was a little structure, about two metres in diameter, made of birch boughs to which ribbons and pieces of cloth had been tied. In another corner there were the poles from a teepee. And then we knew where we were. We picked a few blueberries and then we left because we knew this was not where we should be ... I am uncomfortable in churches where I don't belong."

"The ribbons are to remember their dead ones," says Barbara Nielsen. "The ribbons were mostly fairly new although some were older, and they were all placed along the east, towards the rising sun." The Nielsens learned later the clearing had been used for ceremonies "for centuries". Both say the moment they set foot in the clearing they were instantly overcome with the same feeling of reverence and awe people have upon entering a cathedral. "We were very quiet. We did not want to disturb. We knew we shouldn't be there, shouldn't intrude," Barbara Nielsen explains. "It was so peaceful, the same as if you step into a church." [19]

The Ojibwe have many legends about Lake Winnipeg. One, Nanabush Flies with the Geese, tells why the lake is so turbid or muddy.

Nanabush at last came to a land that was very different from what he had been accustomed to. Its people

DENNIS FAST

WANIPIGOW RIVER

Wanipigow Sipi means "Hole River". The name reflects a natural phenomenon: in a strong north wind, the water level at the south of Lake Winnipeg drops, speeding the flow at the river mouth where it passes through a narrow rock gate. A big whirlpool is created on the left side of the river. The early people called it "the river with a hole" or hole river. Over time, this became "Hole" or "Hollow" Water, the name of the nearby reserve. [20]

Each August the Anishinabe from Hollow Water gather on a lovely crescent bay on Black Island's west shore, for a week of cultural renewal and blueberry picking.

had not yet given it a name. The land was one mighty prairie, Mishkodae, without hills or forests, inhabited by animals and birds he had never seen. For all its endlessness and changelessness, the plain was bountiful and its animals, rich in fat and flesh, were beyond counting.

The people were harvesting wild rice for the coming winter when large flocks of geese descended upon this unnamed lake to feed and rest for a while before resuming their migration. Learning that they were bound for the land of perpetual summer to escape the winter, Nanabush received permission to accompany the geese. In order to fly the chief of all the geese gave Nanabush a pair of wings, a rudder and then feathered him. The main rule in flight is not to look down, warned the chief goose before takeoff.

When the flock lifted into the sky, likewise did Nanabush, as if he had been doing so all his life.

There was gloom in the Anishinaubae lodges and villages the entire winter. The people longed for the return of Nanabush. Never had they looked for the coming of spring more anxiously than they now did. Long before the geese were due to arrive, crowds of Anishinaubaeg gathered on the shores of the lake to welcome Nanabush and celebrate his return with a festival.

Nanabush was in the first flock that appeared in the southern sky and the people, recognizing him, set up a mighty cheer of welcome. When he heard the acclaim, Nanabush was moved by the affection of his brothers and sisters and he looked down.

At that moment he fell to earth, legs and arms flailing, feathers fluttering in the air as they were stripped from his wings and rudder. Nanabush plunged into the shallow waters of the lake and was imbedded in the mud. After rescuing him, the Anishinaubaeg cleansed him of the

muck, but in washing Nanabush, the waters of the lake were forever begrimed. From that day the Anishinaubaeg called it Weenipeeegosheeng, the murky-watered lake, or Winnipeg. [21]

The 19th-century geologist, Henry Youle Hind, was the first European to describe the role Lake Winnipeg's limestone cliffs played in aboriginal legends.

There are many places on Lake Winnipeg and Manitobah which the Indians who hunt and live on the shores of those inland seas dare not visit. There is scarcely a cave or headland which has not some legend attached to it, familiar to all the wanderers on these coasts. On the west side of Lake Winnipeg, in the long, dark and gloomy chambers formed by fissures in the limestone, bad spirits are supposed to dwell, according to the belief of the Indians who hunt on the coast ... Near Limestone Cave Point, on Lake Winnipeg, are several of these supposed fairy dwellings. When an Indian approaches them in his canoe, he either lays an offering on the beach or gives them as wide a berth as possible. [22]

Another legend recounted by Hind involves Lake Winnipeg sturgeon:

Sturgeon are also numerous, and, according to the belief of the ... natives who fish here [Big Grindstone Point] during the winter, the deep part of the lake is their great place of resort at that period of the year, where they lie with Mis-ke-na, "the chief of the fishes", in the southern portion of Lake Winnipeg. [23]

44

An illustration of how animals and the natural world molded aboriginal belief can be found in the legend of the thunderbird, told by the Ojibwe of Berens River.

When there was a storm on the lake, the people didn't think of black clouds and lightning bolts, the rumble of thunder and the sudden, white water. They imagined the thunderbird, whose eyes shot out the flashes of lightning and whose giant black wings were the billowing, threatening thunder heads. Slow, rolling thunder signalled the presence of old thunderbirds. The sharp claps were made by the wings of the younger ones. [24]

Waves didn't make the water roil. Its agitation was caused by the Great Lynx (*Misipisiw* in Cree or Missipisi in Ojibwe) or the Sea Serpent or Great Snake (*Misikinipik* in Cree or *Missikinepik* in Ojibwe.) The Great Lynx was the master of all underwater creatures in lakes or rivers, including snakes. The Great Snake was thought inimical to human beings. [25] Every storm was considered a battle between good and evil. The thunderbird represented good and defended humankind against the beast in the water. A revered being, almost a deity, the thunderbird was able to take on human form at will. James Redsky gives this account of what the mythic bird meant to his people:

> To the Ojibweys, the thunderbird is one of the most powerful spirits. These winged creatures obtained their power from Manitou to look after everything in the world. Their power is formidable. When a thunderstorm is coming up you cannot see anything moving ... They [the animals] hide in the presence of the thunderbirds; even the fish stay still until the thunderbird goes by.
>
> The thunderbirds reside at sacred places upon the earth ... Great big rocks and boulders are piled up on each other, making a round place. My family used to live about four miles from one place and at night we could see the red lightning flashing around the nest.
>
> In the moon of berries, when the young thunderbirds go by, they cause destruction because they don't know any better. They are like children ... When they go by in August and September, they are pretty rough on the Ojibweys. They knock down trees with lightning from their beaks. Houses are struck and smashed also. The older thunderbirds try to correct these foolish young birds, but they do not learn because they are so young ...
>
> We saw a thunderbird a few summers ago. A huge bird it was ... Many of the people at Shoal Lake saw it go by. It didn't flap its wings, not even once. It was white on the underside and black on the top. A big, big bird. There were some great big thunder clouds making up a storm and out of one of the clouds came this great bird. [26]

COURTESY OF MANITOBA HISTORIC RESOURCES

Three of the nine thunderbird nests found in Manitoba to date are on the Wanipigow River that runs into Lake Winnipeg near Manigotagan. Pottery and other objects unearthed in one have been radiocarbon dated at between 2200 and 1600 years old. The purpose of the thunderbird nest persisted into very recent times in aboriginal culture. The nests were places where boys, and sometimes girls, went at puberty to observe a rite marking their passage into adulthood. There they would neither eat nor drink until they were visited by a spirit being, the spirit of the animal who would be their guardian for life. Eric Robinson says certain islands on Lake Winnipeg also served as sites for "vision quests".

Archaeologist Leigh Syms has seen the thunderbird nests and admits they cast a supernatural aura. "It's typically a huge pile of very large rocks with a depression in the centre," says

Thunderbird nests, which served as vision quest and rite of passage sites for the Ojibwe, have been found in a number of places on the east side of Lake Winnipeg and, less frequently, in the Manitoba Interlake.

the curator of archaeology at the Manitoba Museum of Man and Nature. "They [the rocks] are not natural deposits, at least, not in the form they are now. Whether humans did them, or spiritual things did them, we really don't know." [27]

However, recent aboriginal accounts provide a much more mundane explanation for the thunderbird nests. Chief George Barker has written that they were storage depots for the wild rice harvest. [28]

The pipe was another sanctified object, made out of the sacred *o pwa gun ah sin* (pipestone). Its stem was taken from *o pwa gun a tig* (sumac) and in it was smoked red willow, tobacco, sweetgrass or sage. A pipe would be turned in the four directions of the earth and then passed on. It carried thoughts and prayers to the Creator and sealed peace among all bands, tribes and nations. Pipestone is found at two locations on Lake Winnipeg, the mouth of the Manigotagan River on the east side and the Roche Rouge near the mouth of the Jackhead River on the west. Artisans from the Black River community used saws to extract the gray pipestone from the Manigotagan deposit. Alexander Henry the Elder reported in his journal that the Roche Rouge was "entirely composed of a *pierre a calumet*, or stone, used by the Indians for making tobacco-pipe bowls. It is of a light red colour, interspersed with veins of brown, and yields very readily to the knife". [29]

Even more mystical were the practices of the shaking tent. Ethnologist A. Irving Hallowell witnessed a shaking tent ceremony at Little Grand Rapids in 1942 and came away believing he had observed an ethereal and unearthly event.

In Thunderbird, *one of several variations on the theme, Jackson Beardy conveys the power of these spirits, who are capable of death and destruction as well as an awesome spectacle in the skies.* JACKSON BEARDY / BY PERMISSION OF PAULA BEARDY / COURTESY OF THE GOVERNMENT OF MANITOBA ART COLLECTION

The shaking tent is constructed of a barrel-like framework of poles about two metres high covered with birchbark, skins or canvas. The conjuror, or shaman, enters the tent after dark and invokes his *pawaganak*, or guardian spirits. When they arrive, the structure becomes agitated and sways from side to side. It is at this point that interspecies communication, communication between the living and the dead and between those present and away, can take place. The voices of the various spirits, people and animals can clearly be heard by those outside the tent.

The Ojibwe say winds are responsible for the shaking; the lodge is never shaken by human hands. Conjurors were often bound with rope before entering and were freed by the spirits.

Ceremony and spirituality accompanied all of life's daily tasks. Manomin or wild rice was of vital importance to all the inhabitants of the eastern lake region, humans as well as birds and mammals. A Hollow Water First Nation elder gives this account of the traditions surrounding the wild rice harvest and other food-gathering activities:

> *We didn't start rice picking right away. What the Elders did was first have a big feast and a couple of Elders would ask the Creator for thanks that they made it and that they would have rice. It was never forgotten that the ceremony would be done first before any harvest. The ceremony was used before everything – harvesting, trapping, fishing, blueberry-picking.* [30]

One of the most distinctive characteristics of Woodland cultures is the creation of rock paintings or pictographs. Research among the Lake Winnipeg Saulteaux has revealed much about the use of these paintings by shamans. One

resident of the Bloodvein Reserve on the eastern shore of Lake Winnipeg said the paintings served as hunting medicine.

"A person would dream of the animal that he intended to hunt and if the dream were real and not just made up, the person would get power from the animal."

Another said the paintings were used to cure illness. "You just sort of talk to it. You ask that 'graving to give you the power to heal this. It's said it takes quite a time before this happens and you've got to be very sure to believe this." [31]

Most paintings are representations of animals, though the motifs also include men, man-made objects, mythological figures and abstract symbols. Among the animals, moose were most common around Lake Winnipeg. The Bloodvein River Moose, near the shore of Lake Winnipeg, is one of the province's most famous pictographs. It has been scarred by gunfire because hitting it was believed to bring luck for the hunt. Another pictograph, located on the

Practices and Customs of Lake Winnipeg Ojibwe

The customs and practices of the Lake Winnipeg Ojibwe, from the gathering of wild rice to the method of diapering babies, live on to this day in the stories of the elders. Wild rice was:

Wild rice drying

"...spreade and dried in the sun. Then it was cooked in a large open container over an open fire. It was heated and stirred until kernels were brown. After this part was completed, they 'danced' on the rice. They dug a hole in the ground and a new hide was spread in it. The dancers wore moccasins and tied them around their ankles so chaff wouldn't go up their legs. After dancing, rice was winnowed. It was put in pans and tossed in the air. The chaff that was loosened during the dancing blow away in the air. The dark brown or black grains of rice were left." [32]

Babies were diapered with moss.

"There was not such a thing as Pampers. All that was used was moss. Moss was put between two blankets. That was how they used to make napkins a long time ago. People used to find that amazing because the baby would never get wet. During the fall, the old ladies (midwives) would go in the bush and get this moss. They knew exactly who was going to have a baby and how many. They would hang up the moss in the muskeg and pick it up when they needed it." [33]

The blueberry picking season was always launched with a feast.

"They would cook white rice, bread, biscuits and other food. They would invite each other, when you were invited to the ceremony, you took your own plate that you used for eating. A lot of people went to this ceremony because many went picking berries long ago. The Indians believed that by performing this ceremony that there would be lots of berries to pick. And strange enough this was true." [34]

Moose hunting occurred on the shore of Lake Winnipeg.

"When they killed a moose, everybody got his share. The hide was kept so it could get tanned. The person who killed the moose got the same amount as all the other people ... The meat was cut thin, then it was smoked until it went dry. Next they ... pounded it with a mallet. The weapon used to kill a moose was a muzzle loader ... the meat was shared among the co-operative, not like today people have to pay for some meat." [35]

Weather was forecast through the actions of animals.

"Some animals also provided us with information for long-range forecasting. In the fall, if deer or moose scraped the trees up high with their horns that meant lots of snow, but if the scrapes were low there would be very little. If the muskrats didn't make houses, or if they made very small houses, we knew there would be plenty of snow. If their houses were big a cold winter with little snow was a certainty." [36]

Rabbitskin robe

Specific clothing was used on the traplines.

"Our outer garments, coats, mitts and leggings were made of smoked moose hide. The mitts had long cuffs to keep out the snow. The leggings were connected to our moccasins, and at the top were leather strips which were tied to a belt worn around the waist. Every night these garments had to be hung near the fire to keep them dry, smoky and soft. Making the sleeping robes and garments required a great deal of labour, but they were wonderfully warm. To prepare the skins for weaving, the rabbits were skewered on sticks and skinned in long spirals. Each rabbit would provide a one-inch strip, twelve feet long. The strips were hung to dry and soften in the wind and then plaited and sewn ... It took 80 skins to make either a coat or a pair of pants. Small robes were made from 150 to 180 skins, and for a fullsize 90-inch by 90-inch robe we used about 225 skins." [37]

lake opposite Black Island, was of two snakes facing each other. Lake erosion destroyed it around the turn of the century. A whole series of figures can be found on the Rice River, upstream from the lake.

Brother Frederick Leach, OMI, spent 60 years at the Berens River and Bloodvein reserves beginning in 1918. He had occasion to use aboriginal medicine and praised it. When he cut his foot with an axe, a friend applied gum blisters from the outer bark of the balsam tree. They stopped the bleeding and prevented infection. On a long trip one spring, Brother Leach became snowblind, a painful affliction. His companion, William Moose, boiled willow twigs, strained the liquid and put a drop or two in each eye. While the drops smarted at first, soon both the pain and the blindness were gone. Leach also reported that ripe puff balls stopped nosebleeds, tea made from mountain ash roots relieved rheumatism and *wike* or *wikanse* (wild ginger) was akin to aspirin, curing headaches, sore throats and chest colds. [38]

John Fleming, a member of Henry Youle Hind's expedition of 1857 and 1858, gives an account of Ojibwe fishing practices. At Dauphin River, he observed "Indians at the rapids scooping large numbers of excellent white-fish from the eddies". Later on, he writes:

> *The Indians were catching very fine white-fish in large quantites at this point with little trouble. The river seemed to be crowded with them. At various places along the brink of the stream, enclosures of stones were constructed, beside which an Indian stood with a large scoop-net attached to a pole, filling the stone enclosure from time to time as he scooped them from the eddies in his vicinity ... The Indians were curing the fish without salt, by splitting them very thin and drying them in the sun ...*

The Ojibwe also employed wooden weirs. Fleming saw one in the Pike (Jackfish) River. It was a fence of poles reaching from one bank to the other, sloping in the direction of the current.

Near the riverbank on one side, there was an opening that allowed the fish to pass through into a rectangular box with a grated bottom sloping upwards, leaving the fish exposed to the air. Continued Fleming:

> *The fish very seldom entered this pound in daylight, but during the night they poured in in great numbers. In order to secure all that come into the trap ... an Indian sits beside it all night with a wooden mallet in his hand, with which he strikes the larger fish on the head to prevent them jumping out. He is kept busily employed pitching them out on the bank, and in the morning there is a large heap for the women to clean and cut up.* [39]

Sometime in the last quarter of the 18th century, (the exact date is not known), the Lake Winnipeg people formed an alliance to repel a fierce invasion from the south. A large group of Sisseton Dakota swept north from Minnesota and, by force of arms, expelled the Penaymootang (Partridge Crop) Saulteaux from what is now known as the central Interlake region. The survivors, under their leader Metikoo-gewaum, or "Wooden Tent", sought refuge at what is now Berens River on the lake's eastern shore.

Metikoo-gewaum sent messengers to every Saulteaux, Ojibwe and Cree camp on both sides of all Manitoba's great lakes. It took three years to gather the allied forces and a campaign was launched in the early autumn, when saskatoons and other berries were available to supplement the supplies of pemmican. Metikoo-gewaum and his warriors set forth in a large fleet of war canoes from Berens River to Reindeer Island on Lake Winnipeg.

The chief divided his army into two parties. One he sent to Nndookunik-unow-wesepee, now known as Warpath River on Lake Winnipeg's west side. The other went to Saskatchewanoos, or Little Saskatchewan River, now known as the Dauphin River. This strategy hemmed in the Sissetons and after a series of battles on the Warpath, Dauphin and Fisher Rivers and Lake St. Martin, the Sissetons were defeated and driven from the region. [40]

Wild rice, nearly ready for harvest, grows in the shallows along the aptly-named Rice River.

American historian Wilcomb Washburn charts four eras in postcontact aboriginal North American experience. [41] The first was a lengthy period of equality with European newcomers. In the initial years of contact and the early fur trade, Europeans were totally dependent upon North Americans for both geographical and commercial expertise. Their knowledge of the continent's waterways made the penetration of the vast interior possible, and their age-old trading networks served as highways for the rich bounty of furs that Europeans coveted.

The second period began when aboriginal equality was challenged and ended when it was destroyed. Using the North Americans' growing dependence on European tools, weapons and household goods and the devastating toll disease took on North American populations, white traders began by indebting the aboriginal people, compelling them to continue bringing in furs. Finally, Europeans took over the fur extraction themselves, reducing North Americans

to a secondary role as labourers and provisioners of food for the growing number of European trading expeditions. Traditional resource bases were quickly strained to near exhaustion.

DENNIS FAST

Meanwhile, smallpox epidemics had decimated native North American communities on many occasions, beginning with the great pandemic of 1520 on North America's east coast and continuing through the eras of Cartier and La Vérendrye to the terrible devastation of the plagues of 1781, 1837 and 1876. The arrival of the horse on the northern plains around the middle of the 18th century was a mixed blessing. Though it vastly increased the mobility of the plains nations and prompted a flowering of plains culture, it also signalled the beginning of the end of traditional ways and hastened the spread of disease.

In the third era, starting in the mid-19th century and running almost to the present, Washburn says, North Americans "existed on a plane of inequality", their destinies largely shaped by whites. The pressure on the fur population, the decimation of the sturgeon and most other fisheries on Lake Winnipeg by industrial fishing practices and the virtual disappearance of the bison, left the original peoples of Lake Winnipeg not only physically destitute and near starvation, but spiritually and culturally destabilized as well.

On July 12, 1890, Manitoba Lieutenant Governor John Christian Schultz attended an Indian Council at Treaty

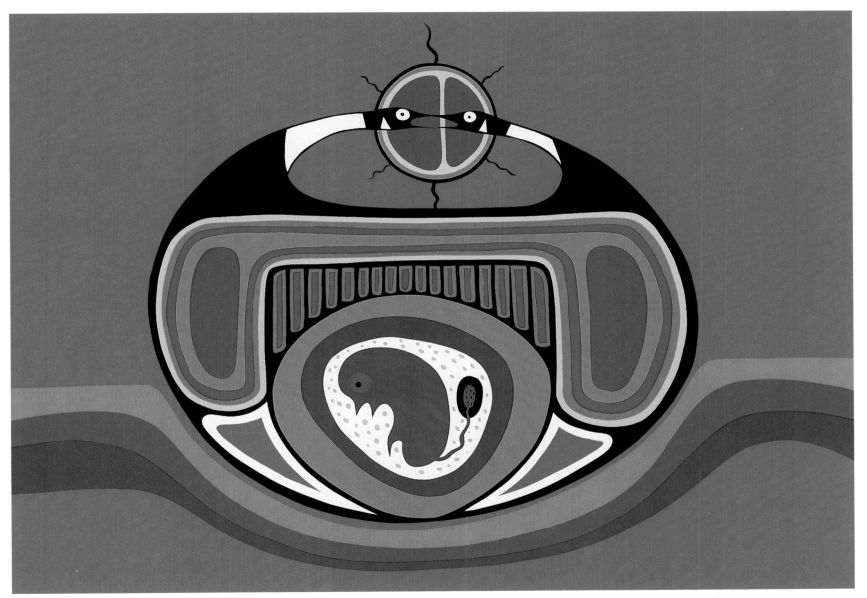

Rebirth *(1976) is a Jackson Beardy classic, symbolizing the universality of life and its link between the material and spiritual worlds.*

JACKSON BEARDY / BY PERMISSION OF PAULA BEARDY / COURTESY OF THE GOVERNMENT OF MANITOBA ART COLLECTION

Rock, Berens River. The chief greeted him with "expressions of welcome" and then delivered this plea:

> We are glad to see you here this day as our people are in much trouble. I must tell you that they have, like myself, lived here from childhood ... We have always had plenty of fish to eat ... In the winter, we used to find a good deal of game in the woods ... Now all this has changed. Fires have run through the woods and game is very scarce. But while we had rice and fish we could get along; but now our fish is going too. There are here tonight Indians from the Poplar River, Black River and other rivers in the same treaty with us and they complain the same as us. We still go down to

Both privation and stoicism are evident in this photo of Saulteaux chief Wekemouskunk and his son taken on Lake Winnipeg in 1888.

J. B. TYRRELL / NATIONAL ARCHIVES OF CANADA / PA–50856

> set our nets but the larger nets outside the river have caught so many fish that little remains for us and sometimes our children cry for food. Why does the white man with his large nets and miles of nets, and his steamboats to tow his other boats, not go out north into the deep waters

> of the lake where we cannot go with our small boats and nets, and catch fish there? Why does he come to spread his nets just at our feet and take away the food from our children's mouths? ... We have complained and complained and still the big fishers comes and we see only starvation for our children ...

Schultz told the people he had "no power of any kind to help you in this matter". He also accused them of being the authors of their own misfortune by catching fish during the spawning season, destroying the whitefish. However, Schultz did turn the chief's complaints over to Interior Minister Edgar Dewdney. [42]

By the end of the 19th century, North Americans found themselves totally dependent, assigned to reserves and under the control of the federal Indian Affairs Department. Hayter Reed, Indian Commissioner from 1888 to 1897, was a firm assimilationist. He launched a plan to turn aboriginal people into self-sufficient subsistence (peasant) farmers. The project was doomed from the start. Local white farmers raised an uproar, fearing unfair competition from government-subsidized operations. Meanwhile, Reed insisted that the prospective farmers begin their agricultural experience as Europeans had centuries before, with homemade hand tools, the hoe, rake, cradle, sickle, flail and hand mill.

As soon as an aboriginal farmer had any success, he naturally bought the most modern farming technology available to improve and increase his output. But whenever Reed heard about it, he had the equipment confiscated. This was the same Reed who was fond of appearing at the governor general's balls at Rideau Hall in full chief's regalia. [43]

Today, after nearly a century of dependence and deprivation, aboriginal North Americans have entered Wilcomb

Washburn's fourth era, one of cultural and political resurgence. Eric Robinson, the provincial cabinet minister, is only the latest example of aboriginal renaissance in Manitoba, often described as Canada's aboriginal province because it has the highest percentage of native Canadian citizens.

Throughout the concluding decade of the 20th century, Manitobans have played lead roles in building aboriginal awareness in Canada. And those Manitobans have all come from communities on or near Lake Winnipeg.

Their interventions are now etched in the national consciousness. Elijah Harper, an Oji-Cree chief and the first aboriginal cabinet minister in Canadian history, sat in his place in the Manitoba Legislature in June 1990 clutching an eagle feather and

said "No" to the Meech Lake Constitutional Accord because it failed to recognize aboriginal rights.

Later that same summer, Ovide Mercredi, a Cree lawyer born in Grand Rapids, was elected national chief of the Assembly of First Nations. His successor was Phil Fontaine, a university trained Saulteaux (Ojibwe) from Fort Alexander, formerly grand chief of the Assembly of Manitoba Chiefs. Men of very different temperments, each in his way thrust the need to deal with Canada's aboriginal injustices onto the national agenda.

Change is coming. Aboriginal enrollment at the universities is up substantially, not only in Manitoba, but across Western Canada, graduating native teachers and lawyers, doctors and dentists. Canada's Supreme Court has upheld native rights in several recent cases and native North Americans increasingly fill positions in Manitoba's civil service and with major corporations.

The cultural and political resurgence of Canada's aboriginal people has been led by a trio of Manitobans – Elijah Harper, Ovide Mercredi and Phil Fontaine. Together they had a powerful impact on Canada in the last two decades of the 20th century.

ELIJAH HARPER AND OVIDE MERCREDI PHOTOS COURTESY OF THE WINNIPEG FREE PRESS. PHIL FONTAINE PHOTO BY PETER ST. JOHN

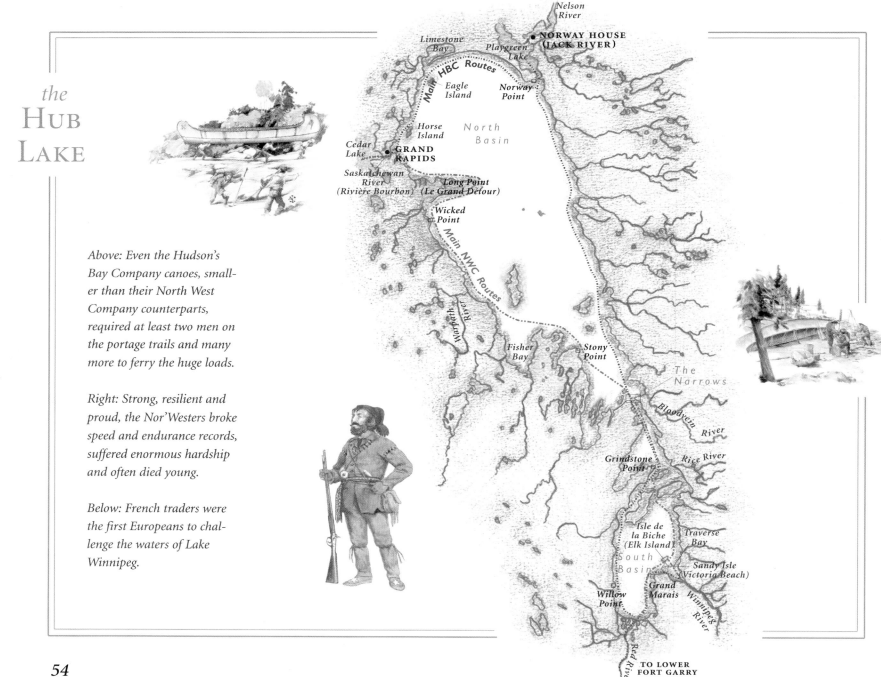

the
HUB
LAKE

Above: Even the Hudson's Bay Company canoes, smaller than their North West Company counterparts, required at least two men on the portage trails and many more to ferry the huge loads.

Right: Strong, resilient and proud, the Nor'Westers broke speed and endurance records, suffered enormous hardship and often died young.

Below: French traders were the first Europeans to challenge the waters of Lake Winnipeg.

Nelson River

Limestone Bay

Playgreen Lake

● **NORWAY HOUSE (JACK RIVER)**

Main HBC Routes

Eagle Island

Norway Point

North Basin

Horse Island

Cedar Lake

● **GRAND RAPIDS**

Saskatchewan River (Rivière Bourbon)

Long Point (Le Grand Détour)

Wicked Point

Main NWC Routes

Warpath River

Fisher Bay

□ **Stony Point**

The Narrows

Bloodvein River

Grindstone Point

Rice River

Isle de la Biche (Elk Island)

Traverse Bay

South Basin

Sandy Isle (Victoria Beach)

Willow Point

Grand Marais

Winnipeg River

Red River

▼ **TO LOWER FORT GARRY**

Lower Fort Garry from the Red River, by Dennis Fast

Illustrations top and centre: courtesy Manitoba Historic Resources; bottom: Barbara Endres

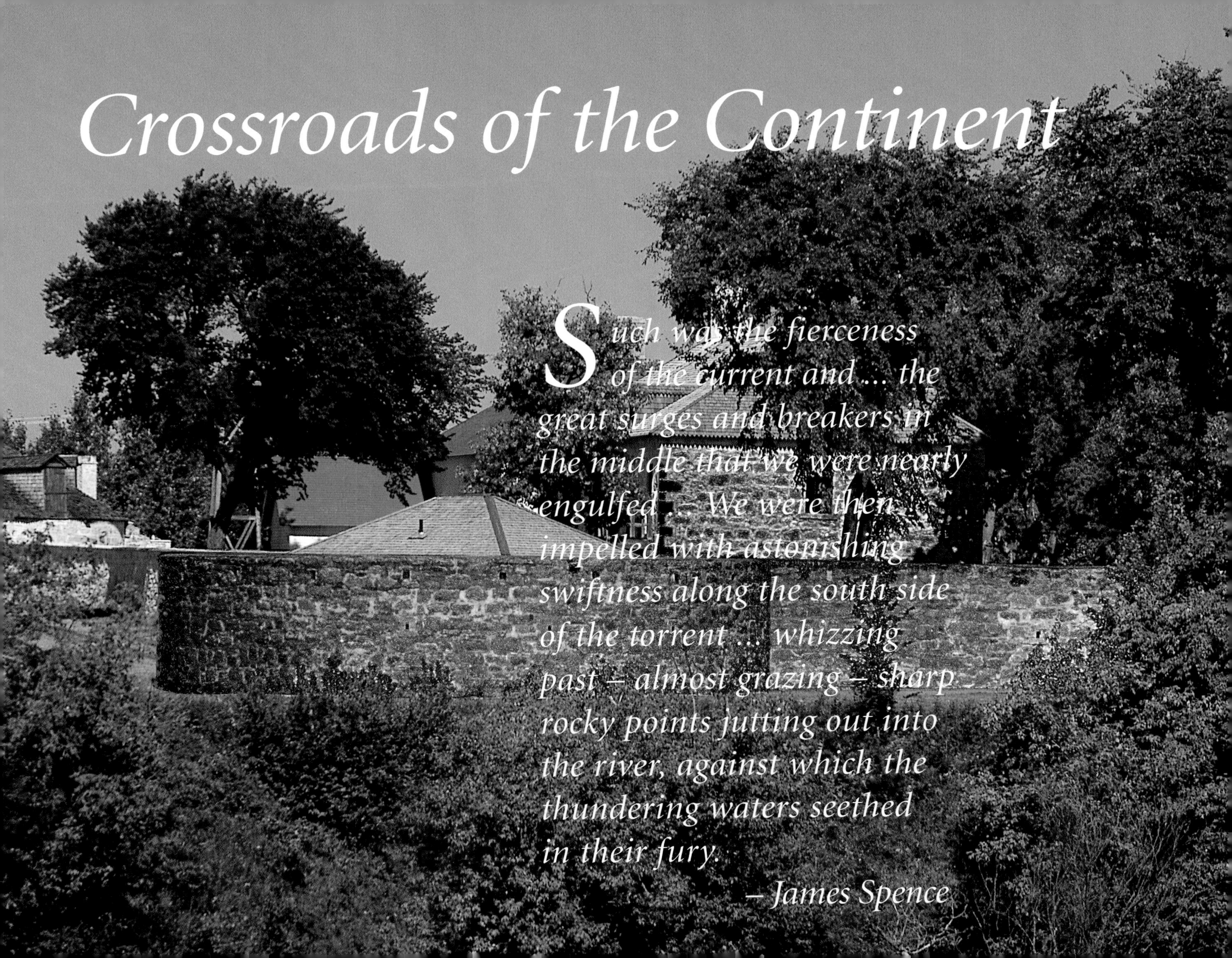

Crossroads of the Continent

*Such was the fierceness
of the current and ... the
great surges and breakers in
the middle that we were nearly
engulfed ... We were then
impelled with astonishing
swiftness along the south side
of the torrent ... whizzing
past – almost grazing – sharp
rocky points jutting out into
the river, against which the
thundering waters seethed
in their fury.*

— James Spence

Crossroads of the Continent

IN THE EARLY 19th century, James Spence guided North West Company canoes down the Saskatchewan River and through the Grand Rapids where the river plunges into Lake Winnipeg. He insisted the best channel was on the south side. Even then, it called for considerable effort, not to mention courage, as his description makes only too evident. [1]

During the 17th, 18th and 19th centuries, Europeans took four routes to reach Canada's western interior. All ran through Lake Winnipeg and all therefore were fraught with enormous difficulty and peril.

The unpredictable, often violent lake and its challenging rivers enticed and repelled Europeans pursuing the riches to be had from harvesting the continent's bountiful furs. They had little choice but to use the lake, but they were forever engaged in trying to find an alternative.

The Saskatchewan River was the pathway to the west. The portion from Cedar Lake to Lake Winnipeg was called the White River by the Cree, who speared sturgeon in the torrent at its mouth. It was, indeed, a white river. There were not one, but three major rapids as the Saskatchewan made its tumultuous descent into the lake: the Rocher Rouge, the Demi-chargé and Grand Rapids, known as Meshea Pow-e-stick, "Large Fall" in Cree. In less than seven kilometres, the river drops more than 21 metres.

The Winnipeg River, the pathway from the east, falls 84 metres within Manitoba and had no less than 26 portages along its 813-kilometre course. But it was so spectacular, the explorers and traders who had to wrestle with it considered it the most beautiful river in northern North America.

"We ... found it to be a most majestic and impressive stream," wrote William Keating on August 20, 1823. He marvelled at

... its immense volume of water, the extreme rapidity of the current, the great variety of form which the cascades and falls present and the incomparable wildness of the rocky scenery which produces these falls and which contrasts by its gloom, its immoveable and unchangeable features, with the bright dazzling effect of the silvery sheet of water, passing from a smooth and unruffled expanse, to a broken and foaming cataract.

Coureur de bois   ARTHUR HEMING / NATIONAL ARCHIVES OF CANADA / C–005746

Niagara, he continued, "is uniform and monotonous in comparison."

The mighty Nelson River, the pathway north to Hudson Bay, was so fierce that only the first 90 kilometres of its 644-kilometre run were navigable. Plunging 220 metres from Norway House to Hudson Bay, the myriad falls and cascades drove the traders to employ the somewhat more sedate Hayes River, "the lower track", to the south. The Hayes presented its own unique difficulty, however, for it didn't flow directly out of Lake Winnipeg. The shallow Echimamish River forged the link to the upper Nelson and the lake, requiring tedious poling and portaging.

Last but not least was the Red River, the pathway from the south and very different than its three wild sisters. So placid and meandering is the Red that it takes 300 kilometres to wind its way along the 96 kilometres as the crow flies from the 49th parallel to its junction with the Assiniboine in today's Winnipeg.

Award-winning historian Gerald Friesen says Lake Winnipeg

represented the heart of this chunk of the world ... certainly to 1900. From North Dakota to the Churchill River and from Hudson Bay to the Rockies, or at least to the forks of the Saskatchewan River, the lake was a giant centre for aboriginal people and later for the fur traders. Water routes were obviously pivotal in this part of the world for both food resources and transportation and people had the

technology to use them. Once the railway came, however, that was the end of water. The routes here were so uneconomic. The lake is dangerous and the rivers are just too long. [3]

This, then, was the dilemma presented by North America's midcontinent watershed. With trade volumes and speed increasingly of the essence, the lake and its rivers offered danger and delay. Little wonder that, despite their initial indispensability to the exploration and opening of western Canada, they enjoyed but a brief two centuries of glory.

During those years, however, Lake Winnipeg witnessed some of the pivotal events of Canadian history. Its shores were walked and its waters paddled by many of the key figures of the age: Henry Kelsey; Pierre Gaultier de Varennes, Sieur de La Vérendrye and his sons; Alexander Henry the Elder; Alexander Mackenzie; David Thompson; John Franklin; Alexander Henry the Younger; Henry Youle Hind and John Palliser, to name but a few.

Not only did these famous personages frequent the lake, they often wrote at length and with eloquence about it. Beginning more than 300 years ago, and in the courtly grammar and idiosyncratic spelling of the day, these writings form a significant piece of the lake's – and Manitoba's – heritage. Buried in archival files and rare books, they let us see the lake we know today through the eyes of the past.

The exploits and chronicles of European adventurers and traders would never have been

Left: More than a century after the first European laid eyes on it, George Back's Fall of the Moving Waters *captured one of the Winnipeg River's many thundering cascades.*

Below: Early maps, such as this Carte Physique des Terreins *drawn by Philippe Buach from information provided by Auchagah, often showed Lake Winnipeg (centre left of map) lying along a northwest-southeast line. Lakes Superior and Michigan are clearly identifiable in the lower right-hand corner.*

possible without the knowledge and assistance of the people who had lived along the shores of the lake for thousands of years. They knew it and every river waterway and stream byway. And they were familiar with the dangers and opportunities each presented.

La Vérendrye's western explorations were greatly inspired by a remarkable map of "the great river of the west" drawn for him by a Cree guide known as Auchagah (sometimes called Ocliagach). Auchagah traced the route between Lake Superior and Lake Winnipeg in a linear style that resembles today's subway or bus route maps. While not as precise as today's highway maps, it provided most of the information a canoeist would need. With the map, their Ojibwe and Cree guides, and information gleaned from other aboriginal sources, the La Vérendryes covered much of today's Manitoba in the 1730s and '40s and travelled far to the south and west.

The age of British discovery was launched during the reign of Queen Elizabeth I (1558 to 1603), which witnessed an explosion of ideas and the rise of English nationalism. Following a series of abortive attempts to find the Northwest Passage and mine the imagined mineral wealth of the continent's northern reaches, Henry Hudson sailed into the bay that bears his name in the summer of 1610. Though his attention was focused on James Bay, where he was cast adrift by mutineers in the spring of 1611, his mysterious journey spurred others to sail the shores of Hudson Bay. These included Thomas Button, who became the first European to winter in Manitoba. Button spent the long, cold months of 1612 and the spring of 1613 at the

mouth of a river he named for Robert Nelson, a ship's master who died there. Button's journal was later lost and we have only general reports of his activities.

In 1619-20, Jens Munck, a Danish navigator, endured a horrendous winter at Churchill, where all but two of his men died, and in 1631 Captains Luke Foxe and Thomas James, on independent expeditions from England, sailed along the coast of today's Manitoba.

Before the deadly cold set in, Munck described the land around the estuary of the Churchill River as "low, flat and wooded" and said there was "scarcely any safe harbour to protect a boat properly ... I myself journeyed up the [Churchill] River to see how far I could get with a boat; but, about a mile and a half up, there were so many stones in it, that I could not advance any further and had to return ..." [4]

On August 10, 1631, Foxe made an entry in his journal concerning the Nelson River estuary: "It was Clay clift on both sides, and of reasonable height; but the fresh came down with great force ... It is also thicke as can stand of Firre and Spruce-trees, but small ones, for there is no ground for the wood to take roote upon, for the thicknesse of Mosse ..." That moss yielded an abundant harvest for the travellers. Foxe reported his party gathered "blackberries", [5] [likely black crowberries] strawberries and gooseberries.

According to geographer John Warkentin, the first journeys into the interior were made, not in pursuit of the Western Sea, but in quest of furs. In 1648 and 1649, the Five Nations Iroquois almost annihilated the Wendat of Huronia, who had served as middlemen between the French traders

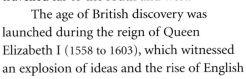

The Wintering Creek   Hayes River

A View of Montagu House from Beaver Creek

These two woodcuts from Henry Ellis's A Voyage to Hudson's Bay, *portraying a pair of 18ᵗʰ-century ships anchored in the Hayes River and a rather fanciful view of early bayside accommodations, make it clear how far apart the two worlds of the fur trade really were.*

of the St. Lawrence and the Ojibwe trappers of the Upper Great Lakes. The destruction of their allies forced the French to travel west themselves. Breaking through the Iroquois cordon, they reached Lake Superior via the Ottawa River and Lake Huron, and established direct contact with the Ojibwe trappers.

One of the most determined of these traders was Médard Chouart, Sieur des Groseilliers. Given to exaggerating his considerable exploits, des Groseilliers reported in 1656 the existence of "... a nation of the sea which some have called stinkards because its people who formerly lived on the shores of the sea called it Ouinipeg – that is, stinking water", leading some to believe that he had actually seen Lake Winnipeg. However, recent research indicates he may not even have reached Rainy River, well east of the great lake. He likely met a party of Cree on the north shore of Lake Superior and used their descriptions of Lake Winnipeg to claim he had been there.

Like the first, des Groseilliers' second expedition of 1659-60 was enormously successful. With his young brother-in-law, Pierre-Esprit Radisson, he returned to Montreal with dozens of canoes full of furs, but his exploits were not appreciated by the authorities of New France, who confiscated the bounty. Spurned, the traders took their energy and ideas about a northern route to the interior of North America to England. There, in 1668, they persuaded an English commercial group to outfit an expedition to trade for furs in Hudson Bay. Two ketches, the *Nonsuch*, carrying des Groseilliers, and the *Eaglet*, with Radisson on board, left London on June 5th. The *Eaglet* was forced to turn back but the *Nonsuch* sailed into southern James Bay on September 29th. The crew wintered there and returned with a large cargo of prime winter beaver, obtained from the Mistassini Cree.

BARBARA ENDRES

In 1669, Radisson accompanied a second successful trading venture and on May 2, 1670, King Charles II signed a royal charter granting "The Governor and Company of Adventurers tradeing into Hudson Bay" monopoly trading privileges and the right to colonize all the lands drained by waters flowing into the bay. The Hudson's Bay Company was born.

The new commercial entity fuelled the rivalry between the English and the French. Beginning in the 1670s, permanent posts were established at strategic points along the Rupert, Moose, Nelson, Hayes and Churchill Rivers.

Ultimately the most important of these was York Fort (later York Factory) at the mouth of the Hayes River, founded by the HBC in 1682 and named after the king's brother, the Duke of York, then governor of the company. It had humble beginnings, only becoming a "factory", (so-called because a factor lived there) much later in its centuries-long history.

Despite their cultural differences, trade was an almost immediate response to every contact between Europeans and North Americans. When the Nonsuch, *above, anchored in the mouth of the Rupert River on the east shore of James Bay, the Mistassini Cree were not only quick to supply the small British wintering party (led by des Groseilliers) with furs, but also provided food and information.*

59

York Fort became a pawn in the wars between the English and the French for control of the bay and it changed hands several times. Pierre le Moyne d'Iberville captured the fort for France in an epic sea battle, but it was returned to the English by the Treaty of Utrecht in 1713. Nearly 70 years later, it was sacked by a raiding party of French marines during the American Revolution. Rebuilt at its present site, it became even more essential to the fur trade when the HBC amalgamated with the North West Company in 1821.

The first European to reach the Winnipeg River from the east may have been Jacques de Noyon in 1689. [6] The first to see Lake Winnipeg might have been Henry Kelsey, who left York Factory in June 1690, and with his Nakota or Assiniboine guides travelled the Hayes and the Saskatchewan Rivers and wintered near The Pas, before striking out on foot westward across the prairies. Kelsey's exact route from the bay isn't known, but Warkentin believes he bypassed Lake Winnipeg on the north, reaching the Saskatchewan River through a series of small rivers and lakes. However, American historian Elliott Coues points to Henry Kelsey's journal, which indicated he was on Lake Winnipeg in the summer of 1692. [7]

In 1720, Nicolas Jéremie, who had served in the French fur trade on the bay from 1694 to 1714, published a book describing the area around Lake Winnipeg. He based his account entirely on information he obtained from the Cree and had many details of geography confused. Jéremie gave the lake several names, including *Anisquaoui-gamou*, meaning "junction of the two seas, for the shores almost meet at the middle of the lake". [8]

The first Europeans known with certainty to have seen Lake Winnipeg were Christophe Dufrost de La Jemerais and Jean-Baptiste de La Vérendrye, respectively the nephew and eldest son of Pierre de La Vérendrye, who had received a three-year monopoly to trade in the area west of Lake Superior in 1731. In 1732, the family established Fort St. Charles on Lake of the Woods and two years later the two young men built Fort Maurepas on the lower Red River about nine kilometres north of present-day Selkirk. A year later, Maurepas was moved to the lower Winnipeg River.

Prior to his arrival in the area, La Vérendrye mentioned Lake Winnipeg in a report to the Marquis de Beauharnois, the governor of New France.

> *Pako, Chief of Lake Nipigon, Lefoye, and Petit Jour his brother, Cree chiefs, reported to me that they had been beyond the height of land and reached a great river which flows straight towards the setting sun [the Winnipeg River] ... They give a great account of that country, saying that it is all very level, without mountains, all fine hard wood ... The wood comes to an end on the shore of a great lake [Lake Winnipeg] formed by the river about 200 leagues from its source; on the left, as you follow down, at the outlet of the lake, you come to a little river [Red River] the water of which looks red like vermilion and is held in great esteem ...* [9]

After La Vérendrye had seen the territory for himself, he had this to say:

> *The whole right bank of the great river as you go down from the Lake of the Woods as far as Lake Winnipeg is held by the Cree and it is the country of the moose and marten, while beaver is so plentiful that [they] place little value on it and only collect the large skins which they send to the English ... The left bank of the same river is inhabited*

by the Assiniboin and the Sioux; the country is rich in metals, and buffalo are abundant. [10]

Pierre de La Vérendrye, the explorer's second son, was commissioned by his father to explore Lake Winnipeg to find a suitable place for a fort. He wrote Governor Beauharnois on June 7, 1735:

I have established a fort at Lake Winnipeg five leagues up the Red River on a fine point commanding a distant view ... I could not establish myself nearer the Lake, because it is all prairie there.

His tour disclosed "a fine wood of high timber, including a great deal of white oak" near the mouth of the Red River. [11] He also reported the existence of a large silver mine along the riverbank.

Between 1740 and 1742, another French trader, the *coureur de bois* Joseph la France, travelled from Lake Huron to York Factory. There, he was taken to England, where he was interviewed by Arthur Dobbs, an Irish aristocrat and opponent of the HBC. In his 1774 book, *An Account of the Country Adjoining to Hudson's Bay*, Dobbs published la France's descriptions, with a map.

> *He [la France] arrived at the great Ouinipique Lake in September, 1740; he was about 30 days in passing it, shooting and fishing as he went. After going half way through it, he joined the Cris or Christinaux Indians, who live on the North-east side, and went on Shore and hunted Beavers all the Autumn. He saw but two Isles in it; one was full of Wood, it was about 3 Leagues long and 2 broad. He called it the Isle Du Biche, or of Hinds, there being several upon it [present-day Elk Island]; the other was sandy, and without Wood, full of Geese and other Water-fowl, which breed there; he called it Goose Isle, but the Natives called it Sandy Isle [today's Victoria Beach].*
>
> *On the West Side of this Lake the Indians told him a River [the Red] enter'd it which was navigable with Canoes ... The Country West of the Ouinipique Lake has dry Islands or Hills with marshy Bottoms, ful of Wood and Meadows. On the East Side is a fine flat Country, full of Woods, until they come to the Bottom of the Mountains, which are betwixt this and the upper Lake.* [12]

Alexander Henry the Elder was born in New Jersey but traded out of Montreal. On his retirement, he corresponded with several distinguished Englishmen about the potential of Western Canada. In his memorandum to Joseph Banks on an overland route to the Pacific, dated October 18, 1781, he makes reference to Lake Winnipeg's stormy habits.

C.W. JEFFREYS / NATIONAL ARCHIVES OF CANADA / C–2146

Though Alexander Mackenzie, above, became the first European to cross North America north of Mexico, like his contemporaries he sometimes found the continent's complex geography confusing.

In places, Elk Island's beaches are sweeps of sand, but here, slabs of limestone dominate.

From the mouth of the Winnipeg River, he writes,

... one must coast along the North [east] Shore [of Lake Winnipeg] for near Forty Leagues, where the Lake forms partly a Strait [The Narrows] and then must Cross to the South [west] side and many Deep bays, which are very Dangerous at this Season, Until you arrive at the Entrance of the River Bourbon [Lower Saskatchewan River] which falls in Lake Winipigon. This lake discharges itself into Hudsons bay at York Fort ... At the Entrance of this River is a Rapid, where the Canoes, and everything, must be Carried over by the men ... [13]

Alexander Mackenzie, the first European to reach the Pacific by an overland route north of Mexico, was also the first to note that Lake Winnipeg lay at the junction of the ancient granitic rocks of the east and the more recent limestone strata of the west. [14]

"Lake Winipic is the great reservoir of several large rivers," Mackenzie reports in his account of his western Canadian travels between 1787 and 1801, "and discharges itself by the River Nelson into Hudson's Bay." He goes on to say:

Along the west banks of [Lake Winnipeg] is to be seen, at intervals, and traced in the line of the direction of the plains, a soft rock of lime-stone, in thin and nearly horizontal strata ... It is also remarkable that, at the narrowest part of Lake Winipic, where it is not more than two miles in breadth, the West side is faced with rocks of this stone thirty feet perpendicular; while, on the East side, the rocks are more elevated, and of a dark-grey granite.

Like many others of the time, Mackenzie termed the Assiniboine River a branch of the Red. He seemed confused about the directions of the rivers' flow and their sources:

The first in rotation, next to that I have just described, is the Assiniboin, or Red River, which, at the distance of 40 miles coastwise, disembogues on the South-West side of Lake Winipic ... The Eastern branch, called the Red River, runs in a Southern direction to near the head waters of the Mississippi ... The country on either side is but partially supplied with wood, and consists of plains covered with herds of the buffalo and elk, especially on the Western side. On the Eastern side are lakes and rivers, and the whole country is well wooded, level, abounding in beaver, bears, moose-deer, fallow-deer, etc.etc. There is not, perhaps, a finer country in the world for the residence of uncivilized man.

Mackenzie gives lengthy descriptions of the Assiniboine, Dauphin and Swan Rivers and Lake Manitoba before describing Grand Rapids at the mouth of the Saskatchewan River:

On entering the Saskatchiwine, in the course of a few miles, the great rapid interrupts the passage. It is about three miles long. Through the greatest part of it the canoe is towed, half or full laden, according to the state of the waters ... The channel here is near a mile wide, the waters tumbling over ridges of rocks that traverse the river ... There is an excellent sturgeon-fishery at the foot of this cascade, and vast numbers of pelicans, cormorants, etc. frequent it, where

Right: People were spearing lake sturgeon in the cascades at the mouth of the Saskatchewan River millennia before Europeans arrived.

they watch to seize the fish that may be killed or disabled by the force of the waters.

Alexander Henry the Younger, namesake of his uncle, was a trader for the North West Company and travelled the Lake Winnipeg country in the summer of 1800. His journal was blended with that of David Thompson, described by J.B. Tyrrell as the greatest land geographer the world has known, and published in 1897 by Elliott Coues.

The younger Henry had barely entered the lake on August 16, 1800, from Traverse Bay, also known as *Baie de l'Isle à la Biche,* when the "fine and clear" weather turned into a gale and a high swell.

We instantly entered Lake Winipic, keeping the last land on the S. shore. The weather being fine and clear, we stood out with the intention of making traverse; but had not gone above a mile when suddenly the wind rose to a gale from the N., followed by a high swell. Before we could reach the shore, we had several sand banks to pass over, where it was almost too shallow for the craft to swim. This occasioned a short, tumbling sea which dashed over us, and before we could land our canoes were half full of water, and all of us wet to the skin. After much trouble, we got everything on shore, though one of my canoes was split asunder from one gunnel to the other ...

Having fine weather, we got everything in order again ... At two o'clock, the wind abated, we embarked, and soon after passed Red Deer [now Elk] island. Here is a narrow strait between the island and the mainland, which some years obliges us to portage about 200 paces, across a neck of sand; but this year the water being very high we got through without unloading ...

The Sturgeon

The lake sturgeon is an ancient and suitably prehistoric-looking creature. In keeping with its unearthly appearance, it has other singular features. It is very large, weighing on average 23 kilograms, but specimens as large as 136 kilograms have been found. It lives to a great age, up to 150 years, but doesn't attain maturity until between 20 and 25 years, making it extremely susceptible to overfishing. In early days at Grand Rapids, sturgeon were most easily speared during the spawning season when they swarmed up the rapids. At other times, they were caught in scoop nets. At O nika pik (the carrying place) the fishers stood on the rocks beside the deep pools to fish. They would move a pole slowly downstream through the deep water until they felt the fish's ridged backbone and then use their scoop to catch it. The sturgeon is very oily and large quantities of fish oil were made from the catch. The fish not only provided a staple food and caviar, but many tools and instruments as well. Jars were fashioned from its skin and needles and hooks from its bones. Isinglass, a kind of translucent gelatine, was manufactured from the sturgeon's air bladders and was used for glue and paint. In 1878, Grand Rapids produced 76 kilograms of isinglass. By the 1890s, Lake Winnipeg and its tributaries produced almost half the annual catch of sturgeon in Canada, but 10 years later the stock was almost depleted. Today, the sturgeon is protected and must be returned to the water if caught.

North Americans also caught whitefish in scoop nets. They smoked and dried them, and then put them into a canvas bag, which was pounded over a smooth rock to produce a fish pemmican suitable for winter and trail use. [15]

63

The treacherous waters of Lake Winnipeg were among the reasons that York boats, portrayed below in Walter J. Phillips' York Boats in Moon and Mist, replaced canoes on many of the HBC routes by the end of the 18th century.

We had no sooner got from behind the island than the wind sprung up from the W. off the lake, accompanied by a heavy swell, which obliged us to put ashore and unload. We remained until sunset when the wind abated. With great difficulty we loaded and embarked, with an aft wind from the N. Our course from Red Deer island was about S. After dark the wind increased. We could find no convenient place to land – nothing but large rocks, over which the sea broke dangerously. Necessity kept us on with our sails close-reefed, until we reached the Point of the Grand Marais. Here the sea ran so high that we shipped a quantity of water, which kept us using kettles to bail it out as fast as it came in. At last we sighted the Grand Marais, and finding ourselves more under a lee, we ran in safely about 10 o'clock. It was some time before all the canoes and boats reached us.

The next day, the wind had subsided but the swell was still very high. Though anxious to proceed, Henry thought

it prudent to wait and went duck hunting. His journal picks up the tale that appears to include one of the first descriptions of the lake's fishflies:

I shot several [ducks] and observed the tracks of moose, red deer, and bears. The beach was covered with grasshoppers, which had been thrown up by the waves and formed one continuous line as far as the eye could reach; in some places they lay from six to nine inches deep and in a state of putrefaction, which occasioned a horrid stench. I also shot a pelican, of which there are a great plenty here. [16]

Eight years later, the younger Henry again found himself on Lake Winnipeg in the month of August, travelling from the mouth of the Red River to Grand Rapids. As before, his trip was one storm after another. The journey took him nine days, from August 12th to 20th. His daily log is a template for generation upon generation of lake sailors, who will instantly identify with every travail. It follows in abbreviated form:

Friday, Aug. 12, 1808 – At 10 o'clock, the wind rose from the N. and this annoyed us much in rounding Presqu'Isle [now Willow Point]. The wind then coming about from the S.E., we hoisted sail and kept on till two o'clock, when there was every appearance of a squall from the S.W. We had some difficulty landing as the rain fell in torrents and the wind blew a gale.

Saturday, Aug. 13, 1808 – The wind continued high from the S.W. We embarked and proceeded along the lee shore in hopes of finding ... a small passage between the mainland and the large island opposite [Big Island, now Hecla Island]. The bay is shallow and overgrown with

WALTER J. PHILLIPS / NATIONAL ARCHIVES OF CANADA / C–110833

rushes; wild fowl of all kinds are numerous. We searched in vain for the passage and were obliged to return to the mouth of the bay and coast along the great [Black] island, the shores of which are covered with huge flakes of limestone. At three o'clock we came to an opening, but a gale from the N.W. obliged us put ashore at the entrance of this large strait. Here we remained until five o'clock, when the wind abated, and we embarked, though the swell was still high. We made a long traverse from this island to the mainland, where the shore was so steep and rocky that we could find no place to put ashore, and were obliged to push on in the dark. In a short time the wind rose dead ahead from the W. and the swell increased. Our position was decidedly unpleasant; the sea dashed with great violence against the rocks, the night was extremely dark, and the wind seemed to be increasing ...

Sunday, Aug. 14, 1808 – At daybreak we embarked. The wind continued strong ahead, and though the men laboured hard against it, we made slow progress along the shore. About two o'clock we found ourselves astray ... We put ashore for a short time and then, the wind having veered to the S.E., we embarked, hoisted sail and steered N. for a high [Grindstone] point about four leagues off. Having doubled this point, our course lay due W. along a steep rocky shore ...

Monday, Aug. 15, 1808 – The wind continued to blow hard from the S.E., making a heavy swell in The Narrows. My guide thought it unsafe to proceed ... As the weather was clear, we spread out baggage to dry, almost every article having been wet since the 13th. During this operation, the men gathered raspberries, which grew in profusion. The N. side of the lake appeared to be rocky, the rocks black and gray. The traverse is about a league

wide; across it appear some snug inlets and coves with a sandy bottom, which would be of great advantage if one were overtaken by a storm ... At 11 o'clock everything was dry and the wind had abated; we hoisted sail ... but a sudden squall from the N.W. obliged us to put ashore ... The wind then came about from the S.E.; we hoisted sail and took the traverse [of Fisher Bay] in which we found a very heavy swell ... We camped on a fine, sandy beach. We soon had a terrible squall with thunder, lightning and a heavy shower ... My tent was blown down, and passed a wretched night, wet to the skin.

Tuesday, Aug. 16, 1808 – At daybreak we loaded and embarked; wind strong, about W. We crept slowly along the shore which partially sheltered us ... We came to the great Reef of Rocks [Stony Point or Wicked Point], a chain of large stones which extends into the lake for more than a mile. We attempted to get around it, but were in danger of being blown out in the lake; we therefore put ashore and unloaded ... I shot a white crane and a few ducks; at four o'clock, we loaded and with great difficulty we got around the reef. As the wind continued to blow hard, we shipped much water ...

High winds can create tides in both basins, which made traversing Lake Winnipeg an almost constant challenge during the fur trade era. This 20th-century photograph shows how elevated water levels could inundate shorelines. A strong south wind could completely eliminate the narrow beach below the clay cliffs at the north end of the lake, leaving the brigades nowhere to shelter.

65

Wednesday, Aug. 17, 1808 – This morning the wind was easterly, but the swell occasioned by the late gale still ran high. After much trouble in loading, we embarked and stood out on the traverse for the Tete aux Pichaux ... The wind increased to such a degree in rounding this point and the sea ran so high while we were under sail, that at intervals we lost sight of the masts of the canoes not more than 30 yards distant ... The shore here is very high, and almost a continuous limestone cliff ... As the sun went down the wind increased; we attempted to get into Riviere aux Guerriers [Warpath River] but passed it unobserved. As the wind was too high to return, we had no choice but must keep on. We soon found that our canoe could not stand it much longer, as we shipped great quantities of

The clear water of the north basin, seen here at Grand Rapids, is very different than the silty south basin.

water ... We ran in close to shore, and, finding no inlet or cove to shelter us from the swell ... we put her about and kept her stern foremost. Almost every swell washed over her ... We hauled her up with some difficulty and camped

for the night, during which the wind continued to blow with great violence.

Thursday, Aug. 18, 1808 – [W]e with great difficulty loaded our canoe and embarked, hoisted sail and kept along the shore; but the wind increased to such a gale that we could scarcely carry two feet of sail ... We shipped a quantity of water, the swell being very high ... [A] heavy swell rolled in, and we were obliged to run in between Egg island and Point aux Gravois, which joins the Détour [Long Point] where the land is very bad when the lake is in the least agitated. Having got into the bay, after shipping a great deal of water, we proceeded under the lee of the point, which forms an isthmus for about two miles before it joins the mainland. Here we put ashore and camped. Gulls of various kinds were numerous and we killed a great many.

Friday, Aug. 19, 1808 – The wind continued to blow hard; at nine o'clock, we had a squall and light shower ... The wind increased; we took in a double reef. Still we had too much sail, and were in great danger. We furled our sail, leaving only about a foot of canvas spread, which even then required two men to support the mast and keep the yard from being carried away. On the shore, which would not admit of our landing, I observed a nine-gallon keg, which I supposed to be empty; but in a short time I saw another of the same kind. I then suspected them to be part of a cargo that had been wrecked in the late gales. We proceeded until we came to the Point of the Detour [the end of Long Point] where the wind was directly ahead ...

Saturday, Aug. 20, 1808 – At sunrise the wind had abated and it soon fell dead calm; but there was still a heavy sea. However, we made out to load and embark, and came on to Moose Nose island where we shot some ducks and gulls, with which the shore was almost covered. The

wind sprang up again. We hoisted sail, came on with a pleasant breeze aft past Horse islands, and soon entered the mouth of the Saskatchewoine ... [17]

Captain John Franklin's Arctic Expedition of 1819-22 travelled from York Factory to Lake Athabasca following the Hayes River, Oxford Lake, Lake Winnipeg, Saskatchewan River, Sturgeon-weir River, Churchill River, Methye Portage and Athabasca River route and returned that way three years later. John Richardson's *Geognostical Observations*, printed as an appendix to Franklin's narrative of the expedition, is the first substantial geological account of Canada's western interior. As had Mackenzie before him, Richardson noted the two distinct rock varieties characterizing and setting apart the lake's shorelines:

> *The primitive rocks disappear under the clay below Norway Point. The north shore of Lake Winipeg is formed into a peninsula by Play-Green Lake and Limestone Bay. It consists of steep clay cliffs, similar to those which preceded the gneiss in Hill River, but containing rather more calcareous matter ...*
>
> *The beach is composed of a fine calcareous sand, and small fragments of water-worn limestone. The same materials form a narrow bank, which running to the S.W. for about eight miles, separates Limestone Bay from the body of the lake. The fragments belong to two kinds of limestone; the one yellowish white and dull with a conchoidal fracture, and translucent edges; the other bluish and yellowish grey, dull, with an earthy fracture and opaque.*
>
> *We did not observe any rocks of the former kind ... but cliffs of the latter appear on the west side of Limestone*

Bay, and continue to bound the lake as far as the mouth of the Saskatchewan, and as we have been informed, down the whole of its western shore. [18]

Captain John Palliser also gave a detailed account of the lake's divided geologic heritage. "[Its] rugged eastern shore is principally composed of primitive rocks, while along the west the headlands are formed of beds of limestone, and the country in their rear is low and marshy," he writes in the journals of his 1857-1860 expedition.

He correctly forecast the lake's coming steamboat era, but not the death and tragedy its shallowness portended.

> *Lake Winnipeg communicates with several other sheets of water, of which Manitoba and Wimpegoors lakes*

From the air, Limestone Point dangles like a pendant into the north basin. For all those who made the crossing from Norway House in small craft, Limestone Bay, upper left, sheltered behind its dunes, provided a welcome haven from bad weather.

are the most considerable. None of these lakes are deep, and many parts of them are extremely shallow, but still they present fine stretches for future steam navigation, and from the facility of access which they give to the timbered districts they will doubtless prove of great value in opening up and settling the country. [19]

Just prior to their merger, Lake Winnipeg almost became the battleground in a war between the Hudson's Bay Company and the North West Company. Though the HBC did not build a post at Grand Rapids during the period of competition with the NWC, the importance of Grand Rapids within the transportation system of both companies was well recognized. It was suggested in 1814 that the HBC governor should locate himself there where, with an armed force he could stop any NWC canoes from passing.

As the competition and the resulting violence escalated, Grand Rapids did become the scene of an armed, though bloodless, coup when HBC Governor William Williams decided to retaliate against the NWC for its actions in the Athabasca region. Williams gathered a force of 30 men at Red River in the winter of 1818-19; 20 of these men were experienced soldiers of the Des Meurons regiment whom Lord Selkirk had brought to Red River in 1817. This selection made it evident that Williams was preparing not for a fur trade expedition, but for war.

On June 9, 1819, Williams left Red River for Grand Rapids by boat accompanied by Captain Mathey and the Des Meurons and armed with a brass cannon and other weapons. The force

As heavy and unwieldy as they were over the portage trails, York boats quickly replaced birchbark canoes on the lake, for they carried far greater loads and handled the open water of Lake Winnipeg better.

JERRY KAUTZ

arrived on June 18th and camped at the Lower Basin, the longer portage trail. They had scarcely set up camp when two North West canoes shot the rapids and landed. Their crews, involved in action against the HBC in the Athabasca, were captured and imprisoned on Devil's Island in the Saskatchewan River.

Charles Racette, an old freeman who also was camped at the foot of the rapids, tried to send his sons to warn the Nor'Westers up the river. The HBC party got word of his plans and confined Racette, his wife, two sons and an aboriginal family. The next day, Governor Williams moved his position to the upper landing (the west end of the portage trail). There, his force seized the crews of eight more canoes as they unloaded to shoot the rapids.

In 1820, the Nor'Westers, whom George Simpson described as a "lawless assemblage of half-breeds and Indian assassins", gathered in force at Grand Rapids, where they planned to capture Governor Williams. Williams heard of their presence at the rapids and detoured to avoid them, but Colin Robertson was not so fortunate. He tried to shoot the rapids past the Nor'Westers but was seized and taken to Montreal, where he was soon released.

By the following year, talk of outright war was at a fever pitch. The Nor'Westers had heard the HBC was building an armed scow at Jack River (Norway House), with which it intended to blockade Grand Rapids. Fortunately for all concerned, the decision was made in London to merge the two bitter rivals and plans for the naval engagement were soon abandoned. [20]

The union between the two great fur companies did not end competition to the HBC, however. Free traders, many of them American, continued to irritate the company. One who set up shop at Grand Rapids around the time of the U.S. Civil War was known as Clemens or Clement. Roderick McKenzie, who was in charge of the Cumberland District for the HBC, called him "the Yankee Clement" and thought him to be the brother of the celebrated American storyteller, Samuel Clemens or Mark Twain. Clemens' presence caused the company to close its post at Cedar Lake and establish one at Grand Rapids in the fall of 1864.

If the HBC didn't like Clemens, neither did Clemens like the HBC. He threatened to break down the HBC trader's house and throw the company's property into the river. He subsequently relocated to The Pas.

Meanwhile, the nature of the trade on Lake Winnipeg had been undergoing dramatic changes, fuelled by the competition between the HBC and the NWC and the advances brought about by the Industrial Revolution. The replacement of the freight canoe by the York boat, which could carry almost four times the load, had led to the gradual decline of the fur trade's northern and northwestern routes. The portaging of the heavy boats, not to mention their cargoes, was simply too difficult and time-consuming. Brigades were plagued with sickness, injuries and sometimes outright mutiny. By the mid-19th century, the HBC had turned to the Red River cart to carry outfits for the northwest districts and trade to the U.S.

The introduction of steam navigation on Manitoba's lakes and rivers, launched by the arrival of the *Anson Northup* at Red River in June 1859, suddenly rejuvenated the value of the northwestern route. By the 1870s, the stage was set for Grand Rapids to again become a busy port, with the HBC's new Saskatchewan River sternwheeler, the *Northcote*, exchanging freight and passengers with the company's Lake Winnipeg steamers, the SS *Chief Commissioner* and the SS *Colvile*.

The advent of the age of steam on Lake Winnipeg gave rise to one of the most unusual railroads in the Canadian West, the fabled Grand Rapids Tramway. Designed to eliminate the arduous and dangerous portage around the famous rapids at the mouth of the Saskatchewan River at Lake Winnipeg, its last spike was driven in 1877, a mere eight years before another, more famous, last spike ceremony occurred on a misty November day in 1885, at Craigellachie in the Canadian Rockies. The Canadian Pacific's transcontinental railroad would launch a generation of railroad building throughout the Canadian West, signalling the beginning of the end of water transport and all its associated connections, including the Grand Rapids tramway.

The tramway was a modest affair: just 5.6 kilometres of frail, narrow-gauge track, mules and horses for motive power, initially only six pieces of four-wheeled rolling stock and a hand car. Its entire cost was $17,389. At its peak, the tramway had 12 flat cars, each drawn by a single horse.

The little railway succeeded a series of portage trails and crude wagon roads that had been hacked out of the wilderness to bypass the rapids. The men (and perhaps even the animals) who had hauled the goods over the portage for so many decades were undoubtedly delighted when the HBC commissioned an engineer, Walter Moberly, to build the tramway. It was completed in one summer. Said the HBC's Alexander Matheson when the last spike was driven, "It will relieve us of an immense amount of trouble and anxiety as well as expense ... as one horse will now do the work of six under the old system."

The tramway operated profitably for 20 years, carrying troops and supplies to and from the North West Rebellion of 1885 and providing a brief sightseeing tour of the rapids for Governor-General Lord Dufferin and Countess Dufferin in 1877 before fading into history. [21]

PLAYGREEN LAKE

Arduous though life was for the Lake Winnipeg people, they had fun, too. Playgreen Lake or Booscoosecaggan, was cited on a 1792 map by the trader Peter Fidler. He noted: "The Play Green derived its name from numbers of Indians assembling here every year and playing at a particular game." Others noted the Cree name as Puskeeskokan Lake, which a local conservation officer stated was from a place where Indians played a game "on the green, like a bowling green". The game was probably lacrosse. Sir John Franklin observed the lake was so named by two bands of Indians who held a festival on an island here. In 1915, J. B. Tyrrell gave two alternate Cree names: Paskoskagan Sakahegan, meaning "Treeless Island Lake", and Notawewinan Sakahegan, meaning " Egg Gathering Lake". [22]

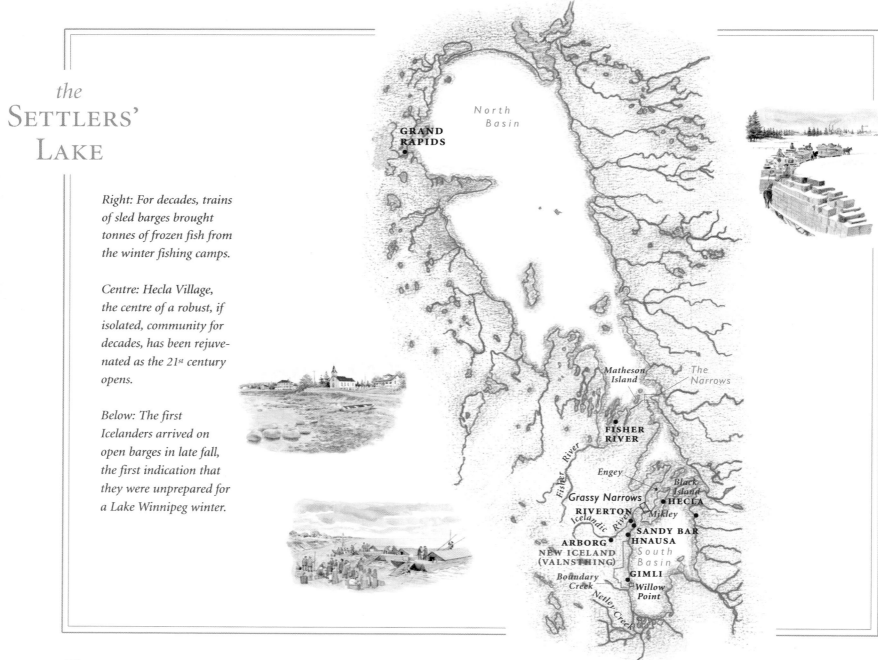

the SETTLERS' LAKE

Right: For decades, trains of sled barges brought tonnes of frozen fish from the winter fishing camps.

Centre: Hecla Village, the centre of a robust, if isolated, community for decades, has been rejuvenated as the 21st century opens.

Below: The first Icelanders arrived on open barges in late fall, the first indication that they were unprepared for a Lake Winnipeg winter.

Illustrations by Barbara Endres

North Basin

GRAND RAPIDS

Matheson Island

The Narrows

FISHER RIVER

Fisher River

Engey

Black Island

Grassy Narrows

HECLA

RIVERTON

Mikley

Icelandic River

SANDY BAR

HNAUSA

ARBORG

NEW ICELAND (VALNSTHING)

South Basin

Boundary Creek

GIMLI

Willow Point

Netley Creek

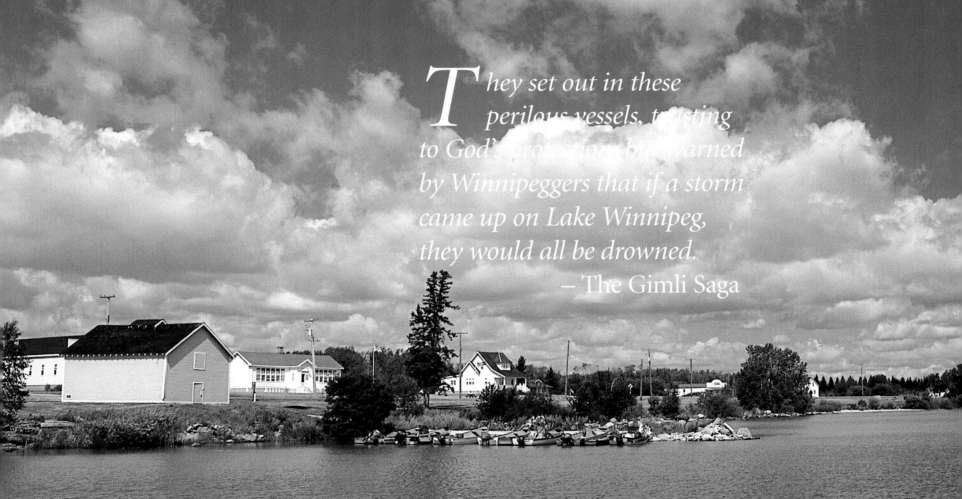

The Icelandic Saga

*T*hey set out in these
perilous vessels, trusting
to God's protection, but warned
by Winnipeggers that if a storm
came up on Lake Winnipeg,
they would all be drowned.

— The Gimli Saga

The Icelandic Saga

O N OCTOBER 17, 1875, the 285 Icelanders who were to build Lake Winnipeg's first permanent European community set sail from Notre Dame Avenue's East Wharf in Winnipeg. Unable to afford passage on the Hudson's Bay Company's lake steamer, the S.S. *Colvile*, they purchased one York boat and several flat bottomed scows steered by giant paddles. Normally used to transport lumber and fuel, one was of such questionable seaworthiness that the settlers dubbed it *Vitfirring*, or "Maniac".

The voyage was slow and difficult and the scows often ran aground. Arriving at the St. Andrew's Rapids (now Lockport) on a Sunday, the boats were moored and a sermon was preached to the flock. Their prayers said, the company commenced the tricky and dangerous task of traversing the rapids, where their baggage was damaged but no lives were lost.

Farther downstream, at the crossing below Selkirk, the boats became entangled in the nets of some Ojibwe fishers, causing one of the women to scream and gesticulate at the newcomers. The incident would prove an aberration. In the years to come, relations between the Icelanders and their North American neighbours were generally as warm and mutually supportive as one might expect among people thrown together in a harsh and often dangerous environment. In one instance, they became the stuff of legend.

Entering Lake Winnipeg, the colonists met the HBC's *Colvile*. It is unclear whether a prior arrangement had been made for the ship to tow the train of boats, or whether the

The church at Hecla BARBARA ENDRES

steamer provided the service as a matter of courtesy. Historians believe it was more likely the latter as the colonists had apparently planned to pole their flat-bottomed boats all the way themselves. They had no idea how perilous that was, a reality subsequent travellers found out, often tragically. During the next 20 years, many people drowned trying to get to Gimli on similar craft.

The Icelanders' original destination was the Whitemud (Icelandic) River, but an unfavourable wind and a ruffled lake changed all that. At about 5 p.m. on October 21st, the *Colvile* cast anchor off what is now called Willow Point, a kilometre south of the present Gimli harbour. The ship's captain said it would be insane to try for the river and equally dangerous for him to bring his ship closer to shore.

As a result, on the first day of winter according to the Icelandic calendar, the York boat manned by eight oarsmen pulled the improbable fleet into a little bay. The settlers walked up and down the sand bar that evening and spent their first night in the boats. During the hours of darkness, their number grew to 286. The birth of a baby boy, Jon Johannsson, was taken by the colonists as a sign that they had staked their claim to New Iceland.

Though the settlers passed that first winter huddled in the scows or in buffalo-hide tents borrowed from the HBC, a warehouse and a store were built and the men embarked on what would be the colony's main industry, fishing. Early attempts proved fruitless, for the nets they had brought from Iceland proved too large-skeined for the lake fish. Cash was added to hunger as an incentive for the first Lake Winnipeg catch. The $5 prize went to Kristmundur Benjaminsson, who landed a goldeye. Contemporary accounts report that "a crowd rushed to inspect this unfamiliar species of fish that later became prized as a delicacy". [1]

Adversity was nothing new to the colonists; it was what had driven them to seek a new beginning in the New World. Icelanders are descendants of Norsemen who left Norway in the ninth century to escape the rule of King Harold Fairhair (Haarfaager) of Norway and of Celts who came later from the British Isles. With this ancestry, the sea was in their blood and ships were their second home. Nor was North America unfamiliar; a group of would-be colonists, led by Leifr Eiriksson (or Leif Ericsson, as we know him today) had landed on the shores of today's Newfoundland about 1000 AD.

Iceland is stunningly beautiful, with its snow-topped peaks, blue fjords, fast rivers and brilliant green meadows, but the earth's crust is very thin and volcanic activity is an ever-present threat. The last third of the 19th century was a dismal period in Iceland. Under Danish rule, the country was mired in poverty.

The crippling impact of Danish trade restrictions was made worse by harsh winters and an epidemic that killed 200,000 sheep. In the early 1870s, the land was wracked by volcanic eruptions, which reached their peak in 1873. The following year, the weather inflicted hardships of another kind. The winter of 1874 was one of the most severe on record, lasting well into summer. In September, the island was devastated by a violent week-long windstorm, which destroyed many homes, ships, crops and livestock. Little wonder many were open to the prospect of emigration.

The Icelanders who founded Gimli were part of a group of 375 who left the homeland in 1874 to come to Canada, settling first in Kinmount, Ontario. There, they were housed in four hastily constructed log sheds where conditions were so bad that almost all children under the age of two as well as a number of elderly people died.

The next year, 1875, was as mild as 1874 had been cold in Iceland. However, just two years after the island had been wracked by volcanic activity, Iceland's numerous volcanoes all seemed to awaken at once. There was a tremendous eruption of Mount Askja and the neighbouring Dyngja Mountains, devastating a 6,475-square-kilometre area. At the end of their tethers, large numbers of people decided to emigrate and embarked for Brazil and various parts of the U.S. and Canada.

With the blessing of the Canadian government, an expedition led by John Taylor, a lay missionary, and Sigtryggur Jonasson, the leader of the Kinmount settlers, went to Red River in the early summer of 1875 to explore the possibility of a colony. Arriving in Winnipeg, they encountered a severe grasshopper infestation. It was so bad, reports of the time claimed, the insects blackened the sky and "were swept up in truckloads on Main Street and piled in mounds up to five feet high on the riverbanks". [2]

Dismayed, the colonists' advance guard bypassed the river valley's rich agricultural land and explored instead the Keewatin district along the west shore of Lake Winnipeg. At that time, Manitoba was the Postage Stamp province, extending north just to Boundary Creek in today's Winnipeg Beach.

The Icelanders were granted exclusive rights of colonization to an 812-square kilometre area running 58 kilometres north of Boundary Creek and inland an average 14 kilometres. Included in it were two islands, Mikley (Mickle

Sigtryggur Jonasson, left, died just four years after leading the original group of Icelanders to the shores of Lake Winnipeg.

The tiny "postage stamp" province that entered Confederation in 1870 was expanded in 1881 to include roughly a third of Manitoba's current mass and enlarged yet again in 1912 to its present size and shape.

73

GIMLI

The name "Gimli" arises from an Icelandic legend. According to the ancient *Voluspa* (Sibyl's Prophecy), found in the *Elder Edda*, the earth is destined to vanish, destroyed in the flames of war. Thereafter will arise a new and better world, inhabited by just and good people, who will live forever at peace in their heavenly abode of Gimli. [4]

While Manitoba lacks Iceland's mountains and glaciers, Lake Winnipeg's ever-changing, ever-challenging waterscapes must have made the newcomers feel at home.

Isle, or Big Island) now called Hecla Island, and Engey (Meadow Island) now called Goose Island. A later enlargement, bringing the colony's length to 67 kilometres, added the Isafold community.

Jonasson and Taylor enthusiastically recommended the site to the Kinmount colonists. But they were financially destitute and there was no provision in Canadian law for assistance to settlers moving within the country. Fortunately for the Icelanders, Governor General Lord Dufferin had visited Iceland and come away a great admirer of the Icelandic people. In his book, *Letters from High Latitudes,* he described them as sincere, honest and peaceful and noted approvingly that in Iceland, crimes, police, prisons and armies were not to be found. [3] Lord Dufferin pledged his personal word that the Icelanders would prove desirable colonists and the Canadian government made a grant enabling the settlers to move west.

They received a warm welcome when they arrived in Winnipeg on October 11th. The next day, the *Manitoba Free Press* commented in an editorial: "They are a smart-looking, intelligent and excellent people and a most valuable acquisition to the population ..."

When the colonists disembarked from their boats that October evening, they were landing in more than a colony. For 12 years, from 1875 to 1887, New Iceland was an independent republic with its own constitution, its own official language, its own civil law and a unique and very elaborate system of social welfare for widows and the indigent.

The republic, called Vatnsthing or "Lake Country", was divided into four districts like the ancient quarter-sections of 10th-century Iceland: Vidinesbyggd (Willow Point District); Arnesbyggd (Arnes District); Fljotsbyggd (River District) and Mikleyjarbyggd (Big Island District). Each

district elected its own council of five members. A regional council of six, called the Thingrad, administered the colony's general affairs. The president (Thingradsgtjori) and vice-president (Vara Thingradsgtjori) were elected annually by all eligible electors. The regional council met once a year on March 11th at Gimli to discuss major issues and changes to the constitution. Records for the republic were kept in five books. Book One contained the minutes of meetings; Book Two, the census figures; Book Three, road-building records; Book Four, vital statistics including births, deaths and marriages and Book Five, records of land transactions and values.

The republic was absorbed into Manitoba in 1881 when the provincial boundaries were extended north. Initial local resistance meant that the republic's constitution remained in force for another six years, after which New Iceland adopted local municipal government forms.

MIKE GRANDMAISON

The lava flows and choking ash of Iceland's volcanoes were hardly worse than the travails and grief awaiting the first colonists of the new republic. During the first winter, the settlers endured bitter cold, scurvy and starvation. One man lost seven of his nine children and many left the colony. Of the 100 or so who remained, about a third died. Nevertheless, three issues of a handwritten newspaper were published, a school was begun and a New Year's feast was held at John Taylor's home, the main course of which was a well-seasoned giant pike.

The next year, another 1,200 souls, the "large group", arrived, driven by the devastation of the ongoing volcanic eruptions. But in Canada, equally harsh fates awaited many. One died from eating a poisonous plant. Two were so severely frostbitten after losing their way and wandering three days on the lake that one of them was forced to clear his land on his knees for the next three years. An elderly widow died of exposure on the lake and two men drowned.

Still, the colonists persevered. Lots were laid out along the lake and named, for naming ceremonies are very important in Icelandic culture. Accustomed to stone and earth as building materials, the Icelanders struggled to learn how to construct log cabins that would keep out the snow, cold and wind. Farming, often on poor rocky soil, clearing the dense forest, they laboured largely with their bare hands. Still, reading and education were paramount. Even the most rudimentary dwellings boasted libraries of 30 or 40 books.

Hunger, cold and exposure soon paled before the little colony's most dreadful tragedy. In the fall of 1876, a smallpox epidemic broke out, brought, it was thought, by the so-called "large group" of immigrants. The Manitoba government put the colony under quarantine on November 27th, establishing the line at Netley Creek. A hospital was estab-

DENNIS FAST

lished in a Gimli storehouse and three doctors were sent in to treat the patients. Over one-third of the settlers contracted the disease and 100 people died. But in the hospital, all but one of the 64 patients survived.

Sandy Bar, an Ojibwe village just south of Lundi, present-day Riverton, was wiped out. During the winter, the pox was carried across the lake where it destroyed entire Anishinabe communities. The few survivors hung the corpses of their loved ones in the trees to keep them from the wolves until the ground thawed and they could be buried. The following spring government agents ordered the burning of what was left of the lake's tiny eastern shore settlements to kill off the disease.

The course of this disaster and graphic descriptions of the colonists' hardscrabble existence are captured for posterity in a document to be found in the Provincial Archives

The first settlers had scarcely erected their borrowed tents, when the first frosts turned Lake Winnipeg to a dazzling ice sculpture, forcing the newcomers to learn about ice fishing.

of Manitoba, known simply as The Smallpox Letter. It was written by Dr. Augustus Baldwin, one of the three doctors commissioned by the government to treat the epidemic, on March 13, 1877. Despite its idiosyncratic spelling and grammar, as well as Baldwin's rather disengaged style, the horror of the times is clear.

My darling Phoebe, I left on Sunday the 26th of November – I got up to Gimli the next day – in the evening. Next morning I went over with Dr. Lynch – to visit the Hospital. It was full of patients, of course all with small pox. They were to be seen at every stage, some dieing and some convalescent. The next day, I went to visit several houses and such a sight you never saw – Every house had somebody down with the disease – The settlement extends about forty-five Miles. And the houses were of the worst discription. I had to stoop to go into nearly every house – There were some doors so low, that I had to go on my hands and knees to get in – And such filth. I cannot describe it ... I always slept with my clothes on, so that I would not get lice on me ...

The houses are all one room. And in some there would be 18 or 19 in them. They would all be huddled together like so many pigs – And then those houses that had room, they would have their cows in them – You can imagin that it would not smell very sweet ...

On my first trip, when I was forty miles north of Gimli, – on one of those large Islands – my guide took the small pox. Well as he and I used the same blankits ... I had to sleep with him and he with the eruption out on him – for four nights. At the end of that time I was able to get another guide. And then

started across again to White Mud River, but night – and a storm over took us before we could reach the land - and we could not see where to go to – And here we were out on the Lake, and no shelter – I quite made up my mind that I would loose either my feet or hands ... But at last my guide found land ... On my third trip I had to amputate three feet that got badly frozen – The poor devils got lost on the Lake in a storm. One has no Idea what a storm is on the Lake unless they have been in one themselves.

For three months I did nothing but treat for small pox – so you can imagin that I have seen enough of it – When I went to some of the houses, I would find perhaps some six or eight sick, some that only had a few hours to live – You would see Old Men and woman, Young men and girls, and poor little infants that would make the hardest heart ache for them.

On my second trip I hear that there was a family on Big Black Island. So I went to see them. And such a sight. The Mother had just got over the small pox and her infant at her breast, dieing and they had not a thing to cover the poor thing – The house was so small that I could not stand up in it. I was compeled to sit down. I brought my tea and pemacan, and me and my Indian guide had to have our dinner on that a lone – after a whole day's travel – They had no flour in fact, had nothing but fish – I left what medicine and nourishment I had – which I brought for the sick– and to see their eyes brighten up, to hopes that it came in time to save their little one can never be forgotten – But alas, the little thing only nine months old, died next day. And then they had to put the little thing on top of the house till they could get some boards to make a box for the little one ...

I had a pretty hard time myself, but when I looked at the poor Icelanders I faired like a King ...

The creation of the Republic of New Iceland and the prospect that steamboat travel on Lake Winnipeg would open the lake's vast mineral, timber and fish potential were the two major motivations for Treaty Five, which extinguished aboriginal title to most of the land around the lake. About 200 families were involved; some of the bands on the east side of the lake had already signed either Treaty One or Treaty Two.

On May 21, 1875, Manitoba Lieutenant-Governor Alexander Morris wrote a letter to the Minister of the Interior outlining the most comprehensive rationale for Treaty Five: "The progress of navigation by steamer on Lake Winnipeg, the establishment of Missions and of saw milling enterprises, the discovery of minerals on the shores and vicinity of the lake as well as migration of the Norway House Indians all point to the necessity of the Treaty being made without delay." [5]

Aboriginal Manitobans had long been anxious for treaty settlement. As early as 1857, the great Chief Peguis wrote to the Aborigines Protection Society:

We are not only willing, but very anxious after being paid for our lands, that the whites would come and settle among us, for we have already derived great benefits from their having done so, that is not the traders, but the farmers. The traders have never done anything but rob us and keep us poor, but the farmers have taught us how to farm and raise cattle. [6]

Sadly, Chief Peguis came to realize how misplaced his faith was in the integrity and honesty of the European settlers and their government. Fortunately, he didn't live to witness the ultimate betrayal of his people.

The advent of steamships on the lake meant the loss of employment for the Norway House Cree as boatmen on the Hayes River. Increasingly, the Hudson's Bay Company preferred to send its goods south via the Red River through the United States. As compensation, the Norway House Band asked for a reserve at Grassy Narrows where the causeway now links the mainland and Hecla Island. They, too, hoped to take up farming. They were refused. Some went to Fisher River and the rest stayed at Norway House.

At Grand Rapids, the Saskatchewan River Cree sought recompense for the negative impact on their fish and fur resources caused by the growing steamboat traffic, a traffic accompanied by shrieking whistles, clouds of black smoke and destruction of the forest to produce timber for the ships' boilers.

The government, meanwhile, was anxious to get the maximum in concessions while ceding the minimum. Morris used the HBC steamer SS *Colvile* to meet with the Lake Winnipeg bands. At each location, the Treaty Five talks began and concluded in a single day. Fully 160,000 square kilometres of land were given up by the Cree and the Ojibwe; in return the people received reserves of 160 acres per family of five and individual annuities of five dollars a year, a settlement that contrasted very poorly with the 640 acres and $12 annual payments provided by Treaty Three and Treaty Four.

The Grand Rapids Band ended up with a reserve comprised largely of muskeg. Nevertheless, the people set about

The continual assistance Chief Peguis, left, and his Saulteaux people rendered early European settlers is recalled on his gravestone in the churchyard at St. Peter's Dynevor Church in East Selkirk.

St. Peter's, built in 1836, is among the oldest churches in Western Canada. Though the Saulteaux left it behind when they were relocated north to Manitoba's Interlake, it still reflects the time they spent along the Red River.

DENNIS FAST

trying to raise potatoes and cattle and attempted to adopt the agricultural life envisaged in the treaty. After much pleading, they obtained additional land in 1896, but the government refused their request to have their reserve include the river and its rapids, which they claimed as their ancestral possession. The strategically located river and rapids were considered to be vital to Canada, Manitoba and the HBC.

One of the most shameful episodes in the long and often tragic history of European and North American relations occurred in September 1907 with the surrender of the St. Peter's Reserve north of Selkirk and the subsequent forced relocation of the people 160 kilometres north to the Fisher River. The yielding of the land Chief Peguis had specifically retained for his people in negotiations with Lord Selkirk in 1817, 90 years earlier, was accomplished by bribery, trickery and an outright denial of due process. Reserve residents were given less than two days' notice of the vote on the sale of their ancestral home and that notice was posted in English only. The schoolhouse where it was held was too small to accommodate the few people – about 200 – who had heard about the meeting and were able to attend. Those unable to get in crowded around the building trying to hear, as those inside attempted to keep them informed of the proceedings.

As a final act of treachery, the government agent, Frank Pedley, threatened those present that they either gave up their title or they would get "nothing", a reference to the $5,000 cash he had brought with him in a satchel to give out on the spot.

The people of St. Peter's lost 48,000 acres of prime agricultural land for less than one-tenth its value at the time. With winter coming on, they were taken up the lake on the SS *City of Selkirk* and the SS *Frederick* to Fisher River, where they were confronted by raw, hardscrabble land, no seed, no agricultural implements, no houses, no schools, no road and no opportunities for employment. [7]

This was how the Government of Canada repaid the people of St. Peter's and Chief Peguis, without whose countless acts of generosity and assistance the fledgling Red River Colony would never have survived.

Though contested land titles almost invariably ended in disaster for aboriginal people, in one instance they laid the foundation for a cross-cultural legend that forged a unique and lasting bond between Manitobans of aboriginal and Icelandic descent. During the winter of 1875-76, three Icelandic families decided to settle at the colony's original destination, the Whitemud, or Icelandic, River. When they commenced construction of a hut on the river's north shore, an Ojibwe whom they would come to know as John Ramsay attempted to push their boat away from the bank. One of the colonists drove him off, threatening him with an axe.

Determined to defend what they considered to be Ojibwe territory, a number of men began rowing rapidly up and down the river, ostensibly shooting at birds, but, the three Icelandic families believed, trying to intimidate them into leaving.

The tense episode culminated with the Ojibwe striding into the hut with their guns, sitting down in a silent semi-circle and glaring at the colonists, who stood opposite them, equally silent, glaring back.

At dusk, Ramsay returned with an interpreter. After some discussion, the two sides decided to allow the Indian agent to settle the issue. The agent said that the colony's land did indeed include the river's north bank. In fact, it did not, but the Ojibwe immediately abandoned their protests.

By all accounts, Ramsay was a striking figure, tall, lean and handsome, with shoulder-length hair, a mustache and a close-cropped beard. Once the land controversy was over, he became a friend and even a saviour to the settlers, giving them wild meat, teaching them how to chink their log cabins with moss, waterproof their boats and shoot with a bow and arrow. Whenever he found a family short of food, he invited them to his cabin for a meal of venison, bannock, syrup, dried berries and tea. A skilled hunter, he often hunted solely to put food on the colonists' tables. Repeating a pattern that had accompanied European contact across the Americas, Ramsay's kindness was to cost him dearly.

In the smallpox epidemic of 1876, Ramsay's wife Betsey and two little sons contracted smallpox and died, while his daughter Mary survived but was badly scarred. Ramsay buried Betsey south of Sandy Bar, as the story goes, "near the lake and the sounds she loved – waves beating against the shore, the cries of seagulls wheeling overhead, the haunting call of the geese winging their way northward." [8]

The grieving husband then trekked to Fort Garry where he traded his furs for a tombstone to mark Betsey's grave. The clerk misunderstood and Ramsay became "Rumsay" on the stone. The inscription on the stone, in a mixture of writing and printing, says: "In Memory of Betsey, Beloved Wife of John Rumsay Who Died September 1876 Aged 35 years".

Ramsay pulled the tombstone on a sled from Fort Garry to Sandy Bar, laid it on the grave and encircled the site with a stout fence. He then closed his cabin and fled north to Matheson Island with his little daughter.

IAN WARD

When spring came, the remaining residents of Sandy Bar moved away too; leaving behind their deserted cabins and their many graves.

The years rolled by. Sandy Bar became a farm and the fence around Betsey's grave was broken and trampled by farm animals. On Matheson Island, John Ramsay, now grown old, learned from fishers that the fence had disappeared, leaving the grave exposed. He sent word to the settlement, asking for the fence to be replaced, but no one heeded his request. And so he died, his plea unanswered.

According to the legend, in 1910, a young man named Trausti Vigfusson took a homestead in Geysir (today's Arborg) and built himself a cabin. Shortly after his cabin was completed, he had a strange dream. He was standing near his cabin "when a tall, handsome Indian strode out of the forest and held up his hand in greeting, giving his name."

Vigfusson, too, extended his hand. He had heard of Ramsay and also of his kindnesses towards the settlers.

John Ramsay would undoubtedly be happy to see the state of Betsey's gravesite today, surrounded as it is by a stout fence amid the ripening grain.

79

HECLA

Mikley's biggest community was christened Hecla by its first residents. The name came from Iceland's Mount Hekla, a volcano often mentioned in old writings as "the entrance to hell". Hekla erupted in 1845-46 and again in 1878. The original meaning of the word, Hekla, is a hooded cloak knitted in diverse colours. The volcano was black on top, with normally black sides except in deep winter when, white with snow, it looked like a figure dressed in a hooded cloak of black and white. The town's name was extended to encompass the entire island in 1903. [9]

Ramsay asked Vigfusson to build a fence around Betsey's grave. Vigfusson knew about the suffering at Sandy Bar in the winter of 1876, acknowledged that it was a small request and promised to fulfill it. But on waking, it slipped from his memory. Months went by and then, one night, Vigfusson again dreamed that Ramsay visited him, this time chiding him. Filled with remorse, Vigfusson took Ramsay's hand in both his own and again promised to build the fence to repay Ramsay for all the kindnesses he had shown the Icelanders many years ago. Pleased, Ramsay departed, adding enigmatically, "You will not forget. Ramsay will not forget either."

The next day, Vigfusson set to work carving the pickets. When the haying season was over, he piled the pickets and the lumber for the framework on a wagon and set off for Sandy Bar. But Vigfusson was not without his own troubles; he had no money and was almost out of food. He hoped to obtain groceries on credit from the store at Hnausa. First, though, he headed north, towards the gravesite, now part of Gestur Gudmundsson's farm at Sandy Bar.

The Gudmundssons didn't think his errand a strange one. They showed him Betsey Ramsay's grave and the next morning, as he had promised Ramsay, Vigfusson built the sturdy fence. Just as he was preparing to set off for home, Gudmundsson put two huge bags of fish on his wagon, declaring, "One good turn deserves another. This is for Ramsay."

The story goes that never again was Vigfusson's lot as hard as it had been that day. He became the master builder of the community. The houses and churches he built still stand there, mute testimony to his craftsmanship.

As a centennial project, the town of Riverton had the grave covered with concrete and decorative stones. And in 1998, the story of Betsey Ramsay's grave and Trausti Vigfusson's dreams, which were verified by his daughters, became the subject of a documentary film co-directed by Phil Manaigre and Claude Forest.

Despite its traumas and tragedies, the colony developed a rich cultural and social life. On September 1, 1877, the inaugural issue of *Framfari*, (Progress) the first Icelandic newspaper in the colony, came off the presses. It was published by a public company, The New Iceland Printing Company, which was formed by the sale of $10 shares. Four-page issues were printed three times a week. Subscribers paid $1.15 annually if they lived in the colony, $1.35 if they lived elsewhere in Canada and the U.S. and seven Icelandic crowns if they lived in the mother country. The creation of a newspaper in a community of just 1,500 souls less than two years after its founding and in the year of a devastating epidemic is considered a unique achievement in the annals of journalism. But, plagued with financial problems, the paper ceased publication in 1880.

The lively intellectual life of the colony produced, in 1877–78, an unlikely clash, a religious "war" between the supporters of Hecla's Reverend Jon Bjarnason, "Jonsmenn", and the those of Reverend Pall Thorlaksson, "Palsmenn". Thorlaksson was the uncle of the doctor who began the Winnipeg Clinic, Paul Thorlakson.

The Jonsmenn were Icelandic Lutherans, religious free-thinkers who largely became Unitarians, while the Palsmenn were Norwegian Lutherans, religious fundamentalists. The Jonsmenn welcomed non-Icelandic settlement and thought the future for the Lake Winnipeg colony was bright. The Palsmenn wanted all the Icelanders in North America to come together in the U.S., to continue to hew to traditional ways and preserve their links to the fundamentalist Missouri Synod.

According to Gimli historian and author David Arnason, the two opposing factions "were fighting for the soul of New Iceland. Pall Thorlaksson nearly wrecked the settlement by convincing a large number of people to leave and follow him to North Dakota. [The departure] put the settlement in real danger. But in 1883, came this huge influx of 6,000 to 8,000 people who suddenly made it really viable."

Arnason says the Gimli settlement also caused hard feelings in the mother country. "There was this feeling in Iceland for years that the people who left had abandoned the battle for independence and had they stayed, Iceland would have got its independence in the 1880s rather than having to wait till 1943 when Hitler invaded Denmark." [10]

Mikley, or Big Island, was settled by the second "large group" of Icelanders who came to Canada in 1876. One account has it that some colonists were travelling farther north up Lake Winnipeg in a flatboat when one of their cows, weary of the journey, jumped overboard and headed for the nearest land, which turned out to be Mikley. Landing on the island to retrieve the cow, the settlers liked what they saw and decided to stay.

They were not, by any means, the first to set foot on the island, which nestles in the lake immediately south of Grindstone Point and west of Black Island. For centuries, it had been used as a stopover point for aboriginal fishermen and a Scot, Thomas Hillgrow from Selkirk, was operating a sawmill there when the Icelanders arrived. Relations between the newcomers and Hillgrow were strained until he married an Icelandic girl.

The Mikley settlers were generally better off than those in the other parts of New Iceland

PROVINCIAL ARCHIVES OF MANITOBA / N–11432

because they had greater access to timber, pastures and fishing on the lake. Hillgrow taught some of the Icelanders how to fish through the ice.

The colony was relatively isolated until 1954, when a regular ferry service was commenced linking the island to the mainland. Prior to that, leaving the island meant a nine-hour trip by steamer to Selkirk or a four-hour trip around the north of the island to Riverton. The ferry was replaced by a causeway in 1972.

Socials and all-night concerts were the order of the day to break the feeling of isolation during the long winters on the island. One resident recalled:

We would dance all night and when the sun came up young and old alike would pile into horse-drawn sleighs and we would go for a trip around the island. When they went to socials or concerts people would dress up their horses smartly with colourful handmade blankets and decorations on the horses' harnesses.

We had our own cows, and we produced our own butter, milk, cheese and meat. We didn't go to the market for much in those days and those things that we had to buy like sugar, coffee and flour would come in large bags and wooden pails.

Fish were so plentiful off-shore that you could wade out to

PROVINCIAL ARCHIVES OF MANITOBA / N–11430

After its initial years of hardship, Gimli grew steadily. The village, seen from the roof of the Lyric Theatre in 1912, left, became a bustling town by 1942, when this photograph, above, looking west along Centre Street from the dock, was taken.

DENNIS FAST

Manitoba's Icelandic community remembers its Nordic roots in many ways, including this statue of a viking, in Gimli.

American white pelicans, sometimes dubbed "the Icelandic airforce", gather in large numbers on the islets in the lake.

your waist in the water and within an hour you would have plenty for that day and some to put away as well.

If anyone ever got sick on this island, or disabled, it was accepted in the community that someone just had to do his share of the work for him. [11]

The island's population grew steadily until, by the 1920s, more than 500 people made their homes there. In 1969, most of the inhabitants of the island were bought out when Hecla was included in a provincial park along with Grindstone Point and the undeveloped islands of Deer, Little Punk, Punk and Goose. The creation of the park coincided with closure of the lake fishery for two years due to mercury contamination.

About half of the families on Hecla sold willingly and most of the rest were expropriated, but four simply refused to leave. All told, 60 families, largely descendants of the original settlers, moved away. The wisdom and fairness of the expropriation prompted bitterness and divided opinions for more than a quarter-century until, in 1997, the government allowed those who had owned property on the island or their descendants to repurchase their land. Initially, 35 ex-landowners or their families signed $5,000, 21-year renewable leases for two-hectare parcels of land. By 2000, the province had released 47 of the 50 lots to their original owners or relatives. The remaining three were sold by public draw and all were bought by a single family from Gimli. A small group of cottagers at Gull Harbour also were able to reclaim their properties.

Despite strong objections from the Manitoba chapter of the Canadian Parks and Wilderness Society, the province has permitted 65 cottage lots to be developed on the island's northwest shoreline, again on the 21-year renewable lease system and, as of mid-2000, was considering making more lots available along the shore at West Quarry. [12]

The first Islendingadagurinn, a festival celebrating the Icelandic culture and the colony's survival in a new land, was held in 1889, in Winnipeg's Victoria Gardens. It became an annual event, and moved to Gimli in 1932. Now it is one of the biggest and most famous summer festivals in Manitoba. Lasting three days, it features a variety of activities including a social, a parade, fine art displays, a variety of contests, a celebrity concert, fireworks, community singalongs, beer gardens, the naming of the Maid of the Mountain and the hilarious Islendingadunk in which two people, suspended on a pole over water hit one another with pillows until only one is left standing.

Each year, the festival plays host to an honoured guest from Iceland. Presidents and prime ministers have been among the attendees, testament to Gimli's importance as the largest settlement of Icelanders outside the mother country. Further testament to the pride and strength of Manitoba's Icelandic community and the significant contribution it continues to make to all walks of provincial life was the opening, in October 2000, of the New Iceland Museum in Gimli.

PETER ST. JOHN

Today, Gimli Harbour draws a mix of pleasure and commercial craft. DENNIS FAST

The Lake's Year-round Fishery

From the very beginning, Lake Winnipeg was fished year-round. Aboriginal fishers cut holes in the winter ice and taught the Icelanders and other Europeans the intricacies of ice fishing.

Lake Winnipeg has the largest inland fishery in Canada. The lake's fecundity is attributable to its shallowness, which allows the water to warm quickly, encouraging fish growth. It also means the

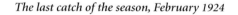

The last catch of the season, February 1924

lake mixes readily, drawing nutrients from the bottom. The famous goldeye is not the only valuable catch from its waters. Lake Winnipeg pickerel, fried in butter, is considered a delicious delicacy. As well, Lake Winnipeg whitefish is exported all over North America.

The Freshwater Fish Marketing Corporation, the federal body that markets the lake's output, restricts the catch by quotas alloted to fishers in three defined areas: the north basin, the centre or channel basin, extending from Berens River to Hecla Island, and the south basin.

There have been many attempts over the years to track fish movements in the lake. The fisheries branch began tagging whitefish in 1938 and by 1976, 10,000 had been tagged but no discernable movement was discovered between the north and south basins. A total of 22,000 pickerel and 14,000 sauger were tagged from 1954 to 1970, but this, too, revealed little movement between the two basins. Most fish migrations are attributed to spawning when the fish swim towards the shore and into the many streams. Whitefish spawn in the fall, while pickerel and perch lay their eggs in the spring. Those who fish the lake are certain

of one thing: wind is a major factor. According to one longtime Matheson Island fisher, northwest winds bring in the fish, while southwest winds make them disappear.

Winter or ice fishing was not just a simple matter of drilling a hole in the ice and putting down a line. To make it commercially feasible, fishers had to find a way to set their nets under the frozen lake, just as they set them on the open water in summer. A delightful description of the ingenious tool that makes it all possible appears in a childrens' book written by Gimli author W. D. Valgardson and illustrated by Ange Zhang. Thor is visiting his grandfather, a Lake Winnipeg fisherman, for the Christmas holidays. Grandfather and grandson set out in the family's Bombardier which carries a big auger to drill the ice and hauls a cozy caboose heated by its own cookstove.

As they drive onto the lake, they confront a long pressure ridge as tall as a house. Grandfather tells Thor the ridge is caused by the same process that makes his soft drink swell when he puts it in the freezer. "The ice expands and gets too big for the lake and pushes up," he says. Just as they reach a place where the ice is clear and dark, they hear a booming noise like a huge explosion. "That's the ice cracking. Sometimes the ice pulls apart and leaves open water. We have to watch for cracks," Grandfather warns. He starts the auger to drill through the ice.

Grandfather wants to set his nets a distance of forty fathoms. After drilling the hole he takes a long plank of wood with a spring and a piece of metal in the middle and pushes it under the ice. "This is a jigger," he tells Thor. "It walks under the ice." The wood's buoyancy presses it tight against the bottom of the ice surface. A running line is attached. Alternately, he pulls it and lets it go.

"When I pull, this piece of metal catches on the ice. When I let go it pushes the board forward. It'll pull the running line along.

Your job is to walk above it and listen. The ice is too thick to see the jigger, but you can hear it. You have to listen closely. When the string is at forty fathoms, the jigger will stop. Then we'll dig a hole there."

Thor stood where Grandfather had put the jigger. Grandfather pulled the running line and let go. Thor heard a click. Then another one. Thor walked along the ice listening carefully, leaning against the wind to keep from being blown away. He wondered if maybe he shouldn't have put some rocks in his pockets to keep his feet on the ice. [13]

Ice fishing became commercially viable in the late 1800s and persists to this day. In its early years, a unique way of life developed around the industry, complete with fishing camps, freight gangs, teams of horses, dog sleds and, of course, bitter cold and ever-present danger.

The danger came in two forms. Storms on the lake are as sudden in winter as they are in summer and just as lethal. In summer, the lake is whipped into a white-capped frenzy in minutes, while in winter the snow can simply bury a small campsite, leaving its occupant alone and exposed in an immense white wasteland. Another peril arises from the nature of the lake ice. Freezing and thawing produce expansion and contraction. The winds shift the ice pans. All these factors mean that, without warning, giant cracks can open, cutting a fisherman off from his camp or even worse, suddenly dumping him into the frigid water. Many have survived a dunking only to die of exposure because their clothes froze, immobilizing them before they could reach shelter.

In his book, *The Icelanders*, David Arnason writes:

In the winter, the lake was the broadest highway in the world ... What was a hard journey in summer was a casual visit in winter ... There were tricks you learned ... Your wife knitted woolen mitts much too large, then coated them with soap and boiled them in hot water till they shrunk and were thicker and warmer than you could believe. You might keep a pail of boiling water on the stove, and throw your frozen mitts into it. The hot, wet mitts would last through the lifting of one net until they froze again. [14]

Campsites on the lake ranged from primitive to reasonably comfortable, from tents to sheltered shoreline log cabins or cabooses on sleighs, complete with cookstoves. Initially, ox teams were used to collect the boxes of fish from the camps, but they proved too slow and were soon replaced by horses. Long freight trains became a familiar sight on the lake, each with its own snowplow. A typical freight sleigh carried 220 57-kilogram (or 125-pound) boxes of fish, for a total load of 15 or 16 tonnes. The most difficult part for the teamsters was getting started each morning. Sometimes it took as many as three two-horse teams to get each sleigh going. Once the runners were freed from the ice, however, they seemed to generate heat and run almost on their own.

In an article in the Spring 1982 issue of *The Beaver*, Karen Magnusson, the daughter and later wife of Gimli fish-buyers, describes the horse-drawn trains:

As the freight train drew near they could see the horses, white with frost, and hear in the cold crisp air their snorting sounds and the creak of the sleighs as they passed over the snow. The lead teams pulled the snow plough, clearing a swath for the sleighs behind. Next came the caboose where the driver usually sat snug and cosy, ensconced in his travelling home ... It had heaters, a table, a few shelves, benches and bunks for sleeping. Tents were extended from the sides of the caboose to shelter the horses at night ...

Once the freighting gang reached the fish camps there was a great bustle while news about the fishing and the journey north was exchanged.

After the empty boxes had been unloaded and replaced by boxes packed with fish, the teamsters yelled out a command to the horses and off they went, either to the next camp or on to the last lap of their journey into town. Once again the freight trains became small black dots on the horizon, then gradually they disappeared from sight. Once again the campsite and the fishers were the only visible signs of life on the vast white lake.

Fishing boats gather at Gimli, c. 1956
PROVINCIAL ARCHIVES OF MANITOBA / N–18234

the WICKED LAKE

Above: George Island and its lighthouse provide welcome sanctuary in the lake's vast north basin.

Right: In her early days, the SS Princess was the pride of Lake Winnipeg.

Below: Stripped of her finery and put to work, the Princess became a casualty of the lake's violent storms.

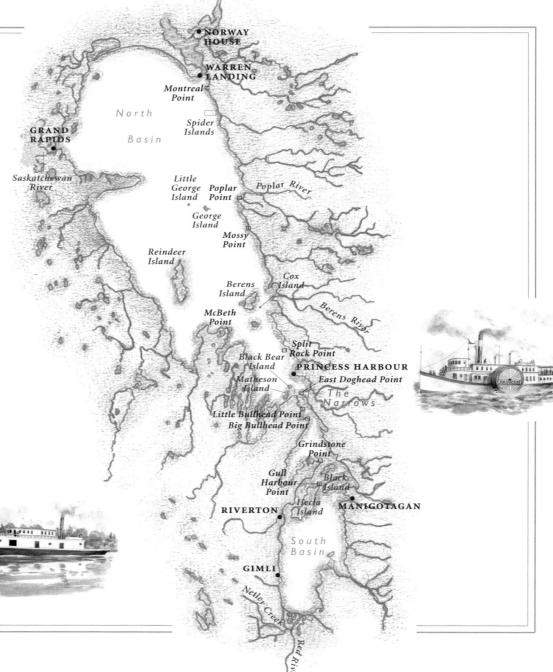

NORWAY HOUSE

WARREN LANDING

Montreal Point

North Basin

Spider Islands

GRAND RAPIDS

Little George Island   *Poplar Point*   *Poplar River*

Saskatchewan River

George Island

Mossy Point

Reindeer Island

Cox Island

Berens Island   *Berens River*

McBeth Point

Split Rock Point

Black Bear Island   PRINCESS HARBOUR

Matheson Island   *East Doghead Point*

The Narrows

Little Bullhead Point
Big Bullhead Point

Grindstone Point

Gull Harbour Point   *Black Island*

RIVERTON   *Hecla Island*   MANIGOTAGAN

South Basin

GIMLI

Netley Creek

Red River

86

Shipwreck!

What had been a mirror-like surface of water a few minutes ago now was a boiling, raging cauldron of unleashed fury, waves tossing high and flooding aboard ... Almost deafened by the roar of the wind and the crashes of thunder, Captain Anderson could only hope and pray that luck would not desert him on this night of nights ...

– Captain Ed Nelson

Shipwreck!

WITH GOOD REASON, Lake Winnipeg has been called "a boiling, raging cauldron of unleashed fury" and "a foaming, raging mistress" by its sailors. Its history is punctuated with tragedy, particularly after the arrival of Europeans. Unlike Canada's first peoples, Europeans have always assumed they could conquer nature. Emboldened by their technology, none but a knowledgeable few treated the lake with the respect that its tempestuous, unpredictable nature demanded. Many paid the price with their lives. Even today, hardly a summer goes by without incaution bred from invincibility finding catastrophe in the quick deadliness of one of Lake Winnipeg's legendary storms.

The first boat to challenge the lake's unfathomable nature was very likely the birchbark canoe. Constructed of cedar ribs, sheathed with birchbark, sewn and sealed with spruce roots and sap, these lissom craft were light to handle, swift on the water and beautiful to watch. Aware from the beginning that the lake was the centre or hub of a vast waterway, early Manitobans used the canoe to travel throughout their vast land. They freely shared their knowledge with European traders when they arrived. Paddling in the wake of the lake's first peoples, the Europeans soon made Lake Winnipeg the pivot of the fur trade's three water hubs.

Over time, French-Canadian voyageurs adapted the canoe to make it carry more. Three types emerged, the 11-metre, 273-kilogram *canot du maître*, the "master" or Montreal canoe, used in the St. Lawrence-Great Lakes region, the smaller eight-metre, 136-kilogram *canot du nord* (the north canoe) better-suited for the lakes and rivers west of the 14-kilometre Grand Portage from Lake Superior and the hybrid *canot batard*. Learning from their Cree and Ojibwe predecessors, the voyageurs hugged Lake Winnipeg's shores, loathe to challenge its deadly open water. By the late 18th century, the Hudson's Bay Company had also developed its own canoes, enlarging on designs used by its Cree trading partners.

Toward the end of the 1700s, fierce competition between the Hudson's Bay and North West Companies led to the invention of the York boat, which became, along with the plains bison and the Red River cart, a lasting symbol of Manitoba. Heavier and larger than a canoe, it was purportedly safer on the lake and carried a great deal more freight. Based on the Orkney yole, which in turn was descended from Norse inshore craft, the York boat was constructed of spruce and varied in length from nine to 12 metres.

The smaller version was manned by a crew of eight – six oarsmen, a bowsman and a steersman. The oars were six metres long and the oarsmen had to stand to push the oars forward and sit to finish the stroke. York boats also carried a square sail, which was unfurled whenever a stiff wind blew in the appropriate direction. The oarsmen were required to pole the boat through the shallows wherever possible, for the portages were brutal. Even the crude "roads" of log rollers did little or nothing to alleviate the backbreaking, lung-crushing labour of dragging and pushing these cumbersome behemoths and their freight overland through swamp and muskeg and across rock outcrops. Nor, really, did the York boats provide much more safety from the "foaming, raging mistress".

The outer light/Red River ED NELSON, COURTESY OF THE WNNIPEG FREE PRESS

The earliest reported fatality in a York boat occurred in 1855. A Miss Greenleaf (her first name was never recorded) was the English sister-in-law of William Stagg, the Anglican priest at Fairford Mission. Entranced as only a Victorian teenager could be with the romance of living on the western plains of North America, she took passage on the annual boat from England to York Factory to teach at the Fairford school.

From York, Miss Greenleaf set out for Red River in the same boat as the wife of another Anglican cleric, Mrs. William Hunter, the daughter of Donald Ross, HBC chief factor at Norway House. Mrs. Hunter was pregnant and just south of Norway House, the trip was delayed for the birth of her baby boy. The party was near Berens River when the weather turned and without warning, a storm struck. The York boat hit a sandbar, capsized and all were thrown into the water. By a miracle, the newborn was saved by his clothes, which kept him afloat. The new mother and her 18-year-old sister were also saved but of Miss Greenleaf there was no sign.

There are a number of references to this tragedy in the letters of the day, preserved in the Manitoba Archives. Henrietta Black, a member of the Ross family, wrote to her brother James, "that part of the lake has been cursed this fall". Mrs. Black's brother, William Ross, also wrote of the tragedy to James. "The boat capsized; the unfortunate lady was never seen ... This is the third casualty this summer, with Mowat's boat and the sloop wrecked." Miss Greenleaf's body was not recovered until the following year. [1]

Chief HBC Trader W. Cornwallis King has left a vivid portrayal of a Red River brigade caught in a fierce lake storm early in the summer of 1863. According to King, three York boats departed Lower Fort Garry to pick up goods from Fort Simpson on the Mackenzie River, a journey of 3,200 kilometres.

Initially confident, King spoke of the boats' "33-foot keel and an eight-foot beam. They were designed to travel over lakes, rivers and rapids." Then he looked at the toolbox of one of the men and was told it might mean life or death. "He was so earnest that I examined the contents carefully ..."

After a lazy drift down the Red River, the flotilla reached Lake Winnipeg at 3 a.m. on June 4th. A storm struck. Baptiste Bruce, the captain of King's boat, gave the command, '*Towich!*', and headed out into the middle of the lake.

King's story continues: "What does '*Towich*' mean?" I asked. "But though I stood immediately above the oarsman, my voice came faint through the hoarse wind. 'Out into the open lake. It is Cree,' he answered. Then he roared a curse of defiance as an avalanche of water raked the boat from stem to stern ..."

The wind became a gale and the captain took charge, shouting out his orders over the tumult of wind and water. "I found myself with the men, bailing, bailing," continued King. "Now I understood the wisdom of Bruce's command, '*Towich*'. Out here on open water, the waves were less treacherous than inshore. They were longer and heavier, more like sea-waves. Nearer shore, the backwash would have swamped the boat."

The men laboured and swore as the heavy combers struck the boat fore and aft, roaring over the bow and drenching them to the skin. The night was pitch black, the cold cut like pain and the seas continued their relentless

Lake Winnipeg lived up to its reputation for trouble in 1821, when Peter Rindisbacher and his Swiss relatives traversed the lake in late October. He portrayed the group's dilemma in Shipwreck *and halt on the great* Winipesi Lake, *below.*

PETER RINDISBACHER / NATIONAL ARCHIVES OF CANADA / C–1924

thumping. Finally, a gray dawn broke. Recalled King in grateful awe: "The first-water brand of seamanship of the Red River boatmen is no legend." [2]

Having relegated the canoe to little more than a pleasure craft, the York boat was itself eclipsed within 50 years by the steamship, dubbed the "fire canoe" by the Algonquian people for the clouds of black smoke, often punctuated by live sparks, that billowed from its funnels. This display was accompanied by animalistic snorts and chuffs and a shrieking steam whistle.

The first steamship to ply Manitoba's waters, the SS *Anson Northup*, was a doughty little vessel, short and boxy, with a smokestack like a fat, black cigar sticking up precisely amidships. Critics called her a "lumbering old pine-basket", yet the comic-opera *Northup* was a turning-point in Canadian history.

When the HBC arranged with the U.S. government in 1857 to have its goods brought through that country rather than York Factory, the St. Paul Chamber of Commerce offered $2,000 to anyone who could put a boat on the Red River. Anson Northup, the owner of a small steamer initially purchased for use on the upper Mississippi, took up the challenge. In the early spring of 1859, he dismantled the little boat and hauled her overland to the Red River, where a new hull was built. The steamer then headed downstream to Fort Garry, arriving on June 10th to a gala welcome. Following an excursion out onto Lake Winnipeg, she returned upriver.

As always during the 19th century, the fires of American annexation were burning bright. The prospect of steamboat traffic between St. Paul and Winnipeg caused open talk of union on both sides of the 49th parallel and spurred the nascent Canadian nation into creating Sir John A. Macdonald's "Dominion from Sea to Sea". In 1867, less than a decade

The Anson Northup *cut an unlikely figure for a heroine, but nonetheless made history.*

later, Canadian Confederation was achieved. Manitoba became the first "in" province in 1870, followed by British Columbia, enticed by the promise of a northern transcontinental railroad, a year later.

John H. McTavish, a member of the Manitoba Legislature in the 1870s and land commissioner for the Canadian Pacific Railway, reckoned that "unless a well-organized steam service be inaugurated throughout the country, the transport business of the [HBC] cannot be carried on any longer." [3]

But for all her impact on the course of a continent, the *Northup* didn't last long. In 1861, while wintering at Cook's Creek, she sank and had to be rebuilt. Renamed the *Pioneer*, she was purchased by the Minnesota Stage Company in a secret partnership with Governor George Simpson and the HBC. She operated between a terminal on the upper Red River, (named Georgetown after the governor) and the Red River colony. Her end when it came was

ignominious indeed for such an important player in Canadian history. Her engines were used to run a sawmill.

The *Northup's* voyages ushered in the "Age of Steam" on Manitoba's lakes and rivers, an era that lasted almost exactly a century and gave North America's Great Plains its own unique maritime lore, complete with all the romance, heroism and tragedy associated with the sea down through the ages.

On October 9, 1877, Manitoba's first locomotive, the *Countess of Dufferin*, arrived in Winnipeg on the steamer SS *Selkirk*. Clifford Stevens of Gimli, a retired lake captain, defines the event as portentous, "epitomizing the coming struggle between steamboats and railways on the prairies". [4]

The expansion of the railroad, followed by the automobile and then the airplane, provided ever-increasing – and instantly embraced – competition to the shipping industry on the "foaming, raging mistress" and her one meandering and three nearly impassable rivers. By the end of the 20th century, only three large ships remained on the lake, the MS *Goldfield*, the MS *Poplar River* and the Canadian Coast Guard cruiser, *Namao*. The retirement of the MS *Lord Selkirk II*, Lake Winnipeg's last cruise ship, in 1983, officially marked the close of a unique and storied chapter of Manitoba history.

Ted R. Kristjanson, a Gimli fisherman, catalogued a total of 79 river and lake ships and barges that spanned the years from 1859 (the SS *Anson Northup*) to 1950 (the MS *Keystone*) in his self-published untitled history of Manitoba steamships. Yet, in a disclaimer on his opening page, Kristjanson acknowledges that he may have been able to find only "most" of the vessels. In 1886 alone, the Port of Winnipeg registered 66 vessels plying the province's rivers and lakes.

COURTESY OF THE NIELSEN FAMILY

The Goldfield, *among the last of the large ships to work the lake, sits at the dock at Hnausa.*

Many, perhaps a narrow majority, of these ships ferried fish, lumber, pulpwood, sawdust, gold, bricks, limestone, fishers, miners, prospectors, hunters, traders, businessmen and tourists to and from their destinations on or near Lake Winnipeg in the fortunate obscurity won from safe harbours, safe havens and escape from danger.

But the rest experienced the triumph or calamity that creates legend. For Manitoba, these ships contribute the stark reds and blacks of dramatic suffering and sudden death to the calmer blues, greens and golds that usually weave the warp and woof of a prairie province's history. Vivid though this nautical strand of Manitoba's heritage is, it is all but gone and forgotten.

The stories of these many remarkable ships and their climactic struggles with the lake have been told in graphic

Lake Winnipeg's First Luxury Liner

The ship that ran a close second to the *Anson Northup* in historical importance was the SS *Colvile*, the second steamer to ply Lake Winnipeg. The first was the SS *Chief Commissioner*, built at Lower Fort Garry in 1872 by the HBC and used to transport supplies until 1877 when the *Colvile* took over her duties. The *Chief Commissioner* was dismantled and used as a floating dock at Lower Fort Garry for many years.

Built of solid oak for the HBC in Grand Forks, Minnesota, in 1875 to carry freight to Berens River, Warren Landing, Grand Rapids and other points around Lake Winnipeg, the *Colvile* sailed immediately into prominence with the signing of Treaty Five.

On September 17, 1875, Lieutenant Governor Alexander Morris reported: "The Hudson's Bay Company kindly placed their new propeller steamer, the *Colvile*, at the services of the commissioners ... and declined to make any charge for its employment." Of course, the HBC was as anxious as the Dominion government for treaties to be signed with the first people around the lake, not only to secure the lake's rich resources, but also to take control of a waterway seen to be of prime strategic importance to the company and the nation.

The ship made three stops to secure the treaty. At Berens River, a pilot was needed to steer the *Colvile* around the maze of islands at the mouth. She was the first vessel of that size to enter the river. Canoes crammed with the curious surrounded the steamer and the Berens River residents fired their rifles in noisy salute. The treaty was signed at the Wesleyan Mission schoolhouse.

The Colvile *at the Norway House Landing, 1880*
HUDSON'S BAY COMPANY ARCHIVES / 1987 / 363 C–29–1

The next day, bucking stormy seas, the *Colvile* nosed north to Warren Landing and "into the Nelson River where no steamer had ever before been", as Morris declared. A pilot was again required to guide the steamer through the islands and on to Norway House. Here, the treaty was signed at the HBC post. The *Colvile*'s next stop was across the lake at Grand Rapids. She tied up before the chief's log cabin while terms were negotiated.

Two years later, during the first vice-regal visit to western Canada, Governor General Lord Dufferin and Countess Dufferin, anxious to see as much of Manitoba as possible, took the *Colvile* up to Grand Rapids and back.

The ship, which had the distressing habit of pitching sideways and rolling in heavy seas, making all aboard violently seasick, steamed across the national stage once more in July 1885. When the North West Rebellion ended, more than 1,000 men and 400 horses were transported from Saskatchewan's battlefields by riverboat to Grand Rapids where they shipped aboard the *Colvile* and the SS *Princess* bound for Selkirk.

When she wasn't making history, the *Colvile* carried freight and passengers for the HBC. Her lading included furs and other "country goods", including an esoteric cargo of porcupine quills used in the making of pens and toothpicks.

But at 4 a.m. July 15, 1894, the *Colvile* burned to the waterline while lying in dock at Grand Rapids. Her captain, an experienced Scottish seaman by the name of G.S. Hackland, a veteran of several trips around Cape Horn, lies buried in Winnipeg's Old Kildonan Cemetery. [5]

and compelling tales by two of Lake Winnipeg's captains: Ed Nelson and Cliff Stevens. Nelson, who captained most of the big boats at one time or another during his 45 years on the lake, spun "Lake Winnipeg yarns" illustrated by his own pen and ink drawings on the pages of the *Winnipeg Free Press* in the 1950s and early 1960s. Son of an English "Bayman" and an Ojibwe woman, Nelson was born at Manigotagan about 1890 and educated by the Oblate Fathers in St. Boniface. He was destined for the priesthood before he ran away to "sea" in 1905.

Stevens, grandson of one of Gimli's original Icelandic settlers, was the third generation of his family to captain on Lake Winnipeg. For more than 100 years, from the 1870s to the 1970s, there was at least one Captain Stevens on the lake. In 2000, Clifford Stevens wrote a self-published memoir of his family's life and experiences, entitled *Steamboat Days Revisted*, which he kindly shared, along with personal reminiscences, with the author.

Lake Winnipeg's old salts were convinced that its geological bipolarity, limestone on the west and granite on the east, influences its behaviour. The Icelandic settlers believed the lake was more dangerous for small boats than the Atlantic Ocean. Certainly, boats that navigate without difficulty on the Great Lakes have been found to be useless on Lake Winnipeg. Nelson called it "the roughest lake in North America. Its waves run short instead of long. The storms can come out of nowhere."[6]

Stevens says many lake boats adopted a design in use on the Caspian Sea, which has a similar wave pattern to Lake Winnipeg. "I've heard about the design coming from the Caspian Sea. They're called a better head sea boat, narrower to handle the waves, sharper on the bow. But a good head sea boat would roll more than a more stubby vessel."[7]

Its sailors also say the lake has a strong undercurrent which, if combined with gale-force winds from any direction, can turn it into "the boiling, raging cauldron of unleashed fury". Two more factors contributing to the lake's unruliness are its north-south axis and the narrow channel between its two basins. The prevailing winds in Manitoba are from the northwest and the southeast. Particularly when the northwest wind blows, it forces a large volume of water through The Narrows into the south basin. This phenomenon is known as wind tide and can vary from a half-metre to almost two metres.[8]

According to the lake's mariners, the dirtiest seas occur at The Narrows between East and West Doghead Point, the Black Island narrows, north of Black Bear Island, between Black and Hecla Islands, around Berens Island, at the mouth of the Manigotagan River and out in the north basin. The north basin has stretches of more than 160 kilometres of open water where an angry sea can build waves topping eight metres in height.

DEATH DUE TO EXPOSURE ABOARD THE *KEEWATIN*

T HE DISASTER OCCURRED in the early morning of September 8, 1890 when the two-masted North West Mounted Police sailboat, *Keewatin*, labouring in a heavy sea,

FRANCES RUSSELL

Two of Lake Winnipeg's best-known "old salts", the late Ed Nelson, above, and Clifford Stevens.

ran aground on a reef not far from the Spider Islands north of Poplar River in the lake's north basin. An NWMP corporal and private drowned after a day of clinging to the wreck and the ship's captain died of complications arising from exposure after eight days of drifting, bound to the wreck, on the open lake.

The *Keewatin* was Manitoba's first recorded major maritime disaster and it featured a stellar cast of characters including the lieutenant governor of Manitoba, who had won his laurels with Ottawa by confronting Louis Riel in 1870, the North West Mounted Police inspector for the Keewatin District, a reputable lakeman and an experienced Great Lakes shipbuilder. The three deaths triggered an investigation by the House of Commons' public accounts committee and prompted the lake's first hydrographic survey a decade later.

John Christian Schultz had had a colourful career prior to being chosen by Prime Minister Sir John A. Macdonald to be lieutenant governor of Manitoba and Keewatin, assuming office on July 15, 1888.

Schultz had arrived in the Red River Colony in 1860 and in his early years augmented his meagre earnings from his first profession, law, by dealing as a free trader in fur, Saskatchewan gold and land. He acquired the *Nor'Wester* newspaper and he and Walter Bown, the man who would become his personal secretary when he was appointed Queen's representative, founded the Canadian Party. It sought union with Canada and responsible government for Red River. During the 1869-70 Rebellion, Schultz was briefly imprisoned in his own house by Louis Riel.

Schultz was "a red-blonde giant, powerful of body and crafty of eye and mind", according to Manitoba historian William L. Morton. One who knew him once observed that

A storm gathering on Lake Winnipeg MIKE GRANDMAISON

"Fate had manufactured a scoundrel out of material meant by nature for a gentleman". [9]

In October of 1888, Schultz commissioned James Stewart, a former HBC employee and lakeman of good repute, to investigate what was feared to be widespread smuggling of liquor into Lake Winnipeg's east shore communities made possible by the growing steamboat traffic on the lake and its rivers. Stewart was also to assess the condition of the lake's fishing stocks. In a report to the lieutenant governor for which he was paid $50, Stewart verified the local fishers' complaints that the commercial fishing companies operating on the lake were destroying the stock and the livelihoods of local residents. "Unless this wholesale exportation of whitefish to the U.S. is stopped," Stewart wrote, "in a couple or three years Lake Winnipeg will be completely denuded of fish ... Unless some means are taken to stop this wholesale slaughter of fish now carried on, the Government will have to feed all the Indians and half-breeds around the shores of Lake Winnipeg, apart from the Icelanders who have settled there ..." [10]

As well, Stewart's report confirmed "there must be a considerable amount of intoxicating liquor carried around the shores of Lake Winnipeg. I noticed that at every point we called there was some, more or less, to be had if wanted." Much of it was in the form of what Stewart called "vile stuff ... essences of peppermint, ginger or lemon". [11]

In a letter to Interior Minister Edgar Dewdney later that same year, Schultz proposed constructing a police patrol boat to bring law and order to the lake, avoiding the cost of establishing permanent constabularies. A boat would offer "the greatest efficiency at the least expense", he wrote. [12]

Matthew Watt, an Ontario shipbuilder, was commissioned for the job and set about designing a boat similar to ones he had built for the Lake Huron fishery. As Schultz

stated in a letter to Dewdney on August 31, 1891, "To give her increased steadiness and lighter draught, he [Watt] added one foot extra beam. The boat was, as you know, for the special service of watching the broader and deeper waters of the north end of Lake Winnipeg; and Watt guaranteed her qualities as a good sea-boat while giving her light draught enough to chase skiffs and canoes supposed to contain intoxicants near shore and into shallow harbours." [13]

The boat was built in Selkirk during the winter of 1888-89. In early June, Stewart gave it a trial sail to the mouth of the Red River, a voyage Stewart later claimed included the lieutenant governor as a passenger. Nevertheless, Stewart formally reported to Schultz by letter that the *Keewatin* was "found to work very satisfactorily in sailing qualities and seems to be well suited for the purposes for which she is intended".

The *Keewatin*, however, had some peculiarities. She was 10.2 metres long and had a beam of three metres amidships. Her rigging would end up an intense subject of controversy. She had two masts and an unusual bowsprit that included a fixed jib. Her foremast was placed in the bow. It was 30 centimetres at the low end and 11 metres in height. The main mast was somewhat less in diameter and 10.2 metres in height. The bowsprit, rather than being round, was made from an four-centimetre plank, 2.5 metres long and 10 to 15 centimetres wide. [14]

As Stewart was later to state, "when in position pointed downwards, [the bowsprit] reminded one very much of a spoonbill duck. The bowsprit in a heavy sea was invariably pitched under water, causing no little danger. Whether this was intended by the inventor [whom he claimed was Schultz] to smash up the waves in order to make a smooth passage for the boat, I cannot say, but ... I wonder that he did not get out a patent for it." [15]

The north shore of Long Point is a rarely-visited sweep of sand and shore, the preserve of many species of wildlife, including black bears of almost every color in the black bear rainbow – blond, cinnamon, brown and blue, as well as black.

COURTESY OF ROGER TURENNE

That was not all. According to Stewart, the fore and mainsails were too large for the craft and the gaff-topsails were actually nailed to the yard, making them impossible to take down in a storm. As the final dangerous feature, the flat bowsprit, lacking a ring or traveller, made it extremely dangerous to bring in the jib, particularly in a gale.

The *Keewatin* set sail on her maiden voyage from Selkirk to Grand Rapids on June 15, 1889. Stewart was the sailing master and his passengers were NWMP Inspector J.V. Bégin, Corporal Morphy, two privates and seaman James Monkman, then nearly 80 years of age, but familiar with the lake. In his October 29, 1890, declaration, Bégin noted he personally had had some experience as a captain of a steamer on the St. Lawrence River below Quebec. "I soon found that while Monkman was familiar with the boat routes and the shore, Stewart knew little of the lake ... and while he might have known something about small boats when he was young, he was now so nervous and excitable as to be in any emergency or storm almost useless."

When the *Keewatin* was making the passage from Reindeer Island to Long Point, she encountered a heavy gale. Stewart, Bégin reported, was unable to steer the boat. Later, when anchored on the north side of Long Point, the *Keewatin* was again placed in jeopardy when the wind suddenly changed direction in the middle of the night.

"I ... asked Stewart what he intended to do for the safety of the boat," Begin said in his declaration. He was very excited and told me he did not know what to do; he agreed with me that we must get away from what was now a lee shore, but he seemed to be like a man half-

crazy, and made no move whatsoever. Seeing this I took command myself." [17]

Bégin, who stayed on in Grand Rapids, sent the boat back to Selkirk with "a strong young man" to oversee Stewart. According to Bégin's subsequent testimonial, the "strong young man" reported that Stewart left Long Point on a fine, bright night with a slight breeze and sailed all night. But in the morning, the party found they had arrived back at the same spot they had left the night before. On another occasion, Stewart became so excited and nervous, he fell overboard.

Stewart was removed from his captaincy by Schultz after Bégin's complaints and Watt was engaged as sailing master.

The fateful journey occurred at the end of the *Keewatin's* second summer of service on the lake. Watt received orders from Bégin to cease his patrols on the lake August 30, 1890 and to take the *Keewatin* from the mouth of the Nelson River to the first post-office in Red River (St. Peter's) for orders and supplies.

According to Watt's story, given to the *Manitoba Evening Free Press* on Sunday, September 25, 1890, just prior to his death, the *Keewatin* set sail with Corporal Morphy and Private René de Beaujen on September 2nd, reaching the boat harbour at Spider Islands the same day. Storm and adverse wind kept the boat and its passengers at Spider Islands for five days until September 7th.

That day, the *Keewatin* left harbour early in the morning under an overcast sky with a north wind blowing fitful gusts. The boat landed at Poplar Point where the crew made tea and had lunch. Watt wanted to remain there until the next day because it was a long run to Swampy (Berens) Island light and harbour. However, his companions opted to press on to try to make up for the time lost at Spider Islands and to take advantage of the fair wind. The *Keewatin* road the waves "like a gull ... going with the speed of a racehorse and shipping no seas," Watt recalled. They sighted Swampy Island at dusk, about 16 kilometres off. But squalls of rain had started and with the night closing in, Watt worried that they wouldn't be able to see the light. He thought it safer to get under the lee of the island and drop anchor.

Watt recalled in the newspaper interview: "The boat acted well when brought close to the wind and shipped only the spray ... [B]eing well acquainted with the difficulty of a night entrance to the boat harbour, I let go the anchor in three fathoms of water ... At about nine p.m., a furious squall struck us with rain; the chain snapped and we were adrift."

Something else snapped at the same time. The young private, René de Beaujen, went "more or less out of his mind". Watt and Morphy paid out an entire coil of towing rope to try to bring the boat's bow to windward and slow her down. This way, they drifted all night.

"At daylight, Morphy said he thought he saw a shoal ahead. He had scarcely spoken when our centreboard struck twice in the trough of the sea and we seemed to be over the shoal when the tow-line caught and jerked the boat violently, careening her and filling her with water to the thwarts."

Although the *Keewatin* was now drifting helplessly with its masts down nearly to the water, Watt knew it wouldn't sink because it had air-tight tanks partially filled with water for ballast. He stretched a life-line from bow to stern along one side to which he lashed himself and urged the others to do likewise. However, Morphy and de Beaujen instead chose to perch on the side of the boat out of the water.

Because of de Beaujen's mental state, Morphy had to keep one arm around the young private to hold him up while grasping the life line with the other. Watt couldn't reach to help Morphy and Morphy continued to resist Watt's entreaties to lash himself and de Beaujen to the life line.

I think Morphy's struggles to keep René from falling over exhausted him a good deal, for in the forenoon of that day [Monday] when the boat gave a lurch, René slipped from Morphy's arm and went down without a struggle. This affected Mr. Morphy very much and I noticed that he began to wander in his mind, talking of Regina and Toronto, and directing me to dry and pack his clothes as though we had reached port. All this time we had not eaten ...

The morning of Tuesday was clear and bright ... Still, Morphy spoke in a rambling way and twice slipped off and was pulled back by me. The sea becoming smoother we both tried to sleep lying along the side of the boat, and from one of those fitful naps I was awakened by a splash

Small and apparently insignificant, the Spider Islands have played an important role in the shipping and surveying life of the lake. In 1890, a combined Geological Survey and Mounted Police party established this camp on a protected cove and began a survey process that continues today.

NATIONAL ARCHIVES OF CANADA / PA–50903

Treacherous shores, whether of granite or limestone such as these, prompted the first hydrographic survey of the lake in 1901 and led to the erection of a series of lighthouses on some of the lake's most dangerous points. These included "the watched light" at Cox Shoal, right, and the lighthouse at Gull Harbour Point.

MIKE GRANDMAISON

and to my horror saw it was my companion who had slipped off again. I made a clutch at him, striking the tip of his sinking head and nearly fell in myself, but it was too late and he sank to rise no more. [18]

Watt floated, lashed to the wreck, for eight more days and nights until he was found by local fishers about a kilometre from shore near Split Rock. They believed him dead because he was unable at first to speak. He was lying crosswise, his head and breast hanging over the inner side of the boat and his legs limp over her bottom. The rescuers took him ashore, rubbed him with coal oil they found in the boat and ministered to him until the steamer *Aurora* arrived five days later. He was taken to Selkirk, suffering from severe exposure blisters and burns on his face and damage to his feet. The doctors were preparing to amputate them when he seemed to recover. Soon thereafter, however, Watt succumbed to his trauma and injuries. He was 66 years of age. Private de Beaujen's remains were found in October near Doghead Point, disfigured by gulls and foxes. Corporal Morphy's body was never found. The *Keewatin* sustained little damage, was repaired and put back on the lake the next year.

Stewart immediately seized on the opportunity provided by the disaster to take his revenge. In letters to the editors of newspapers in Winnipeg, Selkirk and Ottawa, he attacked

Bégin and Schultz and the unseaworthiness of the craft's outfitting. He sneered at Bégin's marine experience, stating the NWMP inspector had "probably crossed the St. Lawrence River a few times ... [but] clothed with a little authority as the inspector of three men ... fancied himself a thoroughbred sailor of the first water. Like the boat herself, he was somewhat cranky." [19] Stewart also derided the *Keewatin's* rigging as "unseamanlike and bizarre" and went on to state he had the "assurance of Mr. Watt himself that she was rigged by the direction of Lieutenant-Governor Schultz". [20]

The tragedy and Stewart's accusations sparked an inquiry by the Commons public accounts committee. Schultz defended himself with letters and testimonials from Bégin and others swearing to the *Keewatin's* seaworthiness. But the committee's attention soon focused on one letter in particular, from Captain J. Bergman of the *Aurora*. Lake captains had long complained about the lack of proper navigation charts for Lake Winnipeg and the almost total absence of lights and buoys.

The *Keewatin* wasn't the only accident that year. The tow freezer barge *North Star* was totally wrecked on a rocky shoal and the steam barge *Red River* was damaged, delaying the boat and its passengers for 10 days. [21]

Bergman wrote that navigating the lake was difficult and dangerous in the best of weather, but at night and in storm, it was perilous. The absence of any proper navigational aids not only risked lives, but impeded commerce, he warned. "The masters of steamers navigating the lake have to depend entirely upon their personal knowledge of these waters, based upon soundings and observations made by themselves." [22]

Bergman proposed at least six lighthouses between the mouth of the Red River and Warren Landing in addition to the only one then in existence at Swampy (Berens) Island:

at Gull Point, Black Bear Island, Cox Shoal, George Island, Mossy Point and the mouth of the Saskatchewan River. He also asked for buoys in the bay outside Warren Landing on the way to Norway House. [23]

ED NELSON / COURTESY OF THE WINNIPEG FREE PRESS

Adam Black, who worked in the Lake Winnipeg lumber and freight trade, also wrote to Schultz to suggest lighthouses on Gull Point, Big Grindstone Point or Berry Island, the east end of Black Bear Island and Cox Shoal for vessels passing eastward of Swampy Island for Berens River or Norway House as well as at the east end of George Island and at Grand Rapids on the west bank of the Saskatchewan River. Finally, Black requested a hydrographic survey and chart of the lake.

Sir Clifford Sifton, Sir Wilfrid Laurier's minister of the interior, commissioned just such a survey in 1901. William J. Stewart, head of the new Canadian Hydrographic Service, began work in the south basin that summer. Over the next three years, the work was done by hydrographic surveyors Frederick W. Anderson and R.E. "Ted" Tyrwhitt, aboard the SS *Frank Burton*. The survey was completed in 1904.

THE S.S. *PRINCESS*: TORN ASUNDER BY A WRONG ORDER

BUILT IN WINNIPEG in 1881 by Jarvis and Burridge, the SS *Princess* was the finest and largest inland passenger vessel in the west and the pride of Lake Winnipeg in her day. A sidewheeler with 40 state rooms, she looked every bit the part of a Mississippi river boat the day Governor General Lord Lorne launched her at the foot of Lombard Street. Her great side paddles gave her an average speed of 25 kilometres an hour and made her bow wave a hazard to every little boat along the Red River.

Her proudest moment came in 1885 when her owner, Captain William Robinson, was called upon by General Middleton to move 1,000 troops down the lake following the North West Rebellion. They had been conveyed from the Saskatchewan battlefields to Grand Rapids by river boats. The *Princess* and the *Colvile* then transported the men and their horses and equipment to Winnipeg.

DENNIS FAST

The decks of the *Princess* were filled with red-coated soldiers with General Middleton and his high-ranking officers on the foredeck when she docked at Selkirk. Mayor James Colcleugh and the officers and men then feasted on a fine meal laid out by the "good ladies of Selkirk" who set up "3,000 feet of table ... for the occasion". [24]

Soon after her finest hour, however, the *Princess* was humbled and shorn of her looks. Stripped of her paddle-wheels, her engine assembly replaced with a steeple compound engine driving a single, four-flanged propeller and her hull lengthened to 49 metres, she was converted to a bulk cargo freighter. The main deck housing now reached to the bows, while nine metres of the deck aft housing was cut away to allow tow-line freedom. These changes left only six cabins with a kitchen and dining room on the upper deck. The *Princess* was put to work freighting fish and railroad ties, often with a barge in tow.

At noon on August 24, 1906, she left Spider Islands carrying only 1,600 boxes of fish, hardly enough to stiffen her hull in case of heavy weather. She set course for Little

The Princess *in 1900, not long before she was "shorn of her looks" and converted from passenger steamer to work horse.*

George Island, the route travelled by all boats to avoid the Poplar Point Reef before it acquired a lighted bell buoy.

The weather, which had been ominously calm, suddenly broke at 6 p.m. with a sharp breeze from the northwest. It increased as the *Princess* passed Little George at 9 p.m. and set a course for Swampy (Berens) Island.

An hour later, the gathering storm caused the crew to urge Captain John Hawes to take shelter in an anchorage at George Island, but Hawes held his course. The wind was then blowing at 64 kilometres an hour. At midnight, the engine was throttled down to half-speed to conserve steam for the pumps. Still, the *Princess* seemed to be taking the storm in stride.

A deep-sea sailor, Captain Hawes was always nervous in the restricted areas of inland waters. Perhaps it was because he was fearful of navigating the passage between Swampy Island and Berens Bank in the darkness that he ordered wheelsman John Bird to bring the *Princess* around and simultaneously signalled the engine room for full speed ahead.

Whatever the reason, his double order spelled death for the *Princess*. As she came around slowly, the wind driving up mountainous eight-metre waves, the tooting of the whistles and the tearing-out of the rolling-stays warned of the punishment she was taking.

Suddenly, above the roar of the elements, the hull tore asunder at the gangways with a splintering crash. Three deck hands were trapped below. Luckily, a fourth man was in the pilot house assisting the wheelsman.

The next few minutes were described by Douglas Everett, a passenger, who had the presence of mind to put his wife and child in a metal lifeboat:

"In the life boat, I waited and shouted for the others and wondered where they could be, as the life deck was now awash with the breaking combers. As each succeeding wave was coming up higher, and there was still no sign of the others, I cut the bilge lashings lest the next wave fill the life boat. I prayed and hoped that the next wave would be high enough to send the lifeboat clear of the deck railing astern, to avoid capsizing."

COURTESY OF THE WNNIPEG FREE PRESS   INSET COURTESY OF CAPTAIN CLIFFORD J. STEVENS

Everett and his family made it safely ashore on Swampy Island and were picked up several days later by fishers from Berens River. Meanwhile, the rest of the crew had cut loose the yawl. Desperately clutching its painter, they shouted for Hawes, stewardess Flora McDonald, 17, and cook Yoba

Johansson, 20. But just as the captain and the two young women came out of the kitchen door, knee-deep in water, the heavy lurching of the yawl tore out the ring bolt.

The three hung on to the aft rail as the girls screamed, "Don't leave us!" With just two pair of oars in the yawl, the men tried desperately to reach the trio. Then an oarlock tore out and the yawl was thrown broadside to the wind. Though overloaded with 11 persons, it was brought before the wind without capsizing. Only three of the 11 had life-belts and even these were so old they were worthless. The yawl, too, was in bad repair. It had no air tanks, no sea anchor, compass or oil bag and lacked its full complement of oars.

In the haze of dawn, the survivors could see the captain and the two young women clinging to the deckhouse. In an eerie forecast of another, much greater, maritime tragedy to take place on the Atlantic Ocean six years hence, through the tumult and roar of the wind and waves, the girls' voices could be heard singing *Nearer My God To Thee*. The enormous sea running made it impossible for the yawl to turn back. The three were never seen alive again.

Distraught, the yawl's passengers, bailing furiously, scanned the boiling waste of water each time the yawl was lifted up on a wave. Suddenly, came an excited shout. "Land ahead, boys!"

But between the overloaded yawl and land lay the treacherous deep water funnel between Swampy Point and

This horseshoe of pure white sand on the north shore of George Island has been called "probably the finest beach in Manitoba", yet even in the heyday of lake travel relatively few made the trip to the north basin island, for it often meant bucking huge waves like this 35-foot fishing boat.

The Boat with a Silver Tongue

Everyone knew when the SS *City of Selkirk* was approaching. Her whistle, with its melodious yet penetrating three-note chime, could be recognized anywhere. It was a beautiful whistle, and one captain was often accused of unnecessarily prolonging his approach signals just because he "liked to listen to the whistle" so much. And no wonder. The whistle – really three in one – was once part of the luxury appointments of a millionaire's yacht. So was her steering wheel, which was more than two metres in diameter and fashioned of mahogany and oak. [25]

The *City of Selkirk* was built in 1893 as a passenger and freight boat to run on a twice-a-week schedule from Selkirk to the islands in Lake Winnipeg's north basin where cargoes of whitefish were taken aboard. On May 19, 1901, the ship made a 80-kilometre cruise from Selkirk to Lake Winnipeg and return, billed as "the first steamboat excursion of the century – one of the Dominion Fish Company boats on holiday". The fare was 35 cents.

En route to Warren Landing on the weekend of August 24, 1906, she was so buffeted by wild winds and high waves that Captain William Thorburn ordered all aboard to don life jackets. Arriving safely, she took on passengers and freight at Warren Landing the next day and began her homeward journey, though the weather was still poor. At 5 p.m. Monday, she passed the Cox lighthouse. Thorburn, seated with some passengers, suddenly leaped to his feet and reached for his binoculars.

"There's a group of people standing on the rocks," he called to First Mate Parsons. A moment later, a lifeboat carrying three men approached the ship through the rough waters. They were helped on deck and told their tragic story. The *Princess* had been pounded to pieces in a fierce storm the day before and her captain and five others had drowned. That was how poor Parsons learned of the loss of his step-daughter, 17-year-old Flora McDonald, a member of the *Princess's* crew. [26]

Berens Bank. The crowding of the waves in this narrow passage by the northwest gale caused them to pile higher, with a breaker on every crest. There was a hurried consultation and John Bird was chosen to steer the yawl through the stretch of maddened water.

"The dandiest ride I ever had on a boat," he said of it afterwards. "From the crests of the following waves I figured we were still about a mile from the shingle bar at the point. There was an almost irresistible temptation to beach the yawl on the shingle bar, but I think that would have been foolhardy, as the seas opposite the point were really piling up. It was a great relief, I can tell you, when we made the shelter of the island."

The following day, the survivors were picked up by the SS *City of Selkirk*. In all, six people perished. Only two bodies were recovered, one being the captain's. He wore only the ties of his life-belt. The rest had been torn away. [27]

THE SS *RED RIVER*: THE SHIP THAT LOOKED FOR TROUBLE

In the 1890s rafts of syllogize were a familiar sight on Lake Winnipeg as they were hauled from logging camps on the east side of the lake to a sawmill at Selkirk.

One of the vessels engaged in this log-boom work was the steamer *Red River*, part of the William Robinson Lumber Company's fleet. She was well-suited to her plodding task, being underpowered for her 40-metre length. Her top speed when light was just 10 kilometres an hour.

One early August day in 1900, the *Red River* was pressed into service moving whitefish from the north end of the lake. She left Selkirk with her hold filled with package freight for the HBC trading post at Norway House and her decks loaded with lumber for a new fishing station at Warren Landing.

DENNIS FAST

Many felt the underpowered Red River *belonged here, among the south basin islands.*   IAN WARD

The owners of the Red River insisted she tackle the huge distances and fierce storms of the north basin. Little wonder she wound up here, on the rocks of George Island.

Passing Little George Island on the third day out, the weather seemed perfect for making the remaining 96 kilometres to the Warren Landing channel buoys. At the midnight change of watch, all was still well. But at 1 a.m., a slight breeze sprang up from the northwest. It rapidly quickened and in less than an hour, the mate realized it was no ordinary breeze and alerted the captain.

When the skipper came on deck, the *Red River* was labouring in a heavy sea. Captain James Marshall realized that with the waves breaking over the heavy forward deck load, there was danger the chain fastenings would tear out. The chief engineer's report was also disquieting. The bilge syphons below could not keep the water below the danger level and the steam pressure was going down as the stokers couldn't gain their footing on the heaving floor plates.

COURTESY OF ERIK NIELSEN

It was plain the *Red River* couldn't stand this pounding for long. Marshall ordered all hands on deck and signaled the wheelsman to bring the wheel hard to starboard, turn around and try to get under the shelter of George Island, some 48 kilometres to leeward. With steam pressure very low, the ship answered to her helm, but slowly. She lay on her beam's end, with the seas breaking heavily over her entire length. Then the mishap everyone feared happened. With a splintering crash of the bulwarks, the chain bindings tore out and the deck load shifted to leeward.

The *Red River* was now lying broadside to the weather, completely at the mercy of the pitiless waves. The crew tried to jettison the load, but it was no use. With spume and spindrift flying over the length of the vessel, the officers held a hurried conference. There was only one answer: abandon ship.

The lifeboat was lowered, all hands got on board and, after a six-hour ordeal battling the chaotic elements, steering and bailing while the storm continued at top gale, they made it to the lee of George Island. They were picked up two days later by the SS *City of Selkirk*.

Then Marshall had a different storm to face. While on the island, he had to mollify his crew, who kept telling him in emphatic terms that the feeble *Red River* had no business on the north end of the lake at any time of the year. At Selkirk, there was the inevitable investigation complete with the boat's owners trying to pick holes in the crew's testimony that the *Red River* was not seaworthy for any part of the lake, particularly the north basin.

In the end, the captain and his officers were commended for their skill in abandoning ship in such a storm without one life lost. The *Red River* crew's brush with death resulted in stricter inspections of ships going out on Lake Winnipeg. As for the boat herself, after she sank, her hull broke in two. The forward part of the ship, her hold still full of lumber, finally came ashore on the north side of George Island, a warning even today to those who might underestimate Lake Winnipeg's angry moods. [28]

THE SS *PREMIER*: A FEARFUL OMEN

THE *PREMIER* WAS a 37-metre screw-type steamer built at Selkirk in 1896 and belonging to the Dominion Fish Company. She was considered the finest and fastest boat on the lake at that time. The SS *Wolverine* and the SS *Premier* would sail Monday evenings. The *Wolverine* would leave Selkirk one hour before the *Premier*, but by the next afternoon, north of Black Bear Light, the *Premier* would pass the *Wolverine*.

On this particular journey, the *Premier* was carrying tourists from across Canada and the U.S. who had enjoyed a fair sail up the lake, dining every evening from the *Premier's* famous cuisine. Her chef was celebrated for his preparation of Lake Winnipeg whitefish.

Passing Spider Islands, a crew member saw a terrifying omen. On the main deck was a mother cat and six kittens. As the crewman watched, the mother cat took her kittens by the neck, one by one, jumped to an open hatch and threw them overboard. Then the mother cat herself jumped into the water.

Nevertheless, the weather was perfect when the *Premier* nosed into Warren Landing on the morning of August 8, 1908. She discharged her cargo and took on a return load of furs, fish and package freight. The ship's master, Captain John Stevens, had planned to sail before it got dark but the owner of the HBC store wanted the ship to wait until morning to receive another load of furs expected later that night.

At the midnight change of watch, all seemed ready for departure. Suddenly, at 3:30 a.m., the fearful call of "Fire! Fire! Fire!" awakened everyone. The flames spread with incredible speed. In no time, all the after cabins were on fire. All passengers on the starboard side of the vessel were rescued, but they had to climb through windows as the passageways were already ablaze. Some were helped to the SS *Frederick*, tied up alongside. Some jumped overboard to be picked up by row boats. A few fought through heavy smoke to the opposite side of the ship and jumped to the safety of the dock.

One woman, of generous build, was jammed in a cabin window. Volunteers were unable to free her. Then the mate noticed that one knee was on the window sill, pressing her shoulders against the upper part of the casing. He hit her knee with all the power he had in his fist. The woman flew out of the window into the water. She couldn't swim, so the mate jumped in and held her afloat until help came.

Now the *Frederick*, too, was burning and began to haul away from the stricken *Premier*. As it did so, a young woman, a schoolteacher from Cross Lake, with all her clothes afire, jumped from the deck of the blazing vessel. She landed

Flags flying, decks full of passengers, the Premier looked the part it was meant to play, as "the finest and fastest boat on the lake" when this photograph was taken in the first years of the 20th century.

COURTESY OF CAPTAIN CLIFFORD J. STEVENS

A Boat to Make a Sailor Laugh or Cry

It used to be said that no Lake Winnipeg sailor's experience was complete until he had spent a season on the SS *Highlander*. Not that she was an aristocrat, far from it. Badly designed, underpowered and cranky, she had many peculiar ways and every one was good for a laugh.

On one trip across Humbug Bay during a storm, she was said to have passed Loon Straits three times, and been driven backwards twice, before finally making the shelter of Big Bullhead Point. Her builder, Roderick Smith from Stornoway, Scotland, modelled her on the York boat. Her keel was hand-hewn and her ribs made of tamarack. She was flat-bottomed, had little or no dead rise, a very bluff bow and wide stern. When sailors laughed at her, her builder simply replied: "If it is made out of wood, it will float."

Adding to her troubles, her one-cylinder, high-pressure engine and wood-fired boiler with just 45 kilograms pressure could drive her at a maximum speed of only five knots in calm weather. Riding lights were never a problem. Any ship within eight kilometres could spot her from the steady shower of sparks which the high pressure exhaust system sent pouring from her stack. In heavy weather, she would take such a pounding her compass often was thrown out of its riding brackets.

DENNIS FAST

A further complication arose from the ingenious method the *Highlander's* sailors had devised to do their laundry. They soaped their clothes and trailed them astern on a line. One day, when several clothes lines were trailing and she was bucking a headwind, the *Highlander* suddenly picked up speed. It turned out the exasperated engineer had simply cut the garments adrift. Perhaps Jim Black could be excused for his high-handed action. During almost every headwind, he would spend anxious hours taking bearings on the shoreline to see if the ship was going forward or being driven back. [29]

on the *Frederick's* deck, but with one foot inside the rail and the other outside. She was grabbed as she fell backwards, but she sustained a fractured leg, dislocated hips and first degree burns. Another young woman jumped into the water and was saved only because she was a strong swimmer, able to stay afloat in the fast current until a rowboat picked her up. She, too, was badly burned.

The dockhands and firemen who were quartered in the after end all escaped by jumping overboard.

Meanwhile, tremendous pressure had been building below decks. It broke through with an explosion that sent the smokestack crashing down and hurled pieces of the deck and burning embers on the roofs of nearby buildings. Men on shore were helpless to fight this new spread of the fire. Of the six lines of hose that were playing water on the blaze, four had to be abandoned. The remaining two, on the tug *Idell* and on the dock itself, seemed to have no effect. Then the roof of the pump house collapsed and the last hose line on the dock became useless.

Rising above the confusion and the roar of the flames came the yelping of 12 sled dogs placed on board for trans-

Before the Premier *burned, the fish station at Warren Landing likely looked much like this one, opposite, on Little George Island. The terrible conflagration, portrayed here in an oil painting by Ed Nelson, lit up the night sky. By the morning of August 9th, not only the ship but the fish station were reduced to charred remnants.*

port. The anguished cries of the doomed animals brought tears to the eyes of those on the dock and in the rowboats and canoes. The dogs weren't the only casualties. Eight people died. Most of the survivors escaped with only the clothes on their backs. Many had singed hair and blisters on their hands, faces and bodies.

Captain Stevens was the last man to leave the ship, climbing down the now-hot anchor chain into a canoe manned by a trapper named Jack Folster. Hardly was the captain off his ship when, with a great roar, the *Premier's* superstructure, pilot house and decks all collapsed. The charred hulk drifted downstream with the current and stranded on a reef. The remaining passengers were taken aboard the *Wolverine* for the return trip to Selkirk.

As for Warren Landing, by morning, two great piles of ice and one lone building were all that remained of its

fish station. It was the end of the road for the Dominion Fish Company. It was never learned how the fire started. The marine investigation's findings suggested no negligence on the part of the engine-room crew or the watchman. It was believed a passenger may have fallen asleep on his bunk with a lighted cigarette. [30]

THE SS *WOLVERINE:*
A HECTIC – AND HEATED – VOYAGE

IT LOOKED LIKE the start of a beautiful, restful voyage when the SS *Wolverine*, known as "The Wolf" to her crews, gave the customary short blast on her whistle and cast off from Selkirk that Monday afternoon in mid-August 1914, with a full complement of freight and passengers on board.

Only the mate and Captain Sandy Vance knew that she carried a veritable time bomb deep in her hold – 120 barrels of building lime that had been left standing in the hot sun at Selkirk dock, then stowed beneath other freight.

The Wolf made her usual stops – at Hecla, Gull Harbour, Big Bullhead, Little Bullhead, Matheson Island

"The Wolf" at George Island in 1927.

(then known as Snake Island because of the thousands of garter snakes that abounded there in early days) and Berens River, en route to Warren Landing.

While freight was being unloaded at Warren Landing, someone noticed smoke seeping up through the forward hatches and quickly gave the alarm to the officer on deck. The lime was smouldering through spontaneous combustion.

The passengers were evacuated from their cabins and assembled on deck. Holes were cut in the forward decks and hatch covers for water lines and to keep pressure from building in the hold.

After an hour, the passengers were allowed to return to their cabins. All that night, water under heavy pressure was poured into the hold and as quickly pumped out again

by the engine room, until it seemed the ship was floating in skimmed milk.

When morning came, the hatches were again uncovered. The sudden inrush of air caused flames to break out, but these were soon quenched with four streams of water that were played on the cargo until it was cool enough to handle. Nevertheless, the pressure inside the hold had served to burst and flatten much of the cargo of canned goods. The Wolf's hold was a sickening mess of tomatoes, peas, corn, fruit and wet lime.

The *Wolverine* arrived safely back in Selkirk some 60 hours late, but with no casualties and with a minimum of damage. And from that day on, shipping companies saw to it that lime was treated as a dangerous cargo. [31]

THE MS *SUZANNE E:*
NINE LOST AS BOAT SINKS

There was little warning. Wakened by the violence of the storm, Clifford Everett had just stepped into the wheelhouse to talk to the Suzanne E's *skipper, Richard Johnson, when the boat "tipped right over". Everett remembers seeing packing cases and wreckage floating about, then "three of us grabbed onto this plywood, a piece of the wheelhouse, and we drifted ..." The only survivor of the tragedy, Everett's eyes were bright with the peculiar light of those who have been through a terrible ordeal and lived to tell the story. [32]*

The plywood saved Everett's life. The other nine members of the crew perished in the last major shipwreck on Lake Winnipeg, during a violent storm on Friday, September 26, 1965.

Captain Clifford Stevens knew Everett. He had shipped with him on the SS *Keenora*. In *Steamboat Days Revisited*,

Stevens writes a poignant memoir of the catastrophe.

At the time, Stevens was captain of the MS *Goldfield*. A week prior to that fateful September day, both the *Goldfield* and the *Suzanne E* were waiting for the Saturday catch of fish at McBeth Point on Lake Winnipeg.

Stevens decided to walk over to the "Suzie", as she was called, to chat with the crew. Although he was fond of Captain Johnson, whom he considered an able deck hand and mate, he didn't feel Johnson had the qualifications to be captain. Johnson had a permit to run the vessel but did not have captain's papers.

Friday, September 26th found the *Goldfield* and Stevens at Princess Harbour. Stevens noticed the barometer was falling fast. The *Goldfield* left Princess Harbour in the morning, went to Two Rivers, where it unloaded fishing supplies and took on fish and then headed back to the safety of McBeth Point, reaching it about 4 p.m. After unloading the cargo of fish, Stevens made the *Goldfield* fast to the ice house main beam using a strong nylon rope. By then, the barometer was so low Stevens knew a major storm was brewing.

At 10 p.m., the storm struck. Furious winds reached 112 kilometres an hour, accompanied by heavy snow. The *Goldfield*, held fast, rocked back and forth at the McBeth dock. But the *Suzanne E* had not been so fortunate. Earlier that day, Helgi Jones, a famous Hecla Island fisher and lakeman, watched the ship pass Gull Harbour Light. Knowing the storm was approaching, he felt sure she would take refuge at Gull Harbour. Jones later told Stevens the sun shone brightly on the vessel as it proceeded north.

But the ship didn't dock. It continued toward Big Grindstone Point with its cargo of gasoline, food and fish boxes. As Everett later testified to a coroner's inquest at Riverton, he was on the noon to six o'clock shift the day of

The Mystery of the Wreck of the SS *Garry*

The *Garry* was a smart-looking ship but she never appealed to her sailors and never lived up to expectations. She was wet and dirty in heavy weather and her operating costs were high. Her untimely end is one of the great unsolved mysteries of Lake Winnipeg's steamship era.

On the morning of October 19, 1924, the *Garry* was finishing her 80-kilometre run from Big Black River to the southern approach to Warren Landing. There was a brisk wind blowing astern, but there was no smoke, fog or mist to impede visibility and her master, Captain Hugh Cochrane, had a good record. Suddenly, the *Garry* ran aground on the boulder-strewn foul grounds off Montreal Point. Crew members later maintained that the *Garry* struck twice before the engines could be stopped and then piled up on a cluster of granite boulders and rocky outcrops. She stuck fast with her decks at an acute angle. Repeated reversing of the engine at full speed failed to have any effect. The heavy sea running made it impossible to put out an anchor with a yawl.

Although her bottom remained sound, it was soon apparent she was doomed. No ship could risk getting close enough to attempt to free her. Her owners wrote her off after salvaging the anchors, chains and deck machinery. She lay on her nest of boulders until the shifting of the winter ice pushed her into deep water, where her hull still remains. Ice and waves sheared off her pilot house and cabins and scattered them along the beach.

The *Garry's* fate prompted much seafaring speculation. The foul ground near Montreal Point is a boiling mass of combers and flying spray, well-known to lakemen. How could her crew have missed the danger signs? When a vessel blunders into shallow water, its hull begins to vibrate loudly. Why didn't this unmistakable sound alert the crew?

One possible explanation was a wind tide. The wind was from the south that day and could have made the area deep enough to let the *Garry* in, but not deep enough to keep her from snagging at the end. A rumour began that a faulty compass had sent her 10 kilometres off course.

Of course, no shipwreck can be without superstition. Sailors recalled that years earlier, a passenger ship had burned to the water line in that locality. Her boiler, engine and other machinery were placed in the *Garry*, cursing her from the start. Deepening the mystery was the fact that an inquiry was held, but the findings were never disclosed and no one involved would speak about it. [33]

the storm. The weather started to turn about 5 p.m. After supper, he went down to bed, but woke with the boat's pitching. A short while later, the boat turned to starboard and began rolling about 40 degrees on either side. Then the rolling stopped, as the boat turned and tried to head back south.

"When I got to the pilot house, the captain was there. Just as I got there, the boat rolled over," Everett continued in his testimony. Moments later, it swamped, smashed and sank. In the pilot house at that moment were three other crew members along with Johnson and Everett. One, the cook Christine Settee, floated away with her face in the water.

Allan Clemons, of Selkirk, grabbed a piece of plywood while Charles Cook, also of Selkirk, got on another piece of wood. Both drifted away in the storm. The other five passengers and crew were trapped inside the ship and went down with her.

The tragedy of the Suzanne E, *seen here in quiet waters, still resonates on Lake Winnipeg.*

Everett and Johnson shared the same piece of plywood. Everett said the captain soon stopped talking. He could not tell him what had happened or why the boat had overturned and sank. Eventually, the two men on the plywood sheet reached Black Island. Everett pulled Johnson ashore, but the captain was dead. The coroner's jury attributed his death to exposure "in the chilly waters of the lake and the below-freezing temperatures above the water".

Everett walked a mile and a half in his stocking feet over snow and rocks until he saw a light in a fishing cabin. After seeing to Everett's needs, the fisherman went to Hecla to report the disaster.

The coroner's inquest was told by a veteran marine investigator that one cause of the disaster could have been that a side hatch had been left open because the boat's skiff was too large to fit in any other way.

The *Suzanne E* was constructed in 1946 by Captain Ed Nelson, but had been rebuilt three times. At the time of her sinking, she weighed 75 tons and was 27 metres long. Purchased by Selkirk Fisheries that spring, she'd had a few minor repairs made before starting her season in May. She ended it sunk in 18 metres of water, her stern buried in mud, defeated by the force of the wind and waves.

Stevens said of the *Suzanne E*: "Many veteran sailors believed her to be too blunt on the bow, as she would shear off when sailing down the river. She was very hard to handle in a big storm. Many sailors said, in such a bad storm and heavy weather, they (the crew) should have held her to the wind and not turned her around. It was in the worst possible place that the captain turned her around, as the big seas come down the channel and also from Humbug Bay." Stevens is also convinced that Johnson didn't heed the warning on his barometer. [34]

THE SS-MS *KEENORA:*
THE SHIP THAT REALLY GOT AROUND

THE *KEENORA* IS the most famous and best loved of all Lake Winnipeg's ships. Her story goes back to 1897, when the Rainy River Navigation Company of Rat Portage on Lake of the Woods needed to expand its freight and passenger service on the Rainy River between Rat Portage and Fort Frances. The Port Arthur Ship Building Company was engaged to build the *Keenora* with metal frames, deck beams and plating. As the sections were completed, they were placed on flat cars and transported to Rat Portage, where shipwrights and riveters, metal workers and carpenters assembled them. She was finished in the spring of 1898.

The unique spelling of her name has always caused curiosity. At first, she was to be christened the Keewatin, "North Wind" in Algonquian. The company, however, thought the name too chilling for a pleasure cruiser so a compromise was reached. The first syllable of Keewatin was joined to the first syllables of Noranda, a nearby gold mine, creating *Keenora.*

But the opening of the Canadian Northern Railway to Fort Frances put the ship out of business. After five years of acquiring rust and the fresh water equivalent of barnacles, the *Keenora* was purchased by a syndicate of Winnipeg lawyers who had her cut up and transported in sections by railroad flatcar to Winnipeg.

For the next few years, she led a chequered life. She was rebuilt in 1918 by the Manitoba Bridge and Iron Works at the foot of Notre Dame Avenue East. A nine-metre section was added amidships, with a hardwood dance floor on the second deck, transforming the freighter into a graceful excursion boat. For one season, she carried an orchestra and featured romantic moonlight dances as she glided up and down the Red River. But her owner, Colin Marland, found she gave too much competition to his Hyland Park dance hall barge. She was purchased by Fred Hilson in 1920 and put in permanent dock, causing her floors to warp.

Her prospects took an upturn in 1923 when she was bought by the Northern Fish Company of Selkirk to help its existing ship, the SS *Wolverine*, meet the increasing passenger

An early taste of winter has often caused tragedy on Lake Winnipeg.

IAN WARD

The SS *Majestic:*
Even the Engineer Got Sick

George Barker was chief of the Hollow Water Reserve from 1926 to 1958 and from 1960 to 1968. He served as president of the Manitoba Indian Brotherhood from 1950 to 1968. In his book, *Forty Years a Chief*, he gives a vivid account of the worst Lake Winnipeg storm he encountered as a young man working on the lake boats during the summer.

While the *Majestic* prepared to depart Victoria Beach for Winnipeg towing a barge with about 400 cords of pinewood, the strong east wind that had been blowing all day suddenly hushed and all became calm. Captain Nelson, also in the port that day and with a lifetime of experience on Lake Winnipeg, warned the *Majestic's* captain that a sudden drop in the wind was an ominous sign and there was danger of a storm blowing up from the northwest. The captain decided to leave anyway.

"We were about five miles from Victoria Beach when the storm hit from the north west. It was terrible, with strong winds, thunder and lightning," Barker writes. "The Majestic was a good boat but it rocked from side to side and sometimes felt as though it would go right over."

Everyone became seasick and most ill of all were the captain's two young daughters who "rolled around the floor, vomiting every few minutes". The boat was pitching so wildly, the passengers who had taken to their bunks found themselves rudely ejected onto the jostling deck. Meanwhile, down below, Barker, desperately trying to stoke the boiler, kept being thrown past its opening by the ship's gyrations.

"Suddenly, a steam pipe broke apart in the furnace room. Immediately the engines began to lose power; we could only get pressure up to 80 pounds whereas we needed 150 ... We couldn't go back because we didn't have enough power to turn around."

Eventually, even the engineer got sick. That left Barker the only one able to take over, "a tough job in a raging storm". The engineer, "vomiting as if he would die right there" sat in a chair nearby to provide what assistance he could.

The storm kept up for most of the night and it was early morning before those on board finally spotted the lighthouse at the mouth of the Red River. In a masterpiece of understatement, Barker concludes: "We were happy to see that light." [35]

and freight traffic on Lake Winnipeg. But there were fears that her shallow draft made her top-heavy in the lake's dangerous waters and that her inserted section amidships would weaken her structurally and handicap her manoeuverability in such intricate channels as Berens River and Warren Landing.

To meet the first objection, several tons of rock and pig iron were loaded as ballast; the rock was placed in her stern hold to deter its magnetic qualities from affecting the compass. The second concern was left to be tested. Cabins were built for 100 passengers, observation lounges were installed fore and aft, with a dining salon on the promenade deck and kitchen, cold storage and crew quarters on the main deck aft of the engine rooms.

By the late 1930s, the *Keenora* was attracting about 1,400 tourists annually. The price was certainly right. In 1949, the week-long, all-inclusive return fare from Selkirk to Warren Landing, her most northerly port of call, was $45. At Berens River, the tourists would watch as supplies for the HBC post were tossed from the hold.

At Warren Landing, two red-topped range lights guarded the narrow entrance to the Nelson River. The *Keenora* was too large to enter the river so her smaller sister, the SS *Chickama*, transported passengers and freight the further 32 kilometres to Norway House.

In 1959, the *Keenora's* steam boilers were replaced by diesel, but by 1966, her long and illustrious career was over. She simply couldn't meet new federal marine transportation regulations. For a time it seemed she would face the fate of so many other Lake Winnipeg vessels, allowed simply to rot away in the Selkirk slough. Then, when the people of Fort Frances offered to buy her, the residents of Selkirk joined forces to save this major piece of Manitoba history. Purchased from her owner, Marine Transportation, for $10,000 in 1972, she became the cornerstone of the Marine Museum of Manitoba.

For all the doubts of her seaworthiness, the *Keenora* was a lucky ship. Even so, she had several close calls and one tragedy. On August 28, 1935, she set out on one of her weekly trips to Warren Landing. Right behind her was the SS *Montgomery*, captained by William "Steamboat Bill" Stevens, whose son Robert Stevens was at the wheel. Steamboat Bill told Robert not to follow the *Keenora's* white riding light, which turned out to be a good thing, for both ships. The *Keenora* strayed 40 degrees off course in a westerly direction in the south basin and ran aground on Hecla Island. Captain John Hokanson set off red flares, the traditional maritime distress signal, assembled all the passengers on deck wearing their life jackets and prepared to lower the lifeboats. The Montgomery saw the flares and steamed towards the *Keenora* at full speed. At first, Steamboat Bill couldn't budge the *Keenora*. He tried first with a line on the starboard side then with a line on the port, but both snapped. He then rigged a bridle around her entire length. Giving the *Montgomery* full steam ahead, he pulled the *Keenora* off the reef.

Steamboat Bill threatened to take possession of her as salvage. Later, Hokanson's mistake was memorialized. The

spot on Hecla where the captain beached the *Keenora* is called Hokanson's Point. [36]

Clifford Stevens Jr., nephew of Steamboat Bill, was first mate on the *Keenora* in 1958, the year one of its crew members, suffering from delirium tremens, the DTs, committed suicide by jumping overboard in a vicious storm.

The ship was late leaving Selkirk. During the voyage across the south basin, the wind increased until it was at full gale from the northwest. "The weather was so bad it was doubtful we were making even five miles an hour. When we changed watch in the morning, Captain [August] Helgason

Built for pleasure, the Keenora *spent years rubbing shoulders with fishing boats, opposite, and taking in the sights and smells of fish nets drying at outposts such as Little George Island, above.*

113

The crewman's body washed up here, beneath the lighthouse on George Island.

told me it was the worst storm he had ever been in on that part of the lake," Stevens recalls.

At one point when he was at the wheel, Stevens' sealer of drinking water resting on the ledge by the compass went flying over his shoulder and smashed in the corner of the captain's room.

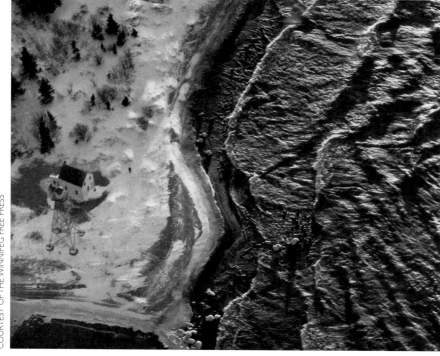

COURTESY OF THE WINNIPEG FREE PRESS

Once again affording pleasure, opposite right, the Keenora *stars in the Selkirk Marine Museum.*

The wind was now a roaring gale and we were in a blinding snowstorm. The sea was heavy with waves over 25 feet high. Captain Helgason knew it was useless to continue under these circumstances and gave me instructions to bring the boat around and go back to Big George. There

was a little break in the sea and I was able to bring the Keenora *around. It was snowing and blowing terribly as we approached the light at Big George and suddenly, without warning, the new deck hand, who had been under constant surveillance since we left Selkirk, made a dash for the railing and jumped overboard. The night watchman had left him for only a few moments to get a cup of coffee.*

The crew made every effort to save the crewman but the terrible weather conditions and high seas made their search futile. "He simply vanished into the snowstorm that surrounded the ship like a white wall." The ship took refuge in the lee of George Island. By the next morning, the *Keenora* had 15 centimetres of snow on her deck. The crew reported the accident to their office in Selkirk and they in turn reported it to the Royal Canadian Mounted Police. The deck hand's body was found the following spring beside the George Island lighthouse. [36]

The *Keenora* had another brush with disaster a year later. On her final trip of the 1959 season, an unusual spell of bad weather choked the channel at the mouth of the Red River with ice and slush and the ship was unable to force her way through. A radio call for assistance brought the icebreaker, the SS-MS *Bradbury*. But even she was unable to clear a passage. For a time, it looked as though the *Keenora* would spend the winter frozen in lake ice with all its associated perils to her survival. Finally, with the *Bradbury's* help, she made it to port at Gimli, where she wintered over in safety. [38]

The *Bradbury* had performed another more heroic service much earlier during her long career on Lake Winnipeg. Built in Sorel, Que. in 1915 for the Federal Public Marine Works as an icebreaker on Lake Winnipeg, she was of steel construction capable of breaking a half-metre of ice with ease.

114

During the Spanish flu epidemic of 1919, she smashed through heavy ice in late November to rescue stricken fishers at the ice fishing posts along Lake Winnipeg's channel area and take them to Selkirk Hospital. She was later used as a dredge tender and to service the lake's lighthouses. She, too, now rests in prairie Canada's only marine museum, in Selkirk. [39]

THE SS-MS *FRANK BURTON –* *MINERVA – GOLDFIELD:* LAKE WINNIPEG'S MOST NAMED SHIP

MANY OF LAKE Winnipeg's ships carried more than one name during their lives. But the record for the ship with the most names belongs to the SS-MS *Goldfield*. Built for the Reid and Clark Fish Company of Selkirk in 1886 to transport fish from fishing stations and tow sail boats to the fishing grounds, she was originally called the SS *Frank Burton*.

Under the command of Captain John Gowell, she was used to conduct the first hydrographic survey of Lake Winnipeg for the Canadian Department of Oceanography (Marine and Fisheries) from 1901 to 1904. When the survey was complete, she was put into passenger and freight service.

Acquired by the Phoenix Brick, Tile and Lumber Company to haul bricks from Manigotagan, she was renamed the SS *Minerva*. The principals of the company

PETER ST. JOHN

DENNIS FAST

The Lake Winnipeg whitefish drives the economy on the lake.

From left, the Lu-berg, Goldfield, Swanne, Luanna, Red Diamond, Betty Lou and Barney Thomas at Gimli Harbour in 1951.

disagreed over the best method to make bricks, and by the time they resolved their differences, their finances had run low. The final blow came when the *Minerva*, towing a barge loaded with freight and 2,000 cases of 40 per cent forcite, a dangerous explosive, was caught in a sudden storm. The tow line broke and the barge drifted to shore and was wrecked on Stoney Point south of Grand Beach. The company went out of business, but its transportation manager, Larry Fisher, took over the ship, rebuilt her and named her the SS *Goldfield*, after a promising gold mine in the Bissett area. He intended to use her to transport passengers and freight from Selkirk to Manigotagan for the Bissett gold fields. But two years later, Fisher was out of business.

In 1916, she became part of the lake's fishing industry. In the spring, she would set out for the fishing areas towing as many as 12 fishing boats behind her. During the fishing season, she made two trips every week from George Island to Gimli with a full load of fish, a feat unequalled by any other lake freighter.

The *Goldfield* sailed out of Gimli from 1919 to 1969. Throughout those 50 years, there was at least one member of the Stevens family in her crew, as captain, wheelsman or mate. When he was a little boy of six or seven, Clifford Stevens Jr. remembers his annoyance when his father would order him down out of the pilothouse during violent storms.

In 1952, the *Goldfield* was rebuilt with steel frames and a Rolls Royce diesel engine and since 1969, her home port has been Riverton. [40] In 1989, she was acquired by the Freshwater Fish Marketing Corporation. In her 114th year, still plying Lake Winnipeg's waters, she smashed a propeller on a reef off George Island in June, 2000.

Sailor's Memories

IN THE FALL of 1940, Clifford Stevens Senior was in charge of fish inspection in the north of Lake Winnipeg and captained a fine little boat, the *Tobermoray*. One morning, on the way from Berens River to Little George Island, he encountered three men rowing south. Their boat had exploded and they were badly burned. Taking them on board, he headed for the nearest port, the Twin Island fall fishing station. Oli Johnson, the least injured, decided to remain there, but Stevens took the two who were more severely burned, Steini Sigmundson of Hnausa and Kari Thorsteinson of Gimli, on to Gimli for medical aid. Stevens sailed all that night battling a strong head wind from the south and two to three metre seas. About eight o'clock the next morning he arrived at Gimli Harbour. There, the men made a full recovery in hospital.

A decade later, Clifford Senior was again called upon to brave stormy seas to rescue a fire victim. Captain of the *Goldfield* by this time, he was docked at McBeth Point when a sudden explosion ripped apart a neighbouring vessel, severely burning its owner Arthur Bristow. Stevens brought him aboard and set out immediately for Gimli. When they left port, the weather was good, but by the next day, a north easterly gale had whipped the lake into a frenzy. Stevens and the *Goldfield* continued on their mercy mission and by the time the ship reached Gimli, the waves were so high that they were washing over the dock and climbing far up the lighthouse. A crowd had gathered, curious to see why the *Goldfield* was sailing in such a storm. Two wheelsmen were required to dock her safely. Bristow was taken to hospital and also recovered from his injuries.

Clifford Junior says his father "like many others, found Lake Winnipeg very dangerous, particularly for the inexperienced". The son also witnessed tragedy.

One summer, when his father was the *Goldfield's* captain and he, its mate, they encountered a violent storm sailing from Selkirk to Hecla. They made port, but three days later were asked for details of the weather by the Royal Canadian Mounted Police. "They were investigating the case of a little sailboat that had left Grand Beach for the river mouth with four boys and an instructor. Their boat had capsized and all its occupants were drowned."

Years later, as a dredge captain during one of the high water periods in the 1960s, he brought his ship to refuge a kilometre and a half up the Red River to escape a storm. Two pleasure boats, heedless of the danger, sailed past him out into the lake. One returned, but the other did not. "It was headed for Grand Beach and was found later drifted on shore in Balsam Bay, stove in by rocks and the four occupants drowned. The waves had risen mountains high and they were unable to make it back to the river mouth." [41]

Awaiting summer   DENNIS FAST

the
HOLIDAY
LAKE

Right: The railways that created Lake Winnipeg's most famous beach resorts were almost overwhelmingly popular for nearly a half-century.

Below: Vacationing at "the lake" quickly became de rigueur, *even for those who did not own cottages.*

Bottom: The enormous dance hall at Winnipeg Beach, like its twin across the water, drew huge crowds every summer weekend.

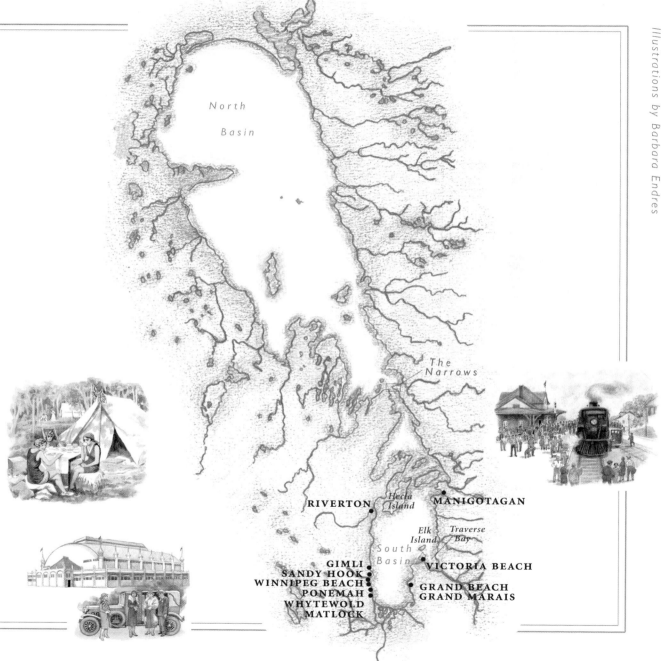

North Basin

The Narrows

RIVERTON

Hecla Island

MANIGOTAGAN

Elk Island

Traverse Bay

South Basin

GIMLI
SANDY HOOK
WINNIPEG BEACH
PONEMAH
WHYTEWOLD
MATLOCK

VICTORIA BEACH

GRAND BEACH
GRAND MARAIS

118

Summers at the Lake

I looked across as far as I
could see. I squinted against
the brightness and saw where
the water touched the edge of
the sky. I had a feeling that this
lake reached all around the
world, that there wasn't any
other land except what lay
behind us ...

— The Corner Store

Summers at the Lake

SUMMERS AT LAKE Winnipeg kindle some of the fondest memories of childhood for generations of Manitobans: the sunlight striking sparks or the moonlight tracing silver pathways on the water; the haunting wail of a steam locomotive whistle just as you're falling asleep; the sand so hot it scorches your bare feet; the hours spent in the water until your skin crinkles like a prune; the soft, soothing sounds of the lake lazily stroking the shore; its deafening roar as white-plumed breakers dash far up the sand to seize you in a watery embrace and carry you out, out, out, for a wild ride in their powerful undertow; cold ginger beer or Hot Lips on the boardwalk; first boyfriends, first girlfriends, the carousel, the screams of terrified delight as the rollercoaster takes its first big plunge, the dodgem cars, the dances, the greasy french fries ... altogether, unforgettable summer idylls.

But these idyllic summers are forever played out against the backdrop of stern parental warnings about Lake Winnipeg's treacherous, untrustworthy character: Don't take the boat far out into the lake. Don't stay out one minute if a wind comes up. Don't ever swim out. Don't try to walk into the waves. Don't. Don't. Don't. Always be careful. Be careful of this lake. It can kill you ...

These are not idle cautions. Police and Canadian Coast Guard records show that not a summer has passed without multiple deaths on the lake. Lake Winnipeg is a Circe. It lures and deceives. Its moments of utter calm

The railways gave life to Lake Winnipeg's beaches. BARBARA ENDRES

usually happen just before it turns into an untameable monster.

In the space of just one season, Peter St. John, the Earl of Orkney and retired professor of political studies at the University of Manitoba, twice risked his life to save people who had paid no heed to the lake's elemental threat. St. John will never forget the summer of 1980, when he rented a cottage at Victoria Beach. His first rescue occurred in the spring of the year. He was sitting alone on the beach in a fairly strong northwest gale, watching two men in a sailboat manoeuvering in the harbour. Without warning, they were suddenly swept out into the lake. They capsized within minutes and he could see them hanging on to the boat. Launching his own boat, he managed to bring them to shore just before hypothermia set in. Later, a friend helped him retrieve their boat.

I remember going out in 10- and 12-foot waves, wondering if I would come up out of the troughs and feeling like I was riding a bucking horse as I crested each whitecap.

At summer's end, the nightmare returned. He was talking to a friend, Rudolf Dyke, on the beach when again he saw two men capsize. Again, there were high waves and wind, and again, it was soon obvious they were drowning. He recalls:

Rudolf said we had two choices – we could literally watch it happen or pile into my 15-foot fibreglass boat with its 50-horse Mercury engine and go and get them ... I don't remember what sort of boat they had, but they were in the water and definitely in trouble. The wind was screaming down and we dove into these giant waves well outside the long pier at Victoria Beach. After what seemed an interminable time, we reached the men and just as we were hauling them into the boat, we hit the Three Sisters. The first wave we knew was a big one and we dragged the guy into the boat. The second one lifted the boat straight up in the air at the prow. It felt as though we were vertical and I honestly thought we would go over backwards ... Then suddenly, as we sat suspended in the air, the third wave hit us, but instead of swamping us, it righted the boat abruptly. I don't know what happened – other than an act of God ... [1]

Lake Winnipeg's role as summer playground, tragic as it all too frequently was and is, still presented the lake in its least lethal form. That's because people treated it largely as a bucolic backdrop for fun and leisure activities associated with but not necessarily on or in it. The lake was there to be seen and be seen at, a place for sitting on the beach, playing in the sand, paddling at the water's edge or swimming just off shore. Its proximity to Manitoba's metropolis made it an obvious magnet for people anxious to escape the heat and humidity of the city in the summer.

The lake's playground era predated cottages and beaches. Winnipeg's *Town Topics*, the society newspaper that boasted of being "read by 15,000 of the best people", enthused about steamboat excursions on the lake.

Under a picture of a ship entitled "Summer Cruise", the June 25, 1898 edition extolled the lake's "incomparable" scenic grandeur and "luxurious and comfortable" steamships, equal to any on Lake Superior. A "perfect holiday jaunt", the paper continued, and available right at the city's doorstep.

One of the highlights of those Lake Winnipeg summer excursions was shooting Grand Rapids. The *Winnipeg Free Press* carried an account of this popular summer adventure shortly after the giant, 480-megawatt Manitoba Hydro dam forever extinguished the magnificent torrent in the early 1960s. The rapids had several channels navigable by canoe. Older funseekers opted for one of the less turbulent ones, but the young and the daring would take the middle channel, white water for its entire length. It was a thrilling trip and a wet one; it was not unusual for a canoe to end the passage with six or seven inches of water aboard. "We go down the middle channel because we like to hear the women screaming," the canoemen would say.

One young lady, a passenger on the SS *Wolverine*, walked back on board drenched to her skin and without her shoes. In her excitement, she had pulled them off and tossed them overboard – why, not even she could remember. Visitors to the rapids would be told they served as a weather forecaster. A muted sound indicated fair winds and skies. But if the roar was deeper and more penetrating, one was to prepare for rain and storms.

The MS *Lord Selkirk II*, the lake's last cruise ship, was the largest ever built between the Great Lakes and the Rockies, with accommodation for 130 passengers and 40 crew. Launched in 1969, she was 54 metres long and 13 metres wide and weighed

In just 15 years, between 1912 when the Winnitoba, *below, took well-heeled passengers cruising on the lake, and 1927, when Peter McAdam caught this athletic quartet performing at Winnipeg Beach, both mores and attire changed dramatically. Summer casual had arrived.*

KRISTIN JOHNSON / PROVINCIAL ARCHIVES OF MANITOBA / N–11410

Mouldering in the Selkirk slough, the Lord Selkirk II *provides a silent commentary on the excursion era.*

1,500 tonnes. She kept to the same ports of call her predecessors had used for nearly a century. Her summer 1970 sailing season advertised a weekly five-day, five-night "Company of Adventurers' Cruise", leaving Winnipeg Mondays at 10:30 a.m. and returning Fridays at four p.m. She dropped anchor at Selkirk, Gimli, Gull Harbour, Matheson Island, Berens River, Warren Landing and Grand Rapids. Passengers were each awarded a fancy certificate, signed by the captain, certifying they had crossed the 53rd Parallel North "into the country of the Company of Gentleman Adventurers".

Lake excursions are no more. The *Lord Selkirk* was pulled out of service in 1983 and sits boarded up, forlorn and abandoned, in the Selkirk slough.

Canadians are among the most enthusiastic cottagers in the world. In 1992, Statistics Canada reported that more than six per cent of Canadian households owned a second or vacation home and a considerably larger proportion either rented a cabin or used one belonging to friends or relatives. According to a 1984 survey by J. C. Lehr, H. J. Selwood and R. Goatcher, 40 per cent of Winnipeggers with summer homes have them at Lake Winnipeg.

In Lake Winnipeg's case, cottage communities owe their origins to the railways. At the turn of the 20th century, Winnipeg was a burgeoning metropolis, bullish about its future and bragging that it was "the Chicago of the North". The railroad was king and Canada's two great rivals, the Canadian Pacific Railway and the Canadian Northern Railway (later to become the Crown-owned Canadian National Railway) were always on the lookout for commercial opportunities.

At the time, the only summer retreats available to Winnipeggers were situated at the much more distant Lake of the Woods in northwestern Ontario. It was a vacation style only the privileged few could afford. The railroads quickly seized upon the untapped potential for tourist traffic and resort hotel development offered by Lake Winnipeg's south basin.

In the summer of 1901, Sir William Whyte, assistant to the president of the CPR charged with extending the railway in the west, and two acquaintances explored the western shoreline of Lake Winnipeg in a motor boat belonging to Captain William Robinson, president of the Northwest Navigation Company. Whyte, who would be named the CPR's second vice-president in 1904, was searching for a location capable of attracting the crowds seeking summer fun, rest and relaxation. Spurring him on was the fact the Canadian Northern was gaining an edge in the recreational travel market with its partially completed line to Delta Beach on Lake Manitoba's south shore. Whyte spied what he was looking for when the boat sailed past a kilometre-and-a-half-long crescent of sand just a few kilometres south of Gimli. The CPR purchased 330 acres of waterfront for $3,000.

Over the next two years, the CPR paid bonus wages to its crews to get the West Selkirk extension finished as quickly as possible. The 64-kilometre stretch of track up the west side of the lake was built in such a hurry the crews laid short rails virtually on the bald prairie, improving the railbed later.

The first Winnipeg Beach train rumbled out of the CPR station on June 6, 1903. In time, the Winnipeg Beach line became the most profitable stretch of track in Canada. By 1910, between 12 and 15 trains a day were ferrying more than 40,000 passengers between Winnipeg and Winnipeg Beach each holiday weekend. Regular weekends had five

IAN WARD

Grand Beach's boom period mirrored that of its sister resort across the water. On the July 1, 1920, long weekend, for example, more than 500 prospective beachcombers had to be turned away due to lack of passenger cars and still the trains carried about 8,000 people in one day, most to Grand Beach. One passenger recalled a trip sometime in the 1930s.

It had about 22 coaches and was filled to capacity with standing room in the aisles and on the ends. I stood on the end the whole trip and couldn't move to a better location. Once the trains reached the Winnipeg yards, they went slowly enough that those from the North End would often jump off to save themselves a couple of miles walk home from the station. [2]

Owned by competitors, Winnipeg Beach and Grand Beach were designed to be almost identical twins, a result of the railways' intense rivalry and the fact they made more money from day-trippers than cottagers. Neither company encouraged a permanent nor even a summer community at these mass resorts. Prospective cottagers were instead direct-

A combination of "grand" beaches, left, and affordable transportation translated almost instantly into throngs of lake-goers. On some weekends, the crush at the Grand Beach station was almost overwhelming.

trains daily, three daytime departures and two evening Moonlight Special excursions. The price of a regular return ticket was 50 cents; one on the Moonlight Special was a dollar, $2.50 if a ticket to the dance hall was included. Over the next few years, the CPR extended the rails to Riverton.

Not to be outdone, in 1914 the Canadian Northern began looking for a site on the lake's eastern shore to rival its competitor's on the west. The story goes that the chosen location acquired its name from a railway official who, picking up a handful of its fine, white, Caribbean-quality sand, exclaimed: "What a grand beach!" That year, the Canadian Northern acquired 80 acres of land and a second parcel of 70 acres was rented, then finally bought, from the federal government in 1930, making a total of 150 acres.

The first passenger train arrived on June 11, 1916, and that same year, the railway was extended to Victoria Beach. By 1919, the CN was providing daily service except on Sundays. Fares in 1934 were one dollar for a day's round trip, $2.20 for weekends and here, too, there was a Moonlight service.

CNR COLLECTION / NATIONAL ARCHIVES OF CANADA / C–34291

ed to the land the railways had to sell elsewhere along their lakeside right of ways. As far as the two big beaches were concerned, the railways' interest was restricted to constructing the major attractions – a giant dance hall and a hotel – to keep the tourists and the money rolling in.

The CPR's Empress Hotel at Winnipeg Beach was built about 1909 and became famous for its lavish bar. In 1923, garden front rooms for two went for $20 per person, lake front balcony rooms, also for two, for $25 apiece. The Empress burned down in the 1930s and was not replaced. Winnipeg Beach also boasted a 51-metre water tower, a midway, a giant wooden roller coaster, a ferris wheel and the Wrigley Pier, named after the chewing gum family. Swimming races were held regularly from the beach yacht club at pier's end.

Meanwhile, across the lake, the CNR was building its own posh hotel, completing it in 1920. The Grand Beach Hotel advertised feather beds, running water, a

Though it lasted only a quarter-century, the Empress Hotel at Winnipeg Beach, seen here in 1910, was nevertheless a landmark on the lake.

PROVINCIAL ARCHIVES OF MANITOBA

library, a huge fireplace, hand-hewn log furniture and the most spectacular view of the beach. Guests were also treated to landscaped grounds, and, on the front lawn, a giant swing in the shape of a boat. The best rooms in the house, with bath and balcony, cost $97 a week, two meals included. Grand Beach also boasted an enormous carousel complete with plunging, prancing horses, several bandstands, Brattson's ginger beer and a deceptively sweet drink called Hot Lips, which burned all the way down. In both, a boardwalk, amusements, and a variety of booths and kiosks created a garish landscape reminiscent of Coney Island, Brighton or Atlantic City.

Over time, differences between Winnipeg Beach and Grand Beach emerged, differences that, as the century wore on and tastes changed, caused each to suffer unique problems, and each to seek its own solution. A town grew up around the railway property at Winnipeg Beach, but it was at the mercy of its one industry in ways even boom-and-bust mining communities don't experience. That's because the boom and bust was annual. In the off-season, its population dropped to 1,000. At summer's peak, it swelled to more than 15,000. Still, it gained municipal status and a main street, a commercial district, a residential area and a settled cottage community.

By contrast, Grand Beach was operated entirely by the Canadian Northern until it was taken over by the Crown-owned Canadian National Railway in 1922. In 1923, the Canada Railway News Company acquired the lease. Because of its public ownership, Grand Beach never became a municipality and therefore never developed beyond its vast stretches of magnificent sand and dunes, marsh and wildlife and the bare essentials required to keep the day or week trippers coming. With the exception of a few mean, run-

Wright Orchestra featuring Paul Grosney. The tunes were Swing Era standards: *Don't Sit Under the Apple Tree, You'll Never Know, I'll Be Seeing You.* [3]

down sheds and cabins the railway eventually grudgingly constructed, those interested in cottaging had to locate at neighbouring Grand Marais.

The two big drawing cards at Winnipeg Beach and Grand Beach were the airplane hangar-sized dance halls unique to the era. Winnipeg Beach's pavilion had turrets and a second-floor balcony from which patrons could gaze out on the beach and the lake. The Grand Beach edifice was plainer, but, initially, much bigger. Winnipeg Beach's dance floor was 10,500 square feet (945 square metres); the one at Grand Beach, 14,000 square feet (1260 square metres). Later, Winnipeg Beach's floor was enlarged to match. Couples bought tickets (10 cents a dance at Winnipeg Beach, five cents at Grand Beach) and stood in line for their opportunity to dance and romance to the music for one "set", exactly two and a half minutes. Then they would be ushered off to buy another ticket and stand in line again. The bands and bandleaders were locally famous: Jackie Hunter, who later made his mark in British dance hall circles; Jimmy Stillwagon and the Syncopated Rhythm Kings; Marsh Phimister, the Don

If the dance halls were integral to the flavour of the period between the two world wars, so, too, were two particular trains, romantically – and aptly – named the Moonlight Specials because they left Winnipeg in the early evening and returned just after midnight. Young people who patronized them usually had more than just dancing on their minds, especially when boardwalks, beaches and sand dunes in the pitch blackness of a summer night were in the offing:

The CNR's Moonlight was synchronized to the same departure time as the CP's ... In fact, in the clear summer evenings you could see the smoke from the two locomotive exhausts juxtaposed across the 20-mile expanse of water ... The dancing was for the same duration on both sides of the lake, and had the same intermission times for refreshments and walking along the shore and mooning at the sparkling lake's surface. On both sides of the lake the train's departure was heralded by the ringing of a loud bell, and was followed by a clamorous rush to the trains for the return journey. Both trains high-balled at 23 hours, and between Balsam Bay on one side of the lake and Ponemah on the other, the youthful passengers vied with the trainmen, putting the lights in the cars on and off eight times. Youth always won, and the trainmen left the cars in darkness,

When these photographs were taken in the summer of 1914, the gleaming floors and elegant orchestra of the Grand Beach Pavilion symbolized an untroubled era that would soon be shattered by strife. But the popularity of the lakeside dance halls survived the Great War and continued to draw thousands to the beaches until the early 1950s.

said "the hell with it" and went into the baggage car to play Euchre ... [4]

The east side of the lake, the CN's, claimed the more stalwart and imaginative because of its later ETA, the extra 10 miles being a challenge for the more virile and ingenious.

Another phenomenon of the beach era was the Caterers' Picnic. Like the dance halls and the Moonlights, it, too, graced both sides of Lake Winnipeg's south basin. Held mainly at Grand Beach, it occasionally shifted across the water to Winnipeg Beach.

The Caterers' Association was formed in 1886 and was composed of food processors, manufacturers, wholesalers, retailers, caterers and their local and travelling salesmen. The picnics began in the 1920s and were held once a summer, always on a Wednesday and usually on the Wednesday following the July 1st Dominion Day holiday.

The dancing was only part of the fun. Refreshments lured visitors outside, where the beaches beckoned and the evening sun would soon turn the lake to crimson.

All the grocery stores in the city would close, many for the entire day. One salesman recalled that there used to be five or six trains, each with 20 or more coaches packed with people, required to take the caterers and all the fun-seekers up to either Grand or Winnipeg Beach. Return fare was 50 cents.

Some years there were about 9,000 people out there, anyone who could possibly take a day off, just to get away from the city. We used to have the train windows open to get some air. With the trains all steam-driven, we'd still come home all sweaty, with soot on our face and sometimes a cinder in the eye.

In addition to the free food and drink, there were attractions for every age, from dances, band concerts and beauty pageants for the adults to sack and three-legged races and pole-vaulting for the children and teens.

The food industry was very discreet, assuming people knew their neighbourhood grocer and would keep patronizing him back in town.

There was no direct advertising at all. We always did have plenty of food to give away. We used to get in touch with the manufacturers and wholesalers and take all their surplus off their hands and then give it away at the lake. [5]

L.B. FOOTE / CNR COLLECTION / NATIONAL ARCHIVES OF CANADA / C-34298

Amid all the laughter, fun and romance, tragedy would occasionally strike as a reminder of the great lake's threat. On July 6, 1912, the *Manitoba Free Press* reported a double drowning at Winnipeg Beach involving one of Winnipeg's most socially prominent families. Carrie Riley, the 24-year-old niece of R.T. Riley, and her beau, Charles Patterson, 23, of the J.K. Moore and Company real estate firm, left Winnipeg on the 9:40 a.m. train for a day at the beach. About 1:30 p.m., they and two friends went swimming in the shallow water near the government pier. The area around the pier had recently been dredged and while the water's usual depth was less than a metre, there was a precipitous three-metre drop all along one side. The murky water obscured the danger, and the four friends, unaware, stumbled over the underwater cliff into what was later described as "oozing, gripping mud, that imprisoned its unlucky victims as in a vice". The other couple managed to get back to shore, but despite the young man's efforts and repeated dives by another Winnipegger camping on the beach, the two couldn't be found in time. Miss Riley's body was recovered later in the afternoon, Mr. Patterson's not for several more days. Reported the paper: "A sad feature of this tragedy is the fact that the last thing that Miss Riley's mother said to her before leaving home was to warn her to stay away from the lake."

The next day, J. K. Moore, one of the dead couple's companions who had nearly lost his own life trying to save them, gave a bitter interview to the newspaper, criticizing the authorities for not posting the danger and the "terrible human indifference" of the many campers and boaters who did nothing to help.

Despite the lurking danger, a trip to "the beach" as the parlance of the day put it, was such a magical event that two of Manitoba's leading writers put personal reminiscences of it in their books. "The Old Man and the Child", part of Gabrielle Roy's collection of short stories in *The Road Past Altamont*, tells of the thrill and awe of a little girl on her first glimpse of Lake Winnipeg at Winnipeg Beach.

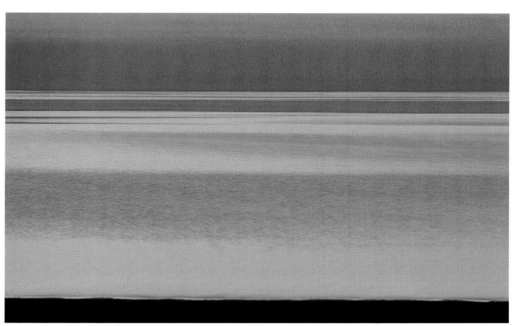

MIKE GRANDMAISON

Then suddenly the train gave a bold and joyous whistle, as if it were announcing: Watch, now, you're about to see something marvellous, new and worthwhile! At the same time, it made a rather quick, sharp turn. I saw then – or believed I saw – an immense sheet of tender blue, deep, glossy, and, it seemed to me, liquid. My soul stretched wide to receive it ... Ahead of us, from one horizon to the other, as the old man had said, was the lake. Nothing but water. But there was something else I had not expected: this was that the lake, even when it made its particular sound heard, also kept silent. How could these be reconciled – this impression of a tireless murmur and, at the *same time, of silence ... All my preparations had been useless; everything surpassed my expectations ... Does one ever, fundamentally, get over a great lake?*

All this time the deep song of the lake penetrated me ... Was it the same breaker that constantly made and unmade itself? Or did they come endlessly from the bottom of the lake? ... I was still struggling to distinguish the slightly melancholy song of the water as it came to spread itself upon the sand ... Had the lake had only this one thing to say since the beginning of time, I wondered ... I surrendered to the same little phrase whose meaning I should have so much liked to know.

For all its impetuous, sometimes savage character, Lake Winnipeg is often "an immense sheet of tender blue", as Gabrielle Roy put it.

The little girl and the old man walk the boardwalk. She is disillusioned "to the point of bitter tears" by the

Sand and ice cream mix surprising well when creating memories.

garishness, the noise, the crowds, the "tinkling of cheap music and the odour of hot grease". He buys her a banana and marshmallow sundae and the two find a place on the sand. He tells her Lake Winnipeg "is older than the soil of Manitoba" and warns her of the lake's danger. "On Lake Winnipeg, I have seen storms almost as great as on the ocean." As their day ends, a storm rises. Heavy, menacing clouds cause the water to take on an evil gray colour.

For a moment longer I struggled to make out what the lake was shouting now that it had begun to be choppy. But everything seemed to merge in a beautiful tumult of air and water ... I was amazed to find myself lying on the sand near a dark mass that heaved and growled dully only a few paces away ... I thought I had had all possible happiness today since, having seen Lake Winnipeg languidly sleeping, I was now going to see it rising in a tempest ... [6]

People of every background were drawn to both Grand Beach, seen here in 1914, and Winnipeg Beach, its twin across the water.

In *The Corner Store*, Bess Kaplan admits she, too, was appalled by Winnipeg Beach when she first visited it as a child. She had expected a paradise but instead found "a slummy sort of town with mud streets and dingy cottages in rows". However, Lake Winnipeg made it all worthwhile for this little girl, too.

Lake Winnipeg made up for everything. As I looked at it I was sure it was as big as the ocean ... There was a vast blueness above and a second, landlocked sky below. Bits of white cloud floated along the ripples, as though they had fallen in ... [7]

From history's perspective, Canada's two great railroads emerge from the beach era as great egalitarians, but for purely commercial reasons. They never cared who patronized their trains or their hotels or their concessions. Winnipeg's ethnic and class cleavages were not to be allowed to get in the way of making a buck. In fact, the railways deliberately priced their attractions cheap to ensure they could pull in the multitudes, regardless of ethnic background, religion or social status.

This, however, was not the case with the cottage developments the rail lines opened, the so-called suburbias in the wilderness. Matlock, Whytewold, Ponemah and especially, Victoria Beach, were WASP (White Anglo-Saxon Protestant) preserves and had "understandings" to exclude the unwanted. In an era when Jews could not be members of the city's posh watering holes like the Manitoba Club, the Winnipeg Winter Club and the St. Charles Country Club, it's not surprising they were excluded from the elite's summer resorts. When the city went to the beach, the city's vertical mosaic travelled along. If Winnipeg Beach and Grand Beach were Atlantic City or Coney Island, Matlock, Whytewold, Ponemah and Victoria Beach were Cape Cod, if not The Hamptons.

Even the WASPS noted it. In his 1980 book, *Wrinkled Arrows*, Howard Dundas wrote about the gentrified scenes the hordes would glimpse from the beach trains as they chugged through Matlock, Whytewold and Ponemah. They had the opportunity to see:

> ... *the younger members of the Establishment in their yellow and black St. John's sweaters and the U of M brown and gold blazers and white flannels playing brisk games of croquet through the twinkling leaves of the aspens, or just sauntering up and down the station platform looking debonair. They also could see the cottages, and the girls in their blue middies and white skirts flitting through the shadows cast by the large elm trees.* [8]

Matlock was named after a town in Derbyshire, England; Whytewold honoured the founder of Winnipeg Beach, and Ponemah is derived from the Cree word *ponematowin*, which means "the end of weeping". From the more open and tolerant perspective of today, it's difficult to comprehend, let alone accept, the prejudices of the past. But they were part of the times. Fortunately, there were enough amenable places around the lake's south basin to accommodate Manitoba's ethnic mosaic. But the past is prologue and these beach communities continue to reflect the predominant culture of those who founded them for the simple reason people go where they feel connected.

CANADIAN NATIONAL RAILWAYS / COURTESY OF THE WINNIPEG FREE PRESS

By the 20th century's end, cottage communities predominated by all the major components of Manitoba's population – Aboriginal/Metis, Anglo-Saxon, French, German, Icelandic, Scandinavian and Jewish – could be found scattered along the eastern and western shores of Lake Winnipeg's south basin and all welcomed all. Still, because of the draw of social and cultural affinity, only the two main beaches, particularly Winnipeg Beach, are, in the words of a newspaper advertisement of the 1920s, "the people's playground". And Winnipeg Beach is the only recreational community on the lake that accurately reflects the province's ethnic composition.

The cultural and social storms perpetrated in those early years at times made even Lake Winnipeg's rages pale by comparison.

Victoria Beach was the creation of a group of private investors who either worked for, or had close ties to, the

Just a few kilometres north geographically, the segregated cottage community of Victoria Beach, seen here in a 1932 photograph, was a great distance culturally from the ethnic mosaic of Grand Beach.

Scenes like this, when the setting sun turns the still water to crimson and imbues the day with a sense of peace, drew city dwellers to the shores of the lake.

IAN WARD

province's land titles office. Over the years, this coterie of insiders amassed a huge tract of land at dirt-cheap prices on one of the most picturesque spots on Lake Winnipeg's south basin. They were determined to create an upper-class haven to rival, if not surpass, the sumptuous island chalets at Minaki and Lake of the Woods. *Town Talk*, the society newspaper that published between 1898 and 1914, agreed the Victoria Beach Investment Company had accomplished its objective.

> *Victoria Beach is an ideal summer resort and a perfect place for rest and recreation. It is one of the pleasantest place for an outing or for a summer residence, to be found anywhere. It has attractions for business men because it gives rest and recreation for mind and body.* [10]

Victoria Beach is located on an isthmus that forms the western shore of Traverse Bay at the mouth of the Winnipeg River. It is marshy at its southernmost extremity. In *coureur*

de bois Joseph la France's time it was an island which gradually connected to the mainland through the action of waves and sand. But much of the remainder of the shoreline of what was then called Sandy or Little Elk Island periodically shoots skyward in a series of almost vertical sand cliffs. Immediately north of the isthmus lies Elk Island, which la France called Isle du Biche. Victoria Beach's interior is well-wooded with forests of birch and pine. The sand on its six pristine beaches, five of which are named after the 19th-century British monarch's children – Arthur, Patricia, Alexandra, King Edward and Connaught, the sixth is called Club Beach – is of the storied talcum-powder grade that made Grand Beach, some 23 kilometres to the south, famous.

The first residents of Victoria Beach boated to their summer homes, either in their own vessels or by steamer, the SS *Pilgrim*, a five-hour sail from Selkirk. The character and destiny of the new resort was shaped by the Victoria Beach Company, which maintained a high degree of control over the development. It advertised itself as everything that Winnipeg Beach and Grand Beach were not. It did not have, nor would it tolerate, public dance halls, boardwalks, large groups of picnickers, Moonlight Specials and noisy midway attractions. Strictly-enforced caveats ensured that high-quality cottages were built on generous lots. By-laws were passed regulating even the removal of trees and rocks. Amusement rides were prohibited and day-trippers actively discouraged, although a golf course and tennis courts were constructed in the early 1920s and the Pinehurst Inn, offering weekly rates of $20, was built on the point near the pier. Later renamed the Victoria Beach Inn, it partially burned in 1953 and was demolished in 1959. Some of its footings are still visible in the grass on Pier Point.

These concessions to resort life aside, the *Victoria Beach News* July 27, 1926, was still able to state:

> *Only private picnics are allowed on the grounds, no public gatherings being privileged to come down, this being the policy of the Company in the interests of those cottage owners who desire to get away from the blare and the bizarre, the loudness and the fantastic of present day outings. [11]*

The company lost some control when it negotiated with the Canadian Northern for train service in 1916. It had to dissolve its original investment company and turn over 50 per cent of its shares to the railway. However, in return, the railroad promised Victoria Beach residents first class Pullman car service, convenient schedules and direct express service.

The First World War and the collapse of the Canadian Northern put an end to all that, but the higher fare for the greater distance and the lack of non-resident facilities achieved the desired effect of maintaining the peace and natural beauty of the resort virtually unchanged, summer upon summer.

At the height of the Second World War, the community's newspaper, the *Victoria Beach Herald*, was publicly upbraided by the *Winnipeg Free Press* for racism. In 1943, a Jewish family showed an interest in buying a Victoria Beach cottage and the *Herald* weighed in with an editorial published August 14, 1943, which said in its least offensive parts:

> *You have an obligation to your neighbours at Victoria Beach. Remember, you have an obligation to see to it that those unwanted people who have over-run beaches on the other side of Lake Winnipeg are not permitted to buy and rent here.*
>
> *Shall we allow our beach to become commonplace? If these people are allowed the run of the beach, it would soon degenerate into a Coney Island and the value of the beach from a pleasure and property standpoint would drop accordingly. Let us beware! [12]*

DENNIS FAST

Until the advent of paved highways, the rail lines were the main avenues to cottage country.

On August 17th, the *Winnipeg Free Press* denounced the *Herald* for what it called "a sanctimonious and cowardly piece of Jew-baiting". That only made the *Herald* more defiant. In a reply published August 21st, the paper pointed out it was merely expressing sentiments that Victoria Beach residents "wish to publicly convey" and warned that "many residents would go even farther than the *Herald* has gone".

The ugly incident made explicit the implicit rigid ethnic class structure that stratified Winnipeg society until the last quarter of the 20th century. Indeed, on the east side of the Traverse Bay isthmus, another exclusive resort based on ethnicity and religion was about to be established. In 1945, the Roman Catholic Parish of St. Boniface began Albert Beach as a children's camp. Soon thereafter, the parish leased additional land from the province, which it sub-let to parishioners for cottages. Albert Beach became a beacon for those Franco-Manitobans who wished to foster their language and culture and find a summer vacation retreat where they could avoid having their children mix socially with anglophones and non-Catholics.

> *As all cottagers sub-leased their land from the church, a "gentleman's agreement" governed the sale or transfer of the lease, ensuring that it was passed on only to the "right" people, thereby enabling the church and Le Club Notre Dame de la Plage Albert to retain some control over the social character of the resort, keeping it both Roman Catholic and French.* [13]

However, in 1975 the gentleman's agreement fell apart. A cottager anxious to dispose of his property found a non-Catholic, English-speaking buyer. When the church and the club objected, the buyer threatened to go to court on the grounds of infringement of his human rights. The Archdiocese backed away and shortly thereafter, sold its land to existing leaseholders and gave up any attempt to control the social character of the resort.

The prejudices of their parents aside, the children of these cottage communities were just out to have fun. In a July 18, 1999 *Winnipeg Free Press* article, Christopher Dafoe, grandson of John W. Dafoe, the paper's legendary editor, captured the idyllic summer months beside the great lake in the 1940s:

> *Matlock, Whytewold, Ponemah, Winnipeg Beach, Boundary Park, Sandy Hook: The railway made the Lake Winnipeg resorts possible and for a generation and more it*

> *dominated them ... The Daddy's Train made two trips a day during the summer, picking up the working fathers just after dawn at the various stations down the line and getting them to jobs in Winnipeg well before nine. It made the return journey at 5:20 and the daddies, hot and*

The "Daddy's train" made it possible for people to work in the city and live at the cottage during the summer months.

frazzled after a day in town, got back to their cottages in time for a drink and a swim before dinner.

Dafoe also recalled that the 5:20 train brought the daily papers.

Back in the 1940s when I helped my older brothers with their Free Press *route at Ponemah we used to listen for the whistle and hoot that told us that the train was leaving Whytewold. On our bikes, bare feet pumping the pedals furiously, we raced the train to the station and always lost by at least five car lengths.*

There was always a crowd at the station at train time and the scene was repeated at stations up and down the line: cars and wives waiting to pick up the arriving daddies; the local postmasters collecting sacks of mail; children waiting for the train to pull out so that they could see what had happened to the pennies and bottle caps they had left on the track to be flattened.

Meanwhile, at Victoria Beach, a favourite childrens' pastime was to jump on the train (there were three a day, including what was called a Daddy's Special) after it had unloaded and drink ice water while enjoying the ride down what is now Gibson Road to the Y-turnaround and back again. Cottagers could treat themselves and their visitors to lake cruises in the *Valtannis*, captained by Walter Thomas. In the 1940s, it took daily excursions from the Victoria Beach dock to Black River, Pine Falls, Elk Island and Grand Beach and back. [14]

The resort's strong community identity led to the creation of the Victoria Beach Club in 1921, an organization that flourishes to this day. Many a parent feels a great debt of gratitude to "The Club" because, thanks to a full-time recreation director, it provides an almost daily answer to that perennial childhood question: What Are We Going To Do Today? The club's summer starts off with a giant flea market on the Canada Day weekend where one cottager's trash becomes another's treasure, all proceeds to the upcoming events. Along with the money raised from an annual membership drive to which nearly everyone subscribes, the club then is in position to begin its season, jam-packed with activities including nature hikes, bicycle tours, swimming, sailing and tennis lessons, bridge, bi-weekly movies, dog shows (every dog a guaranteed prizewinner), sandcastle-building tournaments, a masquerade, a library, a sports day and teen and adult dances.

Among the more vivid memories of Victoria Beach are the delicious smells of fresh-baked loaves and goodies wafting out from the slope-roofed Einfeld Bakery across the street from the store. Long lineups, especially on holiday weekends, sometimes snake right out the door. People gamely put up with standing for lengthy periods in the fierce heat blasting out from the big ovens at the back for their opportunity to buy a vast variety of delights served out of Period-style grocery display cases: Dreams (iced cookie sandwiches with jam in the middle), butter tarts, pies and a wide array of buns, biscuits, Eccles cakes, scones and brown and white Irish bread.

MIKE GRANDMAISON

With Grade 'A' sand to work with, sandcastles become works of art.

133

And who, as a small child or as a parent accompanying that small child, can forget movie night – sitting in the summer heat in the clubhouse while one or another Disney attraction grinds off the projector, swatting mosquitoes and waiting for the intermission to join the mad stampede to the Moonlight Inn to recharge drinks and refresh supplies of ice cream, chips, popcorn and other edibles.

Matchstick piers distinguish the west side of the lake, providing photographers with nearly endless opportunities for composition.

Victoria Beach opened a number of new subdivisions in the late 1980s and 1990s, but the main beach maintains its near-century-old character, thanks to the dogged determination of generations of beachgoers who continue to put nature ahead of personal convenience. Victoria Beach resisted electrification until 1958. The winding, tree-shaded lanes are barely wide enough for a single car, mandating that only permanent residents or those with medical passes are able to drive their cars in the resort during the summer exclusion period from mid-June until Labour Day. Cottagers walk or bicycle and, if they require motor transport, use the taxi service operated by the parking lot. Both the parking lot and the bakery provide much-coveted summer employment opportunities for beach teenagers.

Properties along Sunset – the winding trail that offers a spectacular view of the lake from atop the beach's numerous sand cliffs – often are sold before they are formally on the market. Sometimes, the asking price is bid up by eager

purchasers. Throughout July and August, the parking lot is a testament to the beach's enduring beauty and lure, containing cars with licence plates from all 10 provinces and three territories and most of the 50 American states.

An observer suspended high above Lake Winnipeg in summer would note a singular difference between the beach communities on the east and the west. Matchstick-like piers festoon the shorelines of Matlock, Whytewold and Ponemah, but are less prominent at Winnipeg Beach, Boundary Park, Sandy Hook and Gimli's Loni Beach and entirely absent across the water. The piers, usually two or three planks wide with side rails, are constructed on poplar saplings and are taken down every fall and rebuilt every spring. They are a product of the geology of the lake's west side with its relatively more stoney and muddy shore.

The piers vary in length yearly and among themselves because their builders always test for sandbars before deciding where to put the steps. Sandbars in Lake Winnipeg never stay in one place. In some of the very low-water years in the 1950s, the ends of the piers, sometimes with diving platforms, often barely reached the water. Seasons of high water create the opposite problem. It is not unusual for the frail little structures to be partially or completely demolished in a single storm. Those destroyed in the early part of the summer

IAN WARD

134

A Matlock Treasure

Jim Brennan takes the shiny ice cream scoop with a heavy wooden handle off the wall and points to the lettering on the metal shaft. "See this?" he asks. It reads "# 4 Indestructo". It's not an ice cream scoop you can buy today. It's old, Brennan doesn't know how old. It's been at the cottage for as long as he can remember and he has spent every summer of his life there. His parents bought it in 1949 when he was a year old. As a child, he used the scoop to drive nails — the resulting scars are the only marks that mar its brilliant-from-long-use bowl. It is indestructible, also an apt description of Augdon House, Jim and Nancy Brennan's cherished cottage on the shore of Lake Winnipeg at Matlock.

The two-storey cottage was built in 1910 by Duncan James Ross and Neil Ross and named Durness, after the family's ancestral home in Scotland. The Ross brothers were substantial citizens of Winnipeg. Originally from Pictou County, Nova Scotia, they came west to establish a construction business. It prospered, leading to the summer home at Matlock and a farm a few kilometres east of it. In 1920, they sent for their two sisters, Mary Isobel and Margaret Marjorie, who had been housekeepers, or in the parlance of the day, "in service", in New England.

The two brothers and two sisters, none of whom married, passed 20 happy summers in Durness. In the summer of 1940, one sister passed away there, but that event has not dimmed the Brennans' love for their summer retreat. In 1991, Jim and Nancy bought the cottage from Jim's mother and repainted it in the dark greens, beiges and off-whites indicated in the early photographs preserved in its historic albums. Says Jim Brennan: "There has never been that much to do except general maintenance. Those Scotch Presbyterians built things to last!"

Some concessions to modernity have been made. There is a bathroom and a shower. The screened porch, upstairs and down, has been windowed to extend the cottage's use in the spring and fall. Otherwise, the original furniture is exactly where it always was. A large, slightly watermarked portrait of Queen Victoria hangs over the living room fireplace. "Nancy bought it for me some years ago and in my mind had it

been purchased by the Ross brothers and sisters they would have hung it exactly where I did. They were patriotic in the extreme," Brennan says.

Two years ago, natural gas arrived in Matlock, but the Brennans didn't connect. "It's great, but I'll never use it. I think it's important that cottages be preserved as old things," Brennan says. Heat is provided, as it always has been, by the fireplace, a combination wood and electric stove and Hudson's Bay blankets on the beds. "If you're still cold, you don't belong here," he adds.

Augdon House has had three names. When Brennan's parents purchased Durness, they renamed it Brenwick, to honour their close friends Hilda and Lew Wickett. Some time after Brennan's father passed away in 1965, the cottage was given his middle name. It has now been Augdon House for a good part of its life and, unless something dramatic happens, Brennan doesn't see any reason to change it. He and Nancy have set the original Ross china out on plate racks in their dining room and continue to use all the old kitchen utensils; the cast iron frying pans, two venerable hand-beaters, a wooden-handled egg-flipper and, of course, the ice cream scoop. Upstairs, the four bedrooms contain sets of the rare turn-of-the-century porcelain washbowls, water jugs and "jerry" pots.

Brennan's love for the old cottage is echoed by many others, according to lawyer Allan Adams, whose father was also an early Matlock cottager. Adams says that in his 50 years of practising law, he has learned that nothing causes more grief in the settling of an estate than the transfer of cottage property. The reason is simple.

"Family members connect their good times as children with their parents to summers at the cottage. When an elderly person passes away, the car, the house, the money and all the other bits and bobs, they can be easily divided, but a cottage means so much." [15]

Augdon House then, above, and now   IAN WARD

would be patched together. If the disaster occurred well into August, the task would be left to the next year, much to the sorrow and chagrin of the piers' patrons, particularly the young ones.

Another important aspect of recreational activity around Lake Winnipeg was the summer camp. In 1982, Winnipeggers were served by about 30 childrens' residential summer camps, the antecedents of which lay in the social reform movements of the late 19th century. Summer camps came in two varieties: outward bound ones catering to middle class children whose parents sought to expose them to adventure and character-building; and philanthrophic ones directed at underprivileged children and adults operated by churches, businesses and labour unions.

The first camp on Lake Winnipeg was the Methodists' Deaconess' Fresh Air Camp. Originally set up on the city's fringe in Norwood, it was renamed Camp Sparling and relocated to just north of Gimli in 1911. Over the next few years, many more camps were set up along the western shore of the south basin, drawn by the combination of woods, meadows, beaches, the lake itself and good rail connections to Winnipeg.

In addition to the obvious good works, churches and other organizations saw the camps as a way to acculturate into Canadian society the many nationalities flooding into Winnipeg before and after the First World War.

The camp of the Methodist Church – Camp Sparling – like the other camps which followed in its footsteps was created and operated to save the bodies and souls of the children from the urban ghettos of immigrant Winnipeg.

Quite clearly there was a melange of philosophical concepts embodied in the organization and objectives of each camp, ranging from the practical social concern ... of the social gospel espoused by James Woodsworth to the chauvinistic jingoism of Empire loyalty. [16]

Camp routine was universal. The day began early with the ritual of washing, followed by breakfast, prayers (if it was a church camp), sports, swimming, dinner, strolls or hikes with club or tent leader, boating, supper, a quiet hour and a bonfire with impromptu theatre, story or gospel reading before bed. One of the advantages of the water sport aspect of every day was to instill notions of personal hygiene and cleanliness. The "fresh air camps" pursued physical fitness as a way to build self-confidence and muscle coordination as well as social skills such as cooperation and interaction.

The proselytising aspect of some of the early religious camps spurred other denominations and religions, fearful of losing their religious identity, to create their own summer experiences for their children. It was not long before every religion in the province had a summer camp. In addition to the Methodists' Camp Sparling; the Presbyterians had Camp Robertson; the Roman Catholics, Camp Morton; the Jewish community, B'nai Brith and the Salvation Army, Sunrise Camp. The Workers' Benevolent Association, an offshoot of the Communist Party, also operated a camp near Winnipeg Beach.

Lakeside Camp was somewhat unique. Founded in 1921 by the Union Bank as a memorial to employees who fell in the Great War, it was non-denominational. Among the 824 guests entertained during the 1928 camping season "were children of 19 nationalities ... and 16 religious faiths; among them Church of England, Presbyterian, United,

In many places, the old stone walls were works of art, and have stood the test of time.

DENNIS FAST

Roman Catholic, Christian Science, Jewish, Lutheran and Greek Catholic." [17]

The automobile was a part of beach life almost from the beginning. The first car to be driven into Winnipeg Beach in 1913 was memorable also because immediately upon arrival, it ran over and killed the police magistrate's dog. Intrepid souls could – and often did – drive to the lake in their Model-Ts or roadsters along the dirt and sometimes gravel tracks that snaked across the prairie from Winnipeg. It was not for the faint of heart, however. One determined motoring couple used to install their cat in the rumble seat with a jumbo sweater to chew on as the car made its hair-raising way to and from Matlock in the 1920s. By the time the car arrived at its destination, the sweater was much the worse for wear, as were the cat and its frazzled owners.

Because of the deplorable state of provincial roads in the early part of the 20th century, the car was not much of a threat to the train or to the railway-dictated structure and rhythm of beach and cottage life. The end of the Second World War and the affluence of the post-war boom period in the 1950s changed all that. Paved highways burgeoned. The train retreated in lock step with the automobile's advance. The denouement, when it came, was amazingly swift. In less than two decades, train travel to the beaches on both sides of the lake chugged into history. The Moonlight stopped on the west side in 1956. The next year, Highway 59 to Victoria Beach was paved. In 1961, the last passenger train arrived at Riverton and a year later, the train said its farewell to Victoria Beach.

The car meant personal mobility and much wider horizons for holiday seekers. Both mass beaches went into steep decline. As early as 1943, Winnipeg Beach town council, anxious to air out a growing scent of tough people and rough behavior, passed a bylaw prohibiting anyone from frequenting a public place unless "wearing clothing from the shoulders to the knees". [18] Grand Beach was dealt a major body blow when its dance hall burned down Labour Day weekend in 1950. By the early 1960s, Winnipeg Beach's dance hall was turned into a part-time roller rink to pay its bills. Two years later, the town council passed another bylaw, this one imposing a 10:30 p.m. curfew on everyone under 16 years of age. Soon, the resorts were not only unattractive and unpleasant and perhaps even dangerous to frequent, but eyesores to be avoided.

Motoring to the beach began when automobiles, left, and roads were both rudimentary, and within four decades spelled the end of both train travel and the attractions the railways had created.

NOTICE PARK · AMUSEMENTS · BOARDWALK PICNIC GROUNDS · PARKING AREAS
CLOSED PERMANENTLY
WILL NOT RE-OPEN IN 1965   BEACH ENTERPRISES LTD.

As the 21st century begins, summers at the lake have evolved. Behind old stone walls, many cottages have given way to year-round residences, while the public beaches on both sides of the south basin have become provincial parks, complete with full-service campgrounds and an array of interpretive programming.

DENNIS FAST

Grand Beach climbed out of the pit first because, as public property, it was easy to rescue. It became Manitoba's first provincial park by cabinet order-in-council May 3, 1961.

Winnipeg Beach, however, was a trickier proposition because of its municipal status and private property ownership. Finally, the workings of the market ground to a halt. In 1964, Beach Enterprises Ltd., the owners of its picnic grounds, boardwalk, dance-hall-roller rink, rides, roller coaster, concession stands and hot-dog stands, closed them permanently. The town's multi-year plea for help was answered in 1967, Canada's Centennial Year. Under a Canada-Manitoba agreement negotiated under ARDA (the Agricultural and Rural Development Act) and FRED (the Fund for Rural Economic Development) the beach was purchased and gradually redeveloped by the provincial parks branch.

The turn of the 21st century finds cottage and beach life around Lake Winnipeg both changed and changeless.

Recreational retreats are pushing farther north up both sides of the great lake as more Manitobans not only choose Lake Winnipeg's environs as their summer haven, but as the place they want to call their permanent home. The popularity

of the original cottage communities, now in their second century, is not only enduring, but expanding, as new summer homes are being built and old ones redeveloped or replaced. Still, many families at Matlock, Whytewold, Ponemah, Boundary Park and Victoria Beach find themselves the third or even the fourth generation to occupy the same summer home. These cottages were constructed just before or just at the turn of the 20th century and retain the characteristics, charm and, in some cases, even the furniture, of the late Victorian era. While most cottages have undergone renovations to accommodate modern conveniences like indoor toilets and showers, television, electric heating and insulation, the artifacts from the past have been lovingly preserved: the iron bedsteads; the wooden washstands with their ornate – and priceless – porcelain wash bowls and pitchers from the days before running water; the massive fieldstone fireplaces, and wood stoves that, some say, provide a fragrance and flavour to freshly-baked bread or roast beef and turkey that is unsurpassed.

Meanwhile, Grand Beach and Winnipeg Beach are enjoying a stable, though less frenetic, status as recreation playgrounds. Winnipeg Beach has had the last laugh. Closer to the city, it has emerged as a sought-after bedroom community for affluent Winnipeggers. Freed from the noise and activity of its garish railroad past, it has become one with its neighbouring cottage communities as a somewhat more urbanized location for summer's rest and relaxation. Grand Beach continues to surf on its amazing shifting sand dunes and pristine beauty still astonishing all who come to see and enjoy. Nothing much has changed since that day, almost a century ago, when a Canadian Northern Railway official proclaimed his awe and gave it its name.

The lake itself seems timeless. Walter J. Phillips might have created Fall, Lake Winnipeg *yesterday, rather than in 1919.*

WALTER J. PHILLIPS / COLLECTION OF THE PAVILION GALLERY / GIFT OF JOHN P. CRABB

DENNIS FAST

Grand Beach continues to draw throngs of sun-seekers

Long-distance swimming races quickly became a tradition on Lake Winnipeg, involving many kinds of events, including the annual Wrigley's one-mile race at Winnipeg Beach.

Today, the best remembrance of those madcap summers at the beach during the years between the world wars resides in the lake and its enduring magnetism.

To the generations of fun-seekers who thronged its shores to soak up the sun and the fun, Lake Winnipeg, for all its threat and history of tragedy, was merely a passive presence. But there was one event which recaptured, in immediacy and intensity, the ageless and pitiless story of the lake versus those who dare to challenge it on its own ground – on the open water.

At 5:52 a.m. Friday, August 19, 1955, Kathie McIntosh, a 20-year-old Norwood stenographer, walked into Lake Winnipeg at Grand Marais determined to become the first person to swim the 29-kilometre distance to Winnipeg Beach. Five other swimmers, all of them men and all older than she, had already entered the water and had as much as a two-hour head start on her. One of the five was attempting the swim from the other direction, Winnipeg Beach to Grand Marais.

Almost seven hours later, at 1:07 p.m., the last man still swimming, a Royal Canadian Air Force airman by the name of Camile Filion, 23, was pulled from the water in a state of collapse. "She's On Her Own!" proclaimed the front-page headline in *The Winnipeg Tribune* of that date. Despite persistent bursitis in her left shoulder, she was swimming strongly at 18 strokes a minute.

After almost 17 hours in the water, she touched shore at Winnipeg Beach at 10:40 p.m. As she approached the beach, "a whooping, uncontrollable mob" waded in to greet

her and the flotilla of boats chartered by the media pressed closer, their floodlights picking her out of the black water. "Is my face still dirty?" she asked. Then she instantly fell asleep, awaking the next morning "to find the city was hers". [19]

Her triumph was made all the more sweet because just five days earlier, on August 15th, McIntosh had been beaten by the lake. After a calm start, it became surly. This was how she explained it in a front-page article in the *Tribune*:

> *Those waves were just too much ... it was those huge waves that beat me. To me, they looked about 45 feet high and one of them flipped me right over, just like being on a roller coaster ... I wasn't afraid of anything in the water and I wasn't seasick swimming either ... But the waves kept getting higher and they were pushing me south, off course, and to get straight again I'd have to swim six or eight miles right into them.* [20]

She was pulled out of the water less than seven kilometres short of the west shore. Accompanying her in the track boat, her father and swimming coach, Bruce McIntosh, and her boyfriend, Ed Sokol, who had helped her train at Clear

COURTESY OF THE WINNIPEG FREE PRESS

Lake, were afraid they would lose her as the night closed in. Because of what the *Tribune* called "giant" waves, they often couldn't see her even in daylight.

McIntosh kept secret her plan to challenge the lake again until she appeared on the beach at Grand Marais the following Friday. This time, the lake cooperated and she made it to a pebbly shore just north of the lighthouse at Winnipeg Beach. In the flavourful journalism of the time, the *Tribune* exulted on Saturday, August 20th:

> *Lake Winnipeg said uncle Friday night to human courage and endurance when Kathie McIntosh waded ashore after swimming across its 18 miles in 16 hours and 42 minutes ... Fighting a depth of tiredness few humans have reached, Kathie McIntosh left five male competitors in her wake as she struggled valiantly ... to become the first conqueror of Lake Winnipeg.*

The reporter, who watched the swim from one of the many media boats, wrote of the countdown to landing at Winnipeg Beach:

> *Only one-half mile left to go. We could now hear the chant from the beach. "Come on, Kathie. Come on, Kathie. Come on, Kathie"... And she did in spectacular and*

unbelievable fashion. Her arms just flailed the water. This was the end of the road.

McIntosh's triumph started a trend. On August 21st, 24-year-old Vivian King Thompson, who held almost every Manitoba swimming title and was a former star distance swimmer, dipped into the lake at Grand Marais. She swam fast and strong, covering nearly 26 kilometres in nine hours and 35 minutes. Within three kilometres of her goal, however, a violent storm with winds up to 80 kilometres an hour whipped up three-metre waves and forced her to abandon the effort. Reported the *Tribune*:

> *Vivian (King) Thompson's attempt to conquer Lake Winnipeg almost cost her her life. Mrs. Thompson was being pulled from the lake by her handlers when a giant wave, estimated to be 14 feet high, submerged her. When she came to the surface seconds later, she was gasping for breath and those in accompanying boats had difficulty reaching her in the mountainous waters.* [21]

Though Kathie McIntosh and Vivian King Thompson survived their encounters with the lake, over the years many swimmers were less fortunate. A summer idyll at the lake could, in the blink of an eye, become a summer tragedy.

Kathie McIntosh took the idea a step farther on August 19, 1955, becoming the first person to swim across the south basin. When her five male competitors all dropped out of the race by early afternoon, The Winnipeg Tribune ran the story on Page 1.

141

the
ELEMENTAL
LAKE

Sitting it out, courtesy of Jerry Zaste

Illustrations by Barbara Endres

Upper right: During the fur trade era, lopsticks (or "lopped sticks") were often created on conspicuous points to mark particular waterways or to celebrate the passing of significant visitors.

Below: Advances in watercraft and a desire for adventure travel have increased the number of adventurers on the lake in the past 25 years.

Lower right: Even the latest equipment is no guarantee of victory over the lake, however.

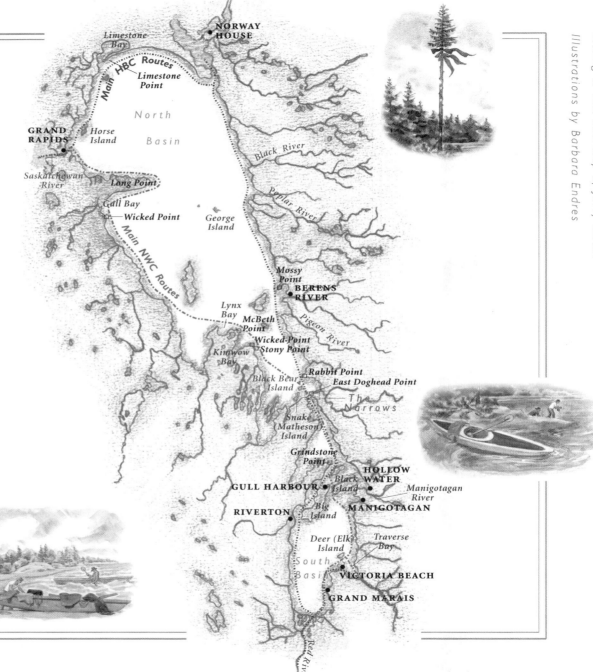

Limestone Bay

NORWAY HOUSE

Main HBC Routes

Limestone Point

North Basin

GRAND RAPIDS   Horse Island

Black River

Saskatchewan River

Long Point

Poplar River

Gall Bay
— **Wicked Point**

George Island

Main NWC Routes

Mossy Point

BERENS RIVER

Pigeon River

Lynx Bay

McBeth Point

Wicked-Point
Stony Point

Kinwow Bay

Black Bear Island

Rabbit Point
East Doghead Point

The Narrows

Snake (Matheson) Island

Grindstone Point

HOLLOW WATER

GULL HARBOUR   Black Island

Manigotagan River

RIVERTON   Big Island

MANIGOTAGAN

Deer (Elk) Island

Traverse Bay

South Basin

VICTORIA BEACH

GRAND MARAIS

Red River

Adventurers on the Lake

I *t's her moods. She is almost like a femme fatale. You're seduced by this beauty. And then those winds come at you. The beauty, the raw energy. It's always there. You have to respect it.*

— Phil Manaigre

Adventurers on the Lake

PHIL MANAIGRE, ADVENTURER, wilderness kayaker, award-winning filmmaker, tries to explain his intense and conflicted love-hate-fear relationship with Lake Winnipeg; how he can talk about it with tenderness and affection one minute, and refer to it as "wicked" and "killer lake" the next. It's the irresistible attraction that human beings have had down through the ages to something that is both beautiful and dangerous, something that offers the bold among us the matchless exhilaration that only comes with daring death and walking away.

Harvard University sociobiologist E.O. Wilson put words to the phenomenon in describing the human enthrallment with predators. "We're not just afraid of predators, we're transfixed by them, prone to weave stories and fables and chatter endlessly about them, because fascination creates preparedness, and preparedness, survival. In a deeply tribal sense, we love our monsters." [1]

Manaigre and Jerry Zaste circumnavigated Lake Winnipeg by kayak in the summer of 1995. In a journey that took them 52 days, they paddled 1,500 kilometres, regularly encountered two-to three-metre waves, had all their food stolen by bears and almost lost their lives in storms. Lake Winnipeg, Manaigre says, is unique.

It's an ocean smack in the middle of the prairies. They say if you can windsurf or kayak Lake Winnipeg, you can do it anywhere. It's considered one of the roughest,

The lake beckons BARBARA ENDRES

most dangerous bodies of water in the world. I have some of the voyageurs' accounts and, in all of their travels Lake Winnipeg was the body of water they feared most. It is often referred to as killer lake. It is a wicked lake. A storm can brew up any minute and if you're not careful, it will kill you. But I've always had a love affair with the lake. I've been attracted by its rugged beauty, the power of all that raw energy, for a long time. It's always that element. You never know what to expect.

In the ocean and other deep bodies of water like Lake Superior, Manaigre continues, the waves are farther apart. But Lake Winnipeg's waves get taken right from the bottom and are close together. "It's so rough because it's so shallow. The waves are steep-fronted and they come at you like a jackhammer. They just keep hitting you."

His most terrifying experience is indelibly imprinted on his mind. Trying to make up time after reaching the north basin on the first leg of the journey up the west side, he and Zaste decided to paddle all one night.

The moon was out. The lake was tranquil. Then clouds came up out of nowhere, obscuring the moon and its light. A wind rose, freshened and, within minutes, began to howl. Suddenly, lightning was stabbing the lake everywhere. Manaigre's kayak, an Aleutian Baidarka, is six metres long. Soon, it was standing straight up and coming straight down on those steep-fronted waves. The two kayakers rounded Stony Point and then Wicked Point, but they dared not try to come ashore. The lightning illuminated boulders well out in the lake. They had no choice but to keep paddling the 18 kilometres across Kinwow Bay to the beacon at McBeth Point. That point, too, was unattainable. Its limestone cliffs plummetted to the water and were festooned with spray and foam from the crashing waves. By the time the kayakers finally were able to put ashore at Lynx Bay, they had been paddling, non-stop, for 24 hours.

Recalls Manaigre in a film he compiled of the journey using a combination of his photos and Zaste's video footage: "Eighteen kilometres of open water in a wicked storm. It was hell. I've never been so scared in my life. I could imagine the hell the crew of the *Suzanne E* must have gone through because I had spent a night in hell on that wicked lake myself."

Another indelible memory Manaigre will always carry about Lake Winnipeg is the wind. "[It] wears you down,

COURTESY OF JERRY ZASTE

physically and mentally. You go to bed, you hear the wind, you get up in the morning, you hear the wind. It's always windy. It just wears you down." [2]

The kayaking duo is only among the more recent of the lake's adventurers. Unlike most, who pitted their skills against the lake of necessity, Manaigre and Zaste tackled it purely for the challenge and excitement. Their lake adventure ended happily, but countless others did not. Over the centuries many paid with their lives and many more left no trace

of their experiences or their particular fates. Often, even the lucky ones who did reach shore carried tales of elemental struggles or terrifying brushes with death.

Of the chronicles reproduced here, two occured during the long, dark months when the lake sleeps in its bed of ice. In winter, Lake Winnipeg is the distilled essence of prairie austerity, habouring the customary dangers of intense cold, freezing winds, blizzards and whiteouts. Yet even then, the lake is capricious; those who traverse it must always anticipate the cracking and shifting of the ice pans that, without warning, confront an unwary traveller with a chasm of frigid open water.

THE VOYAGEURS: THE ANONYMOUS ADVENTURERS

IN HIS BOOK, *Fur Trade Canoe Routes of Canada*, Eric W. Morse notes that no canoe course lay across Lake Winnipeg, in any direction. He calls it "probably the worst lake in North America for small craft".

The French-Canadian voyageurs knew all about Lake Winnipeg's wind. *La Vieille*, they called it, "the old woman". When the old woman battled them to a standstill, the voyageurs retreated, often for days at a time, an enforced pause they termed *dégradé*. Writes Morse, "They spread out the fur bales to air and dry and simply relaxed and enjoyed it, waiting for *La Vieille* to smile on them again." [3]

Those arch-rivals of the fur trade, the Hudson's Bay Company and the North West Company, had to cross paths at two points on Lake Winnipeg, The Narrows and Grand Rapids. Otherwise, they avoided one another by taking the opposite shores up and down the great lake. The HBC's route – along the west side of the south basin and the east side of the north – was somewhat easier and safer. The

Windbound on Long Point, left, Manaigre surveys the pair's charts.

Seymour's Harbour at East Doghead Point provided a welcome haven for fur brigades forced ashore by wild weather. Signs of their passing can still be seen.

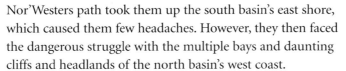

Nor'Westers path took them up the south basin's east shore, which caused them few headaches. However, they then faced the dangerous struggle with the multiple bays and daunting cliffs and headlands of the north basin's west coast.

Entering Lake Winnipeg from the Winnipeg River, the North West Company brigades paddled straight north along the east shore. At the eastern end of Black Island they portaged along the shore of the island to avoid the adverse or even dangerous currents that, depending on the wind, swirl around these confined waters. Farther north they crossed over to the western shore of the Lake at Dog Head (The Narrows).

Possible evidence of the fur brigades' presence at The Narrows has been found by Jens and Barbara Nielsen. "East Doghead Point has a little harbour, Seymour's Harbour, or Lewis Creek, ideal for a stopover," says Jens. Knowing about the voyageurs, he has explored the area. "I thought to myself, if I were to store something here, where would I put it? I found the dugouts, completely overgrown but nicely built with boulders. There were once two houses and root cellars, one and a half metres deep. You only had to go to shore to find old nails that were obviously hand made, pieces of glass and pottery. It's very easy to find things."

From The Narrows, Morse continues:

... the Nor'Westers could not always coast safely close to shore but had to make a total of 10 traverses, across mouths of deep bays or between islands. The minimum distance is five miles (an hour's paddling in bad weather) though to save miles the voyageurs often preferred to make longer, riskier traverses. Two exposed points along the way were significantly named "Maligne" (today's Wicked Points.) Just as they neared safety ... Long Point jutted 25 miles into the lake. This the voyageurs knew as Le Grand Détour, and rounding it was often dangerous. If caught in a squall coming up the Lake, the brigade could land, but the shoreline on the west side was largely inhospitable.

The Hudson's Bay Company's route was the mirror image. From Fort Garry past the mouth of the Red River, the Baymen followed the west coast of the south basin, crossing over to the east side at The Narrows.

Even though the Hudson's Bay Company York boats were more seaworthy, could carry more sail, and chance a longer traverse, they too kept to the coast. They ... held to the east shore of the [north basin], which necessitated no risky traverses such as on the west shore. [5]

Much of the east shore of the north basin is one continuous stretch of Caribbean-calibre sand, but those pristine beaches are defended by a deadly fortress of jagged, half-submerged rocks capable of puncturing any boat's hull.

There were three more subsidiary fur trade routes on the lake. The HBC's eastern trek, from Red River to the Winnipeg River, took advantage of the depression in the narrow neck of land just south of present-day Victoria Beach. At low water, the Baymen dragged or portaged their boats or canoes; at high water, the boats and canoes were floated over. Then their course lay straight across Traverse Bay to the Winnipeg River's mouth.

The most perilous of the HBC's Lake Winnipeg routes was its earliest route to the west, which lay along the lake's

Running before the wind, the crew of Walter J. Phillips' York Boat on Lake Winnipeg takes a well-earned rest from rowing.

treacherous north shore from Norway House to Grand Rapids. For 70 kilometres the shore is lined with clay cliffs. In a strong south wind, the surf beats against the foot of these high banks, denying all a landing place. As a result, the canoes and later York boats waited for any wind but a south wind and sailed day and night to complete the trip as quickly as possible. The north wind, most feared on the lake almost everywhere else, provided a respite for this particular voyage by driving the lake south and exposing a narrow sandy beach where boats could land if necessary. Another salvation along the treacherous route was Limestone Bay, separated from the main lake by Limestone Point, a low-lying, 24-kilometre finger of sand that, some say, resembles a necklace with a pendant at the end. In a strong south wind, the brigades headed for this narrow isthmus, portaged across and proceeded in its lee. Limestone Bay brought the boats to within 70 kilometres of the mouth of the Saskatchewan River.

The North West Company also had a subsidiary route on the lake. To service its posts on the southern plains, its canoes would travel down the east shore of the south basin from the Winnipeg River to the Red River.

Death was a familiar companion of the fur traders. Their pathways were dotted with crude crosses marking where they fell, where lives were extinguished by drownings, strangulated hernias, lung hemorrhages or heart attacks.

> *The early journals speak of seeing as many as eight or ten crosses clustered together. Those ... were nearly all found in specific locations, for what claimed this steady toll of sacrificial victims among the voyageurs were the obstacles along the course: the big lakes, the watersheds and the rapids.*[6]

Morse was writing mainly about French-Canadian canoemen, but the labour required to move the HBC's York boats and their freight through the rapids and portages around Lake Winnipeg could – and did – maim and kill many a crewman. Willy Frog Ross, an Indian boatman on the Berens River-Little Grand Rapids route, recalled that the oars were "so large and heavy that it took a lot of muscle and strength to pull one all day long".[7]

The number of portages on a route fluctuated with changing water levels. Generally, high water reduced portaging but it also made low-lying portages swampy and difficult to traverse. The steersman commanded the crew of seven or eight and he loaded the freight onto men for carriage across the portages. Each man usually carried more than 75 kilograms (about 165 pounds) with the help of a portage strap. York boats were hauled and dragged across portages with the aid of ropes and log rollers.

The Methodist missionary John Semmens critically observed: "Many a man in the North Land today had been

Though many loved the life for its relative freedom, the work of a voyageur was dangerous and often deadly.

W. H. BARTLETT / NATIONAL ARCHIVES OF CANADA / C-2336

crippled by these portages and [are consequently] objects of charity. Many a lonely grave evidences the severity of the work done on these portages ..." [8]

Another missionary, R.G. Stevens, described the work required on northern Manitoba portages in a similar vein: "One day in camp I was concerned to see a man having a bad lung hemorrhage. The next day he was working as usual. Right there I discovered that there were worse conditions of labour than negro slavery."

He also recalled Robinson Portage: "When carrying began, the road was dry. When the work was done the way was muddy, wet with sweat dropped from the faces of the carriers."

Stevens saw men standing around doing nothing and was told they had hurt themselves carrying on the portages. "Their lungs are affected. They will soon die." He was also told "there are no men over 50 years of age at Island Lake". [9]

John Fleming, a member of Henry Youle Hind's surveying party in 1857-58, gave a similar account of the unbelievable travail required to drag a boat through the Grand Rapids at the mouth of the Saskatchewan River on Lake Winnipeg's northwest shore:

The ascent of the Grand Rapid is one of the most laborious duties that has to be performed on a boat voyage from Lake Winnipeg to the Saskatchewan District ... On arriving at the foot of the rapid, every boat discharges one-half its cargo of four to five tons. Thus lightened, they are then tracked [towed] up to the beginning of the portage – the whole of the crew of six to eight voyageurs, with the exception of the bowsman and steersman who remain in the boat being engaged in the labour of tracking.

Each man is attached to the tracking line by a leather belt, or portage-strap, passing round his body; and harnessed in this manner they drag the boat along, running and scrambling barefooted over the slippery and jagged rocks at the sides of the cataract. When the lower end of the portage is reached, the boat is emptied and run back again to the foot of the rapid and from thence hauled up as before with the remainder of its load.

The whole of the lading is then carried over the portage, exclusive of the 15 pieces or about 1,350 pounds, which is left in the boat. With this ballast, the boat is pulled across to the south side of the rapid to be tracked up as the towing path is better there than on the north side.

In consequence of the rapidity and violence with which the upper portion of the rapid flows, in ascending it, it is necessary to employ the main line, a much thicker and stronger rope than is generally used for tracking. To this line the crews of one or two boats are lashed and thus they run along the top of the cliffs of limestone – there being no footing at the bottom of these walls of rock – hauling the heavy craft up the surging cascades. [10]

A JOURNEY FOR FRANCES

IN THE SPRING of 1830, Frances Simpson, the 18-year-old bride of George Simpson, governor of Rupert's Land since 1821, left Montreal for Hudson Bay, a trip of nearly 13,000 kilometres. Her diary of the journey reveals a sharp

Despite the hardships, left, the lure of wild places and the chance to escape class-ridden European society persuaded hundreds of young men into the fur trade. Those at the other end of the social scale, such as Frances Simpson, below, journeyed into the great "Nor'Wast" on the North American equivalent of a safari, an all-inclusive guided tour.

and open mind and a curious and fun-loving spirit alive to the beauty and grandeur of the largely untouched continent unfolding before her canoe.

As the wife of the hard-driving Hudson's Bay Company governor, Frances was treated like royalty. The voyageurs carried her to and from her canoe at every stop. In camp, her tent was carefully screened from the men. Moreover, Simpson sent word ahead as they progressed westward to ensure she never encountered any of his several "country wives" or their children.

The Simpsons reached the Winnipeg River on June 3rd. Frances was enthralled. "Nothing can be more beautifully picturesque than the route of today," she wrote in her diary that night. The next day, she was thrilled by the experience of shooting five sets of rapids, including Pointe de Bois and Chute de Jacob, "the torrent of which foams and boils with a thundering sound for a considerable distance".

Her first experience with Lake Winnipeg left her less impressed. "It blew very hard, occasioning a heavy swell." The Red River fared better. "The beauty of this stream surpasses that of every other I have seen in the interior," she wrote.

After a brief sojourn at Fort Garry, the party paddled north along the Red River towards Lake Winnipeg.

June 11th ... We proceeded to examine the ground for the site of a New Establishment, [Lower Fort Garry] about to be built at this end of the Settlement, and Mr. Simpson having selected a beautiful spot on a gentle elevation, surrounded by Wood, and commanding a fine view of the River, we took leave ... The Sun scorching today, and the Water in Lake Winnipeg, as smooth & clear as a Mirror. Encamped between 8 & 9 O'clock half way between the

Looking much as it might have when Frances Simpson laid eyes on it, the rejuvenated marsh at Grassy Narrows is once again lush and bountiful — and still, especially in June, home to mosquitoes.

Shoal Islands, and the Grassy Narrows [the site of today's Hecla Island causeway].

June 12th... Off at 2 a.m ... On landing this evening, we found the Musquitoes very troublesome, and for the first time during the voyage, used our Musquito Curtains, which are made of a kind of thick Muslin or Gauze, and are fastened so as to enclose the bed, forming a Canopy above.

JERRY KAUTZ

June 13th... Embarked at 2 a.m. The Sun excessively warm during the morning: the scenery along the Lake still bearing the same barren, & dry aspect, the Country having been overrun by fire, which is the case in many parts of the Interior ...

June 14th ... The atmosphere was very hazy, and a small thick rain fell the greater part of the day, which was extremely warm. Between 5 & 6 p.m., a dense fog came on, so suddenly that the Steersman lost his way and bent his course in a direction completely opposite to the one he ought to have taken – considerable time was thus lost ... The Mist, after clearing for a short time, returned with all the darkness of night, entirely excluding any appearance of Land: as good luck would have it, the sharp eye of our Guide hit the mouth of the Jack River, of which we were in search, and that found, we continued our march with great rapidity, and arrived at Norway House at one-half past 10 p.m ...

June 25th ... The Voyageurs agreed among themselves to cut a "May Pole," or "Lopped Stick" for me; which is a tall Pine Tree, lopped of all its branches excepting those at the top, which are cut in a round bunch: it is then barked: and mine, (being a memorable one) was honoured with a red feather, and streamers of purple ribband tied to a poll, and fastened to the top of the Tree, so as to be seen above every other object: the surrounding trees were then cut down, in order to leave it open to the Lake. Bernard (the Guide) then presented me with a Gun, the contents of which I discharged against the Tree, and Mr. Miles engraved my name, and the date, on the trunk, so that my "Lopped Stick" will be conspicuous as long as it stands, among the number of those to be seen along the banks of different Lakes and Rivers.

The party reached York Factory at midnight, June 26th, and Frances penned these reflections of her journey:

"I must here observe, that a Canoe voyage is not one which an English Lady would take for pleasure; and though I have gone through it very well, there are many lit-

tle inconveniences to be met with, not altogether pleasing or congenial to the taste of a Stranger: viz. rising between 1 & 2 a.m. sleeping sometimes on swampy ground, sometimes on hard rocks, and at others on sand (the worst of all materials for a couch, with no other bedding than a couple of Blankets & Cloaks: – living the greater part of the time on salted provisions without vegetables: – exposed to a scorching sun, cold winds, and heavy rain – putting up late some evenings drenched to the skin, and finding the Encampment so wet, as to render it impossible to dry any of our clothes, when it became necessary to wear them the following day in the same state ... [11]

YORK FACTORY TO ST. BONIFACE ON FOOT

IN 1836, PIERRE-LOUIS Morin d'Equilly, a young seminary teacher in Paris, met Bishop Joseph Norbert Provencher during one of his visits to France and was persuaded to come to St. Boniface to serve as a missionary. Bishop Provencher made arrangements for Morin to travel on the HBC ship, *Eagle*, which sailed June 1, 1836. Due to bad weather, the ship arrived two months late, on October 18th. The boats for Red River had all departed in mid-September to avoid the ice, so Morin and a group of HBC employees and Cree guides set out on foot on December 8, 1836. They reached Norway House the day before Christmas and remained there until February 4, 1837, when they started down Lake Winnipeg. Morin arrived in St. Boniface on February 13, 1837, having covered a distance of about 1,000 kilometres.

Here, in part, is Morin's story, translated by Hubert G. Mayes, associate professor of French at the University of Winnipeg:

Frances Simpson's "lopped stick" would likely have stood for years, a reminder to all of her journey.

York Factory, seen here in 1926, was the centre of a sizeable settlement by the beginning of the 19th century, when Morin arrived from France.

151

Our caravan left York on Dec. 8. It was composed of Mr. And Miss Lewis, Mr. Ross and myself. Each of us had a servant. There were also three native guides to drive the sleds, six Scottish tradesmen for work to be done in British Columbia and two Muskegons [Cree] to break a trail for us through the forests, the swamps and the small frozen lakes we would find on our route. Our effects and the equipment essential for travellers who have to journey through these terrible regions during the winter were placed with care and attention to distribution of weight on a sled 2.30 metres long. On this sled I took note of the following articles: clothing, snowshoes, guns, a small set of cooking utensils, tobacco, peace pipe, tea, sugar, rum, moose meat, slices of buffalo hump meat, grease, big biscuits and flour. All these articles were contained in tin boxes and the others rolled up in tarpaulins. The full weight of the sled might have been a hundred kilos, but my two Eskimo dogs pulled it over the snow without appearing tired on our arrival in camp in the evening ...

Their trip south along the Hayes River took them through lands Morin described as "primitive" and "forbidding" and temperatures so fiercely cold that at one point, near Oxford House, their double alcohol thermometer read minus 46.5 degrees Centigrade. They reached "the big factory at Norway" on Christmas Eve. During the 42 days Morin stayed at Norway House, the temperature dropped below the freezing point of mercury (minus 40 degrees Centigrade) no less than six times.

However, when he departed Norway House February 4, 1837, "wearing my snowshoes and accompanied by my

Winter solitude MIKE GRANDMAISON

two guides, liberally supplied with excellent provisions for the crossing of upper Lake Winnipeg", the weather was very favourable, a mere five degrees below Centigrade.

On February 4, Norway to Montreal Point on the [north-east shore] of Lake Winnipeg (48 kilometres). First camp. The 5th, second camp near the mouth of the Black River (106 kilometres). The 6th, we cross the mouth of the Poplar River for the third camp in a wooded area situated beyond Big Rock Point (156 kilometres). The 7th, we go around Point Mossy, cross the estuary of the Berens River and establish our fourth camp between Pigeon River and Catfish Creek (216 kilometres). The 8th, a blizzard which keeps us in camp for 24 hours. Fifth camp at Rabbit Point in dreadful cold (37 below zero ... 265 kilometres). The 9th, after passing through the narrowest part of the lake, sixth camp in a well-sheltered spot opposite a little island close to the shore (317 kilometres). The 10th, still following the south-east side of the lake, we leave ... [the name is left blank] Island on our right and set up our seventh camp on Big Island [Hecla] (359 kilometres). The 11th, the cold, the wind and the snow force us to camp a considerable distance back in the woods (406 kilometres). On the 12th, we press on to Deer Island, [today's Elk Island] crossing the estuary of the beautiful Winnipeg River. From there, we go on to our ninth camp in a frozen marsh broken only by sparse bushes and stunted trees [Grand Marais] (450 kilometres). Finally, on the 13th, we camp in the delta of the Red River of the North, having covered 483 kilometres from Norway House to the head of Lake Winnipeg ...

Before sunrise, and after a substantial breakfast, we broke the tenth camp we had made since our departure to go up the main branch of the Red River delta. About three o'clock, we reached the Stone Fort, 48 kilometres away, a journey which took nine hours ... [12]

Morin went on to become a member of the Geographical Society, Chevalier de l'Ordre du Lys, and director of the Land Titles Service of Canada. His manuscript was annotated by his grandson, the Quebec poet Paul Morin, who read the account to the Royal Society of Canada in 1927. It was subsequently published in the Society's *Proceedings and Translations* for that year.

CROSSING LAKE WINNIPEG BY DOGS

ALEXANDER McARTHUR WAS one of the founders of the Historical and Scientific Society of Manitoba in 1879, precursor of the Manitoba Historical Society. A keen historian and ornithologist, he made many contributions to the society's publications, including articles on the 1869-70 Red River Rebellion and on Manitoba's winter birds.

A Winnipeg businessman and city alderman for one term beginning in 1879, McArthur was the first secretary-treasurer of the Winnipeg General Hospital. However, he sustained heavy financial losses when Winnipeg's boom collapsed in 1882-83. In 1886, he suffered another tragedy when both his wife and son died within a few weeks of each other.

To forget his sorrows, McArthur decided to mount an expedition to the Arctic to study and collect birds. He persuaded Donald Smith, Lord Strathcona, to give him a letter of credit for $500, good at any HBC post, and gathered information from an impressive array of American and Canadian Arctic experts.

He hired an assistant, W.H. Young, and set off by horse-drawn sleigh from Winnipeg at 10:20 p.m. on February 13, 1887, intending eventually to reach Ellesmere Island in the High Arctic. At Rabbit Point on Lake Winnipeg, the two men switched to toboggans pulled by dogs and driven by native drivers. Continuing via Berens River, Mossy Point and Poplar River, they reached Norway House March 3rd.

Exasperated by Young's incompetence, McArthur fired him and sent him back south. On March 8th, he set out for Oxford House but turned back the same day. On March 17th, he decided to return to Winnipeg himself, finally reaching it on March 30th. His stated reason was that he had heard that the Inuit no longer came south to Churchill.

He planned to set off by a different route, but never realized his dream. After a brief illness, McArthur died in his room in the Grand Union Hotel less than five months later, on August 21, 1887. He was buried in St. John's Cathedral cemetery.

While his expedition was a failure, it produced one interesting byproduct, a rough draft of a manuscript entitled "Crossing Lake Winnipeg by Dogs". Here are exerpts:

When chill Novr.'s [November's] surly blast comes navign. [navigation] is at an end and the begining of

Though seemingly stark and lonely, winter on Lake Winnipeg actually heralded a time of considerable activity. Wide white highways, travelled by dog and horse trains, connected otherwise isolated communities.

Just as it was in the summer, Lake Winnipeg in winter was unpredictable. A day of calm beauty could turn deadly in less than an hour.

December, you may go from end to end of this long irregular lake and not see a drop of water.

Then your means of travelling becomes restricted. You can don moccasins and go on foot, or take a cariole and dogs – huskies – trained to the work and doing it thoroughly. Five of these strong, handsome brutes will draw yourself and your bedding and baggage and make day after day forty miles – a total weight of say 300 lbs. And when the road is good your driver will get on behind, light his pipe and smoke it out without a perceptible diminution in the rate of speed. They often bound along at a rate of six miles an hour [but] this is reduced to an average of about four miles, so that 10 hours on the road is required to make 40 miles.

A typical day on the road begins at 3:30 a.m., when the campfire breakfast is made and eaten and the dogs are hitched to the sleighs. The departure time is 5 a.m. The first stop, for tea made from boiling snow, takes place at 9:30 a.m.

Snow requires solid packing and refilling the kettle as soon as space is made by the thawing of the first lot of snow, and even a third filling will not bring the water to the brim. The under crust thawed in the sun or solidified with a shower of rain or sleet is used when it can be got and only a partial refilling is them required. The drivers produce their provisions bag and the frozen pork, without bone and 9/10ths fat is cut with the axe and placed in the frying pan. The frozen bannocks of flour are placed near the fire to thaw and in half an hour or less everything is ready.

Another stop to eat occurs at 2 p.m. and again just before dark, when a longer rest of two hours is taken. The trip continues until midnight, when the dogs get their one

and only meal of the day, four to six kilograms of substandard whitefish.

To have a good camp the first requisite is a point where there is plenty of spruce or balsam and abundance of dry wood for the fire ... The position of the camp is always regulated by the wind, the fire being in front and in lee of the shelter afforded by the back wall [freshly-felled trees] of the camp. In addition to this shelter, the evergreen trees in rear afford protection from the wind ... The diet is always simple, consisting of meat, bread and tea but once in a while when camping early and when the weather is fine variety is obtained by making beef tea or soup ... and if you are lucky enough to have parsed vegetables, you make a soup fit for the Gods ...[13]

NOTES ON A TRIP TO LAKE WINNIPEG ABOARD THE STEAMER *PREMIER*

THIS ANONYMOUS ACCOUNT of a voyage that departed Winnipeg on August 28, 1899, paints a droll picture of the ill-fated ship in her glory days. No expense was spared as Winnipeg's city fathers and Board of Trade were wined, dined and entertained at every opportunity on an excursion designed to convince them of the need to open up the lake to shipping and resource development.

The lake tour was complete with a piper and drum major, who not only entertained the passengers on deck, but piped and drummed them as they marched to and from their onshore festivities. The voyage also featured two storms, one just rough enough to make everyone seasick and another that came close to capsizing the ship.

The first objects of interest [at the mouth of the Red River] were the two light houses, rather unpretentious looking structures although of considerable height ... After entering the Lake, which at this point is a clay coloured peaceful looking body of water, we followed the East shore a distance of about three miles until near a point called Grand Marias [sic] where we entered a small harbour named Victoria Harbour, and turned around and came out again and proceeded on to Elk Island, a pretty Island apparently heavily wooded and showing considerable limestone and sand on the shore ...

The next piece of interest after sailing around Elk Island is Fort Alexander, the Historic Point where Lord Wolseley made his first landing ... apparently a pleasant place, although somewhat secluded, and full of Nature's most beautiful gifts which at the time of our visit were at their grandest and best. We were all struck with the peaceful quietness surrounding the fort, and its fine situation ...

The ship's company enjoyed feasting and festivities at Fort Alexander that evening and night, repairing back to their shipboard beds in the wee small hours. At daylight,

facing a strong headwind, the ship steamed back down the Winnipeg River from Fort Alexander to Traverse Bay and out into the open lake.

Thinking there was a storm on I hurried up about 5:30 a.m. to get on deck, but was told by the Mate that it was only a stiff breeze although it was sufficient to make a number of the passengers conspicuous by their absence, and on being questioned about the state of their feelings, some of them complained about a disturbance in the region of their stomachs. About 10 a.m. we ran on the lee side of Black Island much to the pleasure of those feeling squeamish. We entered the mouth of Bad Throat [Manigotagan] River ... Headed by the Piper, we marched by devious pathways, ravines and rocks for about half an hour when we arrived at Bad Throat Falls. We were indeed repaid for our trouble. We saw there the sight of the trip so far: a fall

Traverse Bay   DENNIS FAST

155

over solid rock about twenty feet in a hundred yards and the ruins of an old saw mill having long since fallen in disuse, one with turbine wheel driven by water ...

Then it was on to Black Island, Gull Harbour and Gull Point, where the passengers watched pelicans and a large number of gulls fish near the steamer. As they sailed north past Big (Hecla) Island, Punk Island, Deer Island, Grindstone Point and Big and Little Berry Islands, the ship's company, apparently bored, formed a procession headed by the drum major and piper and marched around the deck. At Bullhead Point, the ship stopped for wood and everyone went ashore.

The *Premier's* next port of call was Black Bear Island, "a peaceful little harbour", before commencing the 14-hour voyage to Horse Island in the north basin. About 5 a.m., the passengers were awakened by a rough sea and rolling ship. Virtually everyone on board became seasick, or, as the author put it, was "seen making heavings towards the water". He, too, made a hurried trip downstairs, "expecting to be called on to feed the fishes", but escaped with only "a disagreeable feeling" in the morning.

In those days, Horse Island was a major fish station. That evening, the thickest of the fish slime and scales were hosed off the floor of one of the packing houses to make way for a community dance. The *Premier* left at about 5:30 the next morning. While the author again felt a rough sea, he was reassured by the ship's officers

The arrival of passenger ships provided a welcome diversion at island fish stations, where pelicans were more regular visitors.

that it was fairly calm. About an hour later, the ship docked at Grand Rapids. Some of the passengers, the writer included, ran the rapids in canoes.

The water was smooth and swift for about a mile when we entered the rapids, the fall is about forty feet. The banks for a good part of the way had the appearance of being built of solid masonry, being so abrupt and even. The river is about half a mile wide at the rapids and about a mile below the rapids, the running of which, although it did not take a Blondin or a Webb to accomplish it, nevertheless had sufficient danger in it to make it at least exciting and I think the feelings of the different members of our company could be better imagined than described as we dashed along the troubled waters at the rate, as we were told, of twenty miles an hour; past large rocks and shallow places depending entirely on the Indians to guide us through. We passed two Islands on the way down both of which had timber on them, and we also saw a large number of Pelicans.

The experience on the rapids was but a prelude to the voyage's main event – one of Lake Winnipeg's famous storms.

We arrived at the Steamer amid a heavy rain, and at one o'clock we set sail for Berens River, a distance of one hundred and twenty miles, but got about thirty miles on our way when, a storm coming up, caused us to turn back. This time the officers had to admit that it was a "little" rough. The air was filled with a fog or mist when we turned around. About this time some little excitement was caused by turning the Steamer in a strong wind. Our Piper was thrown from the upper berth to the floor but fortunately he landed right end up. Some other little incidents occured here but none worthy of note except the numerous and sudden calls to the side of the boat ...

After a run of about four hours we reached shelter at Horse Island. The storm had continued to rise and was now blowing what I had no hesitation in calling a gale. There was lightning and thunder and very heavy rain, causing some damage to the fishing industry ... Two sail boats came in next day after experiencing considerable hardship, but they did not appear to think much about it, as though it was a common occurrence. We had to stop until evening, when the prospects were a little better, but the sea was yet running high.

We started out again about 4:45 p.m. and reached Long Point, which is said to be the worst place on the lake and, I think, as far as our experience went, it was entitled to the claim. Things were rather lively for a time, tables, chairs and passengers all mixed up. After midnight the storm appeared to abate and we retired for the night, waking up in the morning to find a complete change. The wind and the waves had apparently finished their frolic and we were again able to follow the even tenor of our ways ..."

Storms and "heavings" aside, once safely ashore in Winnipeg, the writer and the rest of his party proclaimed themselves convinced of the lake's commercial potential.

All of the Islands and apparently all of the Coast line are covered with timber, thousands of ship loads of building and lime stone cropping up nearly every place we went,

and I presume, thousands of pounds of fish ... Altogether we saw a good many reasons why the St. Andrews Rapids should be opened up as soon as possible. The resources awaiting development are many and varied ... [14]

LAKE WINNIPEG'S LAST LIGHTHOUSE KEEPER

IN 1905, THE Dominion government came to the aid of mariners in Lake Winnipeg's vast north basin with a light that beamed across 32 kilometres of open water in all directions, beckoning ships to seek sanctuary from storms in the snug harbour on George Island.

George and Little George islands are the continuation of The Pas Moraine as it sweeps in a southeasterly path across the Interlake and Lake Winnipeg before disappearing into the Canadian Shield on the lake's eastern shore. Along with the two Georges, the moraine creates Long Point and the islands called Cannibal, Big Sandy and Little Sandy.

Located about 400 kilometres north of Winnipeg, George Island featured a tourist hotel at the peak of the lake's steamship era in the early years of the last century. To this day, it rewards visitors with fields of wild raspberries, strawberries and mushrooms. It also has long served as a major cog in the lake's fishing industry. Fishers still use the fish station to pack and freeze their catches primarily of whitefish. Seven pristine white sand beaches cover most of the 16-kilometre circumference of the island. At the north end, a thick forest grows right up to high sand dunes on the beach. George is totally isolated, although its beauty rivals the best sand and beach scenery available anywhere in the province. The government of Manitoba is considering making it into a recreational area.

From 1905 to 1981, the George Island light was

COURTESY OF THE WINNIPEG FREE PRESS

Willard Olson, then 64, was honored for 30 years of service on George Island in a ceremony at Selkirk in May 1981.

Seen from the air during a food drop in late 1951, the tiny house and the nearby lighthouse on George Island seem bleak and isolated, but Olsen apparently never felt lonely. Beautiful beaches and forests, bountiful bird life, and the frequent company of fishermen were more than enough.

COURTESY OF THE WINNIPEG FREE PRESS

MIKE GRANDMAISON

manned. For the last 30 of those years, from 1951 to 1981, its keeper was Willard Olson, a bachelor and dog fancier who would arrive in the spring and depart at freeze-up in the fall.

During the intervening five or six months, Olson followed a rigorous daily routine. Four times a day, he climbed the island's 20-metre tower, twice to light the kerosene lamp at sunset and extinguish it at sunrise and twice to clean the reflectors and lenses. Olson would then perform the identical tasks at the island's other three smaller beacons. They mark the shallow, rock-strewn channel to its little, land-locked harbour. In addition, he sent weather reports to Winnipeg every three hours from sunrise to 10 p.m.

In 1968, Olson's burden was greatly reduced with the advent of automated weather and lighthouse equipment.

Olson was the fourth custodian of the George light. When he arrived in 1951, he was one of six lighthouse keepers on the lake. When he left in the fall of 1981, he was the last. He closed that chapter of Lake Winnipeg history. Now, the great beacon turns in silence on an island often empty save for one lonely and oddly-marked grave.

Olson made headlines his very first year. A quick freeze-up followed by a thaw stranded him until December 7th. He was flown out in a daring rescue by a Riverton bush pilot who risked his own life by landing on the barely-solid ice. Until then, Olson survived on food drops from a RCAF Dakota. Winnipeg's newspapers carried daily reports on his condition and he came home to a hero's welcome.

Initially, Olson lived in an uninsulated house exposed to the full blast of the lake's fierce north winds. While the summer months were pleasant, spring and fall brought formidable storms. Eventually, the uninsulated house was replaced with a snug bungalow.

Olson was an avid reader and he often had more than his dogs for company. The fishers and the fish station crews were around, and some Saturday nights when everybody's work was done, cribbage games broke the monotony. Olson could also look forward to the monthly visits of the coast guard bringing his supplies and to his frequent two-way radio and then telephone conversations with the shore and with the ships. In his last years, he had television.

In media interviews over the decades, Olson frequently spoke of his preference for isolation. Born in Selkirk, he was the son of a saw-filer. During the Depression, he and his brother trapped alone in the bush out of Manigotagan and Kinwow Bay, taking with them only a pound or two of tea, sugar, salt, a little flour, a gun and a blanket apiece. "We lived on our guns off the land." It was not the best way to live, but there seemed no alternative during the Dirty Thirties. At 17, he took a job with a fish company on Snake (Matheson) Island.

Olson served overseas during the Second World

158

War, but, like so many other people who have fallen under Lake Winnipeg's spell, he came back to it as soon as he could.

"You have to be a certain kind of person to be a lighthouse keeper," Olson admitted in a 1978 *Winnipeg Free Press* interview. "I've had assistants ever since they electrified the island, but they kept quitting. Some came pretty damn close to going crazy."

In all the years he served on George Island, there were no major shipwrecks. The only event of note was the *Keenora* crewman with the DTs who jumped overboard in that blinding snowstorm in the fall of 1958 (see page 114). Olson found his body the next spring and called the RCMP.

"The guy washed right up under my bedroom window one night," Olson recalled in a 1990 *Free Press* interview. "You are not supposed to move a body like that, but the Mountie sounded like he really didn't want to do it, so I took him out. He wasn't in bad shape except he lost a piece of his nose on the rocks."

Olson buried him, marking his grave with wire pipe. The grateful RCMP officers gave him a case of beer and a bottle of Canadian Club.

In that 1990 interview, Olson, then 74, reflected sadly on the passage of an era on Lake Winnipeg.

I was a good lighthouse keeper. I always knew what was going on for miles around me on the lake, and even with the aircraft, so there were no big accidents while I was around … If you like the isolation like I do, it's the greatest job you could do …

You might say I was the last of the Mohicans. For years after they took me off the island, I had people calling me up and asking me what happened, why I wasn't around any more. I feel for those guys who are out on the

lake all alone now. It's not very damn funny to be out in the middle of a storm at midnight when it's blacker than the inside of a coal sack. The boys tell me they hate not having me there to talk to them on the radio any more. [15]

MEMORIES OF THE BLACK BEAR ISLAND LIGHTHOUSE

M ARGO THOMAS IS an Ojibwe civil servant with some unique childhood memories. Her father, Ralph, was the last lighthouse keeper on Black Bear Island. After 10 years' service, he was replaced by an automated beacon in 1964.

"We actually lived on Matheson Island, but from May until the end of October, we lived on Black Bear and my dad drove us to school by boat," Thomas recalled recently. "It's not even a mile across (at its narrowest point) but it's right in The Narrows where the current is. It's really, really bad at

Automated now, the lighthouse at Black Bear Island was once a summer home for Margo Thomas's family.

COURTESY OF THE NIELSEN FAMILY

that place. You often can't cross there ... In bad weather, my dad would go across to the lighthouse and sometimes he'd be stuck there for days ... We'd be stuck on Matheson or Black Bear, wherever we were when the storm came up or when the ice started moving ..."

She remembers her grandfather telling the children to always be careful on the lake. "I know there are things you do and things you don't do on Lake Winnipeg. My grandfather would tell us, this place you go, this place you don't go and he'd never explain why. But we sort of knew ..."

Ms. Thomas' most vivid recollection is of the hand-operated foghorn she and her little brother manned. "Regardless of whether our parents were there or not, we had to get up in the middle of the night, if necessary, and blow that foghorn. It was a hand-operated foghorn, a bellows. We'd take turns just blowing and blowing that foghorn." The children also took turns lighting the light.

It had to be lit by four o'clock in the afternoon. No later than five. We all knew that. We would climb up the *stairs there. It was a big Aladdin's lamp, the old coal oil lamp, and it had a big reflector ... We would light that light and we'd all take turns blowing that foghorn and we could hear and tell the difference between the boats, even above the storm ... I doubt anybody ever gets to know that lake because it's so unpredictable. But I also know the sound of the waves, the blowing of the wind ... It's so calming. I can get lost in that lake, just riding on the waves, out in a boat, but there were times when I was really afraid of it. So many people I knew drowned. I do remember thinking that I hated that lake because it took so many people.* [16]

STORMY LAKE ORDEALS

A NUMBER OF Canada's leading wilderness and cross-country canoeists have challenged Lake Winnipeg and written eloquently about the experience; it's an eloquence called forth by the lake's ability to elicit from its travellers profound emotions ranging from dread to awe. One described it as "overwhelming"; a second referred to the lake's "terrible splendour"; to a third, the lake was "wild beauty in treacherous

Brooding menace or spectacular sunrise? Lake Winnipeg often shows its split personality.

MIKE GRANDMAISON

places"; but to a fourth, Lake Winnipeg was simply "this bloody lake."

In his book, *Canada's Forgotten Highways*, Ralph Hunter Brine notes the inherent danger of the lake's sudden storms and high-standing waves and also of The Narrows in a north wind.

"Lake Winnipeg has brought disaster to many a canoe brigade of yore ... The north wind ... can be violent, particularly at the change of seasons." The sudden cessation of the north wind causes an immense body of water to rush northward and then oscillate back and forth until its kinetic energy has been expended. "A similar effect could be obtained by rocking a giant bathtub end to end."

The phenomenon was so pronounced, early explorers thought the lake experienced tides, an impression, Brine continues, that led David Thompson and others to call the north basin "Sea Lake". [17]

In 1988, *Kingston Whig Standard* photojournalist Alec Ross's dream of retracing the routes of the voyageurs almost died on Lake Winnipeg when a vicious storm completely destroyed his canoe.

Ross left Lac du Bonnet on June 23rd and encountered the storm that wreaked havoc on the Gimli and Grand Beach areas that year. "I saw the dark, ugly clouds and knew it was a storm so I found a place to store my stuff," he recalled in an interview with the *Free Press*. He hitchhiked into Powerview to spend the night. When he returned in the morning, he found his canoe, dented and scraped, blown several hundred metres down the shore.

Next, he was windbound for five days at Loon Straits where Carl and Anne Monkman took him in and gave him a copy of the New Testament. When the wind finally subsided, he paddled on to Lynx Bay, where he was hit by

another storm. It gave the modern voyageur a taste of Lake Winnipeg at its ferocious peak.

"It was another one of those holocaust-type storms. I was forced to shore on the rocks – trees were bending right over and leaves and branches were being ripped off." While he was trying to build a shelter, the wind took his canoe and blew it 91 metres across the rocks, all but destroying it. "The seat was ripped out, the left gunwale was ripped out, a thwart was gone and it had three holes in it."

But fortune smiled on Ross. He sat out the storm by reading the Monkmans' Bible and later, on a trek along the shore, miraculously found a somewhat rusty red tool kit that had washed in, complete with screwdrivers, pliers, a saw, screws and other gear. Along with his Fibreglass repair kit, it allowed him to make his craft seaworthy again.

"I'd never read the Bible in my life up till then and I find this tool box," he said. "I just don't know: this biblical storm, the tool box – I guess someone or something out there is looking out for me."

However, Ross couldn't suppress his fury at the lake that nearly killed him. "This bloody lake has been hell. I'd been forewarned, but it was still a surprise – it was definitely the worst stretch of the trip. If it wasn't wind, it was the heat. Out of a month on the lake, two weeks were spent sitting out the wind." [18]

Gary and Joanie McGuffin battled one of the lake's storms during the cross-Canada paddle they memorialize in their book, *Where Rivers Run: A 9,600-Kilometre Exploration of Canada by Canoe*. They approached Lake Winnipeg with apprehension, they write, because "few rival its capacity to create totally unnavigable conditions for small craft within minutes" and because of the "almost complete lack of island cover along most of its southeastern and northwestern shores".

The lake answered their dread. Arriving at the mouth of the Winnipeg River, they were welcomed by cumulous clouds billowing into thunderheads on the southern horizon. "A storm was brewing. The surface of Lake Winnipeg was deathly calm. Then the wind began to blow, rising in strength with frightening speed." Within minutes, the lake was boiling and, battered by high waves, they could hardly keep upright. "'Growlers' washed over shallow boulders ...

COURTESY OF ROGER TURENNE

The lake beckons a trio of paddlers at Jackhead Point near Grand Rapids.

In the gathering gloom, pink sheet lightning wavered in eerie formations behind the wall of cloud ... Thunder rumbled ominously ..."

By the time they made land, the lake was running wild with white foaming crests crashing along the shore. The storm left them weatherbound for two days on an inhospitable stretch of the lake's southeastern shore. Finally, they paddled north through The Narrows and past Matheson Island. At Lynx Bay, they again felt vulnerable as they had to journey beneath cliffs rising straight up from the water's edge. "We couldn't help thinking that a rising wind could easily capsize us and dash our canoe to pieces against the cliff face. Lake Winnipeg has already given us a pretty fair demonstration of its capabilities in that department."

However, the two did find "wild beauty in treacherous places". One evening, when the setting sun was bathing the cliffs in orange, they spied a column of white dolomite nearly 10 metres high supporting a solid table of rock covered by a mat of spruce trees. The column, the thickness of a mature white pine trunk, was all that was left of an ancient cliff that had been worn away by eons of storm surges. In time, they knew, the column and its tiny suspended forest, too, would succumb to the lake's elemental force. "What the powerful movement of water is capable of achieving never failed to leave us in awe." [19]

In an article in the June/July 1999 issue of *The Beaver*, Ian and Sally Wilson wrote of their awe at their first glimpse of the lake. "Viewed from canoe level, Lake Winnipeg is overwhelming in its scope. It is a huge expanse of water and the opposite shore is so distant it is merely a pencil-thin line between water and sky." Once, finding themselves more than a kilometre from land, they felt exposed and fearful, recalling the fatal gale that struck the party of Alexander Henry the Elder in 1775, killing four men and destroying a canoe. [20]

Roger Turenne, one of Manitoba's leading naturalists, formerly president of the Manitoba chapter of the Canadian Parks and Wilderness Society, is an inveterate wilderness canoeist. He has always been fascinated by Lake Winnipeg's Long Point, Limestone Point and Limestone Bay which, along with Black and Deer Islands, are being considered for a new national park, the Manitoba Lowlands. Turenne has

Long Point, seen here from the air, is a pristine wilderness of white sand and deep blue water.

COURTESY OF ROGER TURENNE

But for the spruce trees and the absolute dearth of crowds, this might be an island in the Caribbean. Little wonder it's being considered for inclusion in Manitoba's Lowlands National Park.

made numerous visits to prepare a slide show to promote the idea, although he admits to fears that the pristine beauty of the places might be "destroyed by the hordes".

On one visit to Long Point, he stayed for nine days, sleeping in a hammock stretched between two trees and imagining he was alone on a Caribbean island. He didn't meet another human being the entire time. "It's just six hours' drive from Winnipeg. You put your boat in the water and you have your own private paradise. It has beautiful beaches, beautiful white sand, beach ridges with marshland in behind and lots of beaver. The bird life is fantastic, eagles and pelicans, gulls and cormorants, mergansers and white-winged scoters, especially during the fall migration."

COURTESY OF ROGER TURENNE

Long Point is more than sun and sand. It begins at Gull Bay and extends 40 kilometres east into the lake. Not only is it quite wide almost to its point, its interior is impenetrable bush, home to many bears and almost impossible to traverse. While its north shore has, in Turenne's estimation, some of the most beautiful sand beaches anywhere, they, as well as the point's entire south shore are protected by an uninterrupted barrier of fearsome boulders.

Turenne says this was the reason that, of all the places of peril on the lake, the voyageurs feared Long Point most. As they paddled up the lake from the south to Grand Rapids and the Saskatchewan River, it loomed ever-larger on the horizon ahead of them, issuing an ominous, defiant challenge. If they encountered a storm, or even an onshore breeze with waves, Turenne continues,

... they risked disaster. The swells will raise your boat and smash it down on the rocks ... And it's not just the south wind that can get you windbound on Long Point; the north wind can get you windbound on the other side. In fact, you can be windbound anywhere on Lake Winnipeg because it's so shallow.

Lake Winnipeg is very dangerous and it's tricky. It's not the kind of place you'd go for family outings on the water. I have a very simple way to handle the rough lake. I don't go out on it when it's windy. It has so many changing moods and they change so incredibly quickly ... You go when the lake tells you to go and you stop when it tells you to stop. You have to have a relationship with that lake. [21]

On July 12, 2000, Sarah Henderson reported to Canadian Parks and Wilderness Society members on the CPAWS Boreal 2000 Canoe Expedition in an e-mail with the graphic title: "Confronting the Terrible Splendour of Lake Winnipeg".

Her expedition found that "terrible splendour" when it set out to circumnavigate Long Point and paddle the west shore of the lake's north basin despite being warned by "raised eyebrows, concern and knowing smiles" in Grand Rapids.

> Yesterday, we met the legacy of Lake Winnipeg in all its terrible splendour ... Relentless and raging winds, coupled with massive swells have challenged us for the past several days – and yesterday they culminated in conditions that produced strings of exclamations not fit to repeat. We struggled to manoeuvre our boat through the waves, pounded from several sides by alternating wind, wave and foam ... These stretches of remote wilderness are awe-inspiring; beauty framed in sunrise and sunset, we have paddled both ...

If circumnavigator Phil Manaigre thought his life was over in the storm on the lake's west side near Wicked Point, his partner, Jerry Zaste, was certain he faced death in the Black Island narrows.

> We had been windbound on the mainland one kilometre east of Black Island and I was checking our maps. I found a way that was only one kilometre to Hollow Water. The west wind was coming straight on shore, so I figured we could go straight into the waves and we'd be in the lee of the island. Phil didn't want to go, but I convinced him.
>
> Well, we got in there and there was nothing to do but fight for your life individually because if either one of us

 IAN WARD

Though cottages are nearby, this stretch of shoreline at Victoria Beach, with Elk Island in the distance, manages to convey the timeless wild side of Manitoba's great lake.

> went over, there wasn't a thing the other could do. It was a very strong wind and big waves. In fact, after we got ashore, we looked at where the waves were hitting the shore, and they were splashing 30 feet straight up onto the rocks. There we had been, coming down that chute, fighting to stay alive. I lost my hat, my glasses, the wind took them right off me, Phil lost his map. It was a cauldron. The wind would catch my blade when it was in the air. I couldn't move it. We fought like that until we made shore at the mouth of the Wanipigow River. I don't really fear death. I thought, if I go, I'd be going when I was happy. I'd be in Lake Winnipeg ...
>
> I've always loved the lake. I guess it's the uniqueness, the hazard, the sheer power of it. I walk the shores all the time, especially when there's a storm. The bigger the storm, the happier I am. [22]

Satellite image recorded by Moderate Resolution Spectroradiometers / NASA / courtesy of Greg McCullogh

The Lake in Peril

UNIVERSITY OF WINNIPEG aquatic ecologist Eva Pip is one of many prominent scientists who, fortunately for Manitobans, have life-long love for Lake Winnipeg. They are racing against time to save the world's tenth-largest freshwater lake from environmental disaster.

It's not overly dramatic to say that Lake Winnipeg, a major hub of the fur trade and the centre of an immense watershed that helped create Canada, is dying. Saving it is – or should be – a national, or even international responsibility.

The lake's plight arises from yet another aspect of its uniqueness, a uniqueness that makes it so fascinating to those who know and love it. Though it is entirely situated within Manitoba, one of Canada's smaller and less influential provinces, its giant, million-square-kilometre watershed drains four provinces – Manitoba, Ontario, Saskatchewan and Alberta, and four American states – North Dakota, South Dakota, Minnesota and Montana.

When the Great Lakes, particularly Lake Erie, were threatened by pollution in the 1960s, the tens of millions of Canadians and Americans clustered around their shores demanded and got action from governments. By contrast, Lake Winnipeg is out of sight and out of mind for all but Manitoba's one million citizens; in fact, some would say, out of sight and out of mind for most Manitobans, too, at least until quite recently. Relatively few people live around the lake, especially its vast and severely impacted north basin.

Simply put, this means that though Lake Winnipeg's problems originate nationally and internationally, solving them appears to rest solely with Manitoba.

Lake Winnipeg is one of the least-surveyed, least-studied and least-understood large lakes in the world, ranking second-last where research is concerned. Only Great Bear Lake in the Northwest Territories has received less attention among the world's 10 largest freshwater lakes. Lakes Michigan, Erie and Ontario have had 3,085, 2,590 and 1,712 environmental and pollution management studies respectively conducted on them; by comparison, Lake Winnipeg has had 73. When it comes to research on aquatic sciences and fisheries abstracts, the Great Lakes have had upwards of 2,000 studies apiece; Lake Winnipeg has had just 71. The year 2002 saw the first whole-lake survey since 1969 – a gap of 33 years, years when the lake's problems were multiplying exponentially.

This potentially disastrous neglect led one of Canada's most respected scientists to make a passionate plea to save Lake Winnipeg. Interviewed in *Maclean's* magazine in June 2004, Dr. David Schindler, Killam Memorial Professor of Ecology at the University of Alberta, uttered a stark warning. Calling Lake Winnipeg "Canada's Sixth Great Lake", Schindler declared that it is "in a very similar state to that of Lake Erie 30 years ago, when journalists were calling it dead." [2]

It was something Dr. Schindler had said before. Speaking before an audience of senior Canadian and American government officials and corporate decision-makers in Ottawa in December 2003, the former senior scientist at the federal Department of Fisheries and Oceans (DFO) Freshwater Institute in Winnipeg, had begged for intervention on behalf of the lake.

With the co-chairs of the International Joint Commission sharing the platform with him at a meeting

This satellite photo, opposite, taken in August 2003, clearly shows the enormous blue-green algae bloom in Lake Winnipeg's north basin. The image, which would normally appear in the blue tones of the atmosphere, has been altered to approach natural colour, and slightly enhanced.

The north basin is more vulnerable to large algae blooms than the south basin because its water is clearer, allowing sunlight to penetrate more deeply.

The Lake in Peril

We can't sit around and talk about it any longer. We should have acted 20 years ago. It's not like we didn't see this coming.[1]

— *Eva Pip*

of the Summit Institute Society on Managing Canada-U.S. Relations, Schindler, winner of the prestigious Gerhard Herzberg Medal for Science and Engineering, pleaded: "My message to the IJC is please give Lake Winnipeg some attention …We've got to get started." [3]

He listed a multiplicity of threats facing the lake, ranging from super fertilization and low water to climate change and the invasion of exotic species. "Yet no one seems to know or care," he said.

The problems are cumulative and rising, but by far the most important and deadly are the massive, ever-increasing nutrient loads from intensive livestock operations, industrial effluents, fertilized cropland run-off and human sewage from cities, towns and rural septic tanks and fields. Together, they foster an explosion of algae growth that affects the size, health and even survival of the lake's fish and plant species. Already, phosphorus and nitrogen levels in the Assiniboine River exceed provincial objectives for water quality. In the Red River and Lake Winnipeg, fish are harder to find, smaller and sicker, according to those who fish the lake. More than three-quarters of the fishers surveyed by the Winnipeg Game and Fish Association in 2003 for the Manitoba Clean Environment Commission reported a decrease in the number of walleye, sauger, yellow perch and goldeye, and an increase in channel catfish. They also reported fish with more bumps, open sores and backward scales. [4]

The Saskatchewan River, once the source of 60 per cent of Lake Winnipeg's water, has seen its spring and summer flows drop by 80 per cent since 1910, thanks to enormous draws in Alberta and Saskatchewan for agriculture, municipal use and oil extraction. In 2000, Alberta Environment gave the oil industry permission to take 170 billion litres of fresh water, enough to cover 6,475 square kilometers of prairie with an inch of water. A year later, the water used soared to 230 billion litres, sufficient to slake the thirst of Edmonton or Calgary for two years. Injected under great pressure deep beneath the Earth's surface to force the oil upward, the water is, in effect, permanently removed from the planet's water budget.

At the same time, climate change is looming as a major threat. Most of Western Canada's fresh water originates from snow and glaciers in the Rocky Mountains. But as the climate becomes hotter and drier, glaciers are receding at a rate not seen in living memory. Since the mid-twentieth century, Edmonton's temperature has increased by 2.5 degrees Celsius. By the middle of this century, it may rise as much again. The Columbia Ice Fields, the primary source for the Saskatchewan River, are already greatly diminished in size and may be gone entirely within the century. "We will have evaporations exceeding pretty well all the increases expected in precipitation from global climate models," Schindler says. "If you look at predictions for 25 years from now, evaporation is around 20 to 25 per cent higher than in the mid-twentieth century. So it outstrips any projected increase in precipitation. Translated, it's not only going to be much warmer. It will also be much drier." [5]

A 10,000-year core extracted from the bottom sediment of the lake's north basin puts this into alarming perspective. Between 3,000 and 4,000 years ago, during a similar hot, dry period, Lake Winnipeg nearly dried up and Lake Manitoba disappeared entirely.

In May 2004, six months after his address to the Summit Society, Schindler again provided a succinct summation of the lake's situation in testimony before the Senate Standing Committee on Fisheries and Oceans.

The Saskatchewan River, once the biggest river flowing into Lake Winnipeg, is now flowing, in the critical months of May, June, July and August, at only 20 per cent of its flow rates in the mid-twentieth century. It has gone from being by far the biggest river flowing into the lake and a tremendous source of dilution for the nutrients coming from agriculture and cities to the south to being second in size to the Winnipeg River. This is a direct result of drought and the hold-back of water by reservoirs in use for irrigation and other uses on the Prairies.

The second problem is the increase in nutrients coming from the south. That is where … the U.S. comes into play. In the fertile agricultural land of the Red River Valley, probably the biggest source of some nutrients are the cities of Winnipeg, Fargo and Grand Forks; the increasing use of fertilizers in agriculture; the increasing efficiency of drainage of the land to rid it of all water into the rivers quickly in the spring, and the explosion in livestock numbers in that basin. I am quite sure those are all culprits in what we see.

Award-winning science and environment writer Tina Portman says the amount of algae feeding on the phosphorus and nitrogen in the lake is 10 times higher than it was 40 years ago. In a major article published in the *Winnipeg Free Press* in mid-April 2004, Portman wrote that the "huge nutrient flow has caused Lake Winnipeg to suffer from cultural eutrophication – human-caused super-fertilization". [6] As another indication of the dramatic rise in eutrophication, Portman notes that a litre of lake water had 10,000 micrograms of algae in 1969, the first time the lake was surveyed.

In 2003, the same volume of water had as many as 80,000 micrograms of algae, of which 96 per cent were blue-greens. Blue-green algae blooms are not only unsightly, they are potentially dangerous, even fatal, to animals and humans. When they die, they form scum that can cling to shorelines and beaches. Some varieties release liver and/or nerve toxins that can kill animals and cause skin, stomach and lung problems in human swimmers.

In the relatively windless summer of 1999, Lake Winnipeg had an 8,000-square-kilometre algal bloom in its huge north basin. Lake Winnipeg Research Consortium scientists recall that their cruise from Grand Rapids to George Island aboard the retired Canadian Coast Guard ship, *Namao*, was like sailing across a sea of thick green paint. In 2003, a windier year, satellite photos of the lake revealed a 6,000-square-kilometre bloom of the potentially deadly blue-green algae in the north basin.

"When you look into the water, sometimes it looks like a layer of green paint at the surface for kilometres and kilometres," DFO research scientist Len Hendzel says. Windy weather mixes the algae down into the water column so that it resembles grass clippings. Excess phosphorus is to blame for the huge blue-green blooms. [7]

The majority (60 to 80 per cent) of the phosphorus and nitrogen polluting Lake Winnipeg comes from the Red River and the majority (52 per cent) of the Red River's phosphorus originates in the U.S. In his December appeal to the Canadian and American IJC co-chairs, Schindler said Lake Winnipeg "is as eutrophic as Lake Erie was in the early 1970s … We've moved Lake Erie back with our restrictions on nutrient input, but meanwhile Lake Winnipeg has taken off." Lake Winnipeg's 2003 algal bloom produced toxins of several thousand micrograms per litre. The world drinking

AFTER CLAIRE HERBERT / LAKE WINNIPEG
RESEARCH CONSORTIUM

*Dots indicate points where
the lake was tested.*

water standard is one microgram. "Why isn't anyone excited about this?" Schindler wanted to know.

He was also blunt about what he considers one of the chief culprits – concentrated livestock operations. Illustrating his point, he told his audience that Alberta has a population of three million humans and eight million hogs and cattle, each producing waste equivalent to 10 or 11 people.

> *So we have a human equivalent population of 87 million. We control the (phosphorus output) of the three million actual humans with municipal sewage systems. We take out the phosphorus and we treat it for pathogens. To the other 84 million virtual humans we say, 'Well, just go crap on the land or in a pit somewhere and then spray it around and that's OK'. That's why we have Walkertons.* [8]

Lake Winnipeg's chlorophyll concentrations (an indicator of the amount of algae present) in the summer of 2003 were double Lake Erie's at the peak of its eutrophication. Then, Lake Erie not only had the blue-green algal blooms that now clog Lake Winnipeg, it also had a 7,000 square kilometre "dead zone" of chronic low oxygen on its lake bed that seriously impacted Lake Erie's fishery. Coldwater whitefish, cisco and lake trout declined as did low-oxygen-sensitive insect larvae and bottom-dwelling mayfly. Not surprisingly, in 2003 scientists discovered a similar oxygen-depleted zone in Lake Winnipeg's north basin, which smothered somewhere between 7,000 and 10,000 square kilometres – an area equivalent to Lakes Manitoba and Winnipegosis

combined. Oxygen readings were less than two parts per million, sufficient to stress or choke organisms living on the lake bottom and insufficient for most fish. [9]

The effects of this dead zone are large and small. Biologist Eva Pip, for example, fears that the tiny freshwater snail she discovered, *Physa winnipegensis*, may become extinct before it is even officially recognized. It is found only in Lake Winnipeg.

Pip is highly critical of government inaction, saying governments are fully aware of all the science to date and know what needs to be done. "This seems to be the way we approach every issue. We sit around and talk and come up with reports that nobody implements. We know where the problems are, but nobody likes change. " [10]

Lake Winnipeg is a victim of Canada's endless federal-provincial turf wars – and Ottawa's crazy-quilt approach to water policy. In an interview in early 2004, almost 20 years after he chaired a national inquiry into federal water policy, University of British Columbia resource economist Dr. Peter Pearse said that the water policy capacity within the federal government had "disintegrated", victim of a combination of constitutional confusion, budget cuts, interdepartmental rivalry, policy failure, lack of political will and commitment and of course, above all, terror of treading on provincial toes. [11]

Ottawa's first formal initiative in water policy occurred in 1970 with the passage of the Canada Water Act, providing for federal-provincial consultations, cost-sharing and joint planning of water resources. Pearse's water policy inquiry was launched by the Liberals in 1984 and reported to the Conservatives a year later. It made 55 recommendations, resulting in the tabling of a 1987 Federal Water Policy. A major proposal was to update the Canada Water Act to resolve interprovincial conflicts and initiate federal-provincial protection of eco-systems. But two years later, Environment Canada bailed out, embarking instead on an ambitious omnibus approach to environmental protection that lumped water and other resources in with parks and wildlife.

In 1996, Pearse and Frank Quinn, a policy advisor for Environment Canada's water issues branch co-authored a paper on federal water policy. Published that year in the *Canadian Water Resources Journal*, it opens with the consti-tutional quagmire bedevilling Canada's supposed steward-ship of one-quarter of the world's fresh water. Ottawa has jurisdiction over trans-boundary waters; the provinces, over all natural resources, and both share fisheries:

> *The proper role of the federal government in managing Canada's freshwater resources is not easily defined. The constitution offers little guidance. It does not mention water. The government's own view of its responsibilities has changed over time and the attitudes of provincial governments to federal involvement with water resources vary.*

Environment Canada's 1989 omnibus strategy "collapsed under its own weight in 1990," the paper states. The fallout was severe. The Inland Waters Directorate, the body enforcing federal water policy, was disbanded, the Interdepartmental Committee on Water fell dormant, the Federal Water Policy was "quietly shelved" and DFO cut its internationally-respected Freshwater Science Progam by 55 per cent after it failed to have it transferred to Environment.

While the problems affecting Canada's lakes and rivers have multiplied, the government has drifted. Vital arrange-ments with the U.S. and the provinces over international and interprovincial water flows, levels and quality as well as the formulation of strategies for managing floods, droughts and climate change have all been in limbo.

Environment Canada has consistently singled out its water program for the most severe cutbacks. Pearse and Quinn warned nearly a decade ago that unless something changed, "it will be a challenge to maintain a viable compe-tence in water matters, as professional staff with experience, skills and corporate memory are lost in downsizing ... If the decline that began in 1990 continues, the Government of Canada will find itself without the capability to administer even a modest water policy."

The one threat to Lake Winnipeg that is receiving attention at the highest political level on both sides of the Canada-U.S. border is an eloquent example of the vital dif-ference allies can make for a small province like Manitoba in dealing with the menace of national and international pollution. North Dakota's Devils Lake, so named because it has no natural outflow and exhibits spectacular fluctuations in water levels, has swollen dramatically in recent years. The state has decided to ignore protests from its neighbours and forge ahead with an outlet to send the excess water into the Red River and eventually, into Lake Winnipeg. Although the lake is geographically part of the Red River drainage basin, it has been cut off for centuries. But of even greater concern is the state's plan to alleviate Devils Lake's anticipated other extreme – drought – by diverting into it waters from the Missouri River through the proposed Garrison Diversion. Scientists fear the Missouri water could introduce foreign, exotic and potentially dangerous species and toxins – not to mention more nutrients – into the Red River Basin and Lake Winnipeg. Minnesota has linked up with Manitoba to oppose North Dakota's plans for Devils Lake. In the spring of of 2004, the province's case was presented directly to U.S. President George W. Bush during a visit to Washington by Prime Minister Paul Martin.

As for the other environmental threats to the lake, signs are growing that the alarm bells being rung by scientists, lake communities, commercial fishers, the media and the lake's many lovers are at last spurring action – from Canada, Manitoba and the International Joint Commission.

The creation of the Lake Winnipeg Research Consortium in 1998 under the co-ordination of DFO's Freshwater Institute fisheries biologist Dr. Al Kristofferson offers real hope for the lake's future. And it is reaching back to the lake's storied past – its big ships – to carry out its lake-saving work. The *Namao* – Cree for sturgeon – is one of only three large boats still plying the lake's dangerous waters. Thirty-two metres long, with berths for a ship's crew of nine and six scientists, the former Coast Guard Class 900 buoy tender was slated for disposal until she was acquired by the research consortium. Not only does she carry the scientists on their summer voyages to take the lake's pulse, measure its overall health and prescribe treatment, she also tours the lake's ports with her scientific crew, a floating Lake Winnipeg advocate and teaching aid to encourage better stewardship of the lake by those living around its shores.

Gimli-born Kristofferson, whose grandfather was a Lake Winnipeg fisherman, says politicians can no longer afford to regard scientific research on the environment as a luxury. Despite initial setbacks and funding difficulties, he is optimistic about the consortium's future. "Governments are starting to recognize there is a need," he said in an interview in June 2004. "[The consortium] helps us find out how the lake is managing and what people can do. It is a model for addressing the lake's problems because it involves all stakeholders." A passionate lover of Lake Winnipeg who lives near Gimli and commutes each day to Winnipeg, he stopped, smiled and then continued. "You know, there are only three of the big boats left, the *Goldfield*, the *Poplar River* and the *Namao*, all so valuable in terms of preserving our memories about the lake. And here we have the *Namao* assuming a totally different role, but one that is every bit as vital to the future of the lake and the province as the tasks performed by the steamboats of the past." [12]

In 2003, the provincial government created a Department of Water Stewardship to identify and control the nutrient sources polluting Lake Winnipeg. Its first minister, Steve Ashton, announced a Lake Winnipeg Action Plan "to return Lake Winnipeg to where it was 30 years ago", involving the creation of a Lake Winnipeg and Basin Stewardship Board and new rules for farm and municipal sewage treatment. Winnipeg's sewage system will undergo a $500 million upgrade to remove phosphorous and nitrogen from its effluent.

Of particular concern to scientists studying the lake are some regional climate-change models that predict increased flows for both the Red and Winnipeg Rivers. The relatively clean Winnipeg River, currently the major source of water for the lake, could see its flow rise by between 15 and 20 per cent. But the Red, already the main source of nutrients, could experience a 50 per cent increase with the potential for much greater variability. One model forecasts the Red's flows could suddenly swell to levels 200 to 400 per cent above normal, producing more frequent, catastrophic floods and greatly increased nutrient loads from the Red River Basin into the lake.

Rescued from the scrapyard, the bright red Namao *has been refitted for crucial scientific work on Lake Winnipeg.*

MIKE STAINTON / LAKE WINNIPEG RESEARCH CONSORTIUM

The shift towards the Red River as the major source of Lake Winnipeg's water is already well underway, according to Mike Stainton, a chemist with the federal Department of Fisheries and Oceans at Winnipeg's Freshwater Institute. In the last decade, the amount of phosphorus delivered to the lake is double what it has been historically. "Since the Red delivers most of the phosphorus, its flow increase already has had and will continue to have a major impact." [13]

Scientists are divided on what the future holds for Canada's "Sixth Great Lake". DFO biologist Alex Salki says that though the province is now attempting remediation through the Lake Winnipeg Action Plan, "there still remains some uncertainty about appropriate corrective actions, uncertainties that can only be resolved through a concerted effort to bring provincial, federal and university expertise together to resolve the nutrient management questions facing the lake." [14]

Biologist Eva Pip told the Manitoba Clean Environment Commission in early 2003 that it may already be too late to save the lake. "We don't know whether we have already passed the point of no return." [15] Schindler too is pessimistic, but Kristofferson and Stainton are more optimistic.

Kristofferson has one message, above all, for those concerned with the health of our lakes and rivers – and especially Lake Winnipeg. "Although governments do have a responsibility and we are hoping they will act accordingly, all of us must realize that each of us as individuals has a responsibility for helping the lake recover. We must look at our activities and do something positive." [16] From laundry that isn't whiter than white and lawns that sprout the occasional dandelion to better stewardship of industrial and agricultural effluent, each individual choice about everyday items like household cleansers and farm and garden fertilizers plays a role in saving the lake.

Stainton says simply: "The one thing Lake Winnipeg has going for it is that it responds quickly to change." He explains that the average "residence time" of water in the lake is three to four years. "For example, the 1997 flood and all the nutrients those Red River waters brought saw huge growths of algae in the north basin two years later in 1999." [17]

Hedy Kling, retired DFO scientist and one of Canada's leading experts in algae identification, retains her optimism, with these major reservations: "Do I think it's reversible? It's not going to happen fast, but yes, I think it's reversible." [18]

In an interview, she notes, "The lake has a huge watershed. It means everyone in that watershed has to do his or her part. And there have to be legislated restrictions on phosphorous everywhere." [19]

Schindler doesn't believe that the lake's situation is entirely hopeless. He provides a to-do list: phosphorus removal of all effluents from large human settlements and phosphorus-producing industries; improved agricultural practices, including better treatment of livestock wastes, better timing and decreased amounts of nutrient application, restoration of original drainage patterns and less pesticide and herbicide use; and finally, restoration of key wetlands and riparian areas along the Red River and its tributaries. "These act as natural filters for nutrients, silt, pesticides and other pathogens.

"Eutrophication has been controlled at lots of European sites. The phosphorus and nitrogen loading from the Red and Assiniboine Rivers could be controlled. The science of what to do is known. All we need is to recruit some politicians and bureaucrats who are vertebrates." [20]

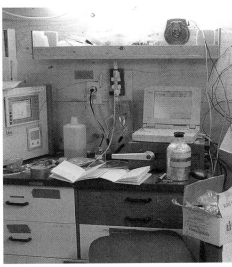

MIKE STAINTON / LAKE WINNIPEG RESEARCH CONSORTIUM

Aboard the Namao, *computers and testing equipment crowd one of the ship's labs.*

Notes

Chapter One

1. *The Canadian Encyclopaedia*, Second Edition. Edmonton: Hurtig Publishers, 1988. Vol. II, p. 1078.

2. *Fur Trade Canoe Routes of Canada/Then and Now*, by Eric W. Morse, Second edition, 1979, p. 109

3. *Encyclopaedia Britannica*, Fifteenth Edition, New York, London, Toronto, etc. 1983. Vol. 10, Macropaedia, pp. 707–708 and Vol. IV, Micropaedia, p. 695 and p. 702–03

4. Ibid., Vol. 8, Macropaedia, p. 301.

5. *Canadian Survey on the Water Balance of Lakes*, published by the Secretariat, Canadian National Committee, International Hydrological Decade, Environment Canada, 1975 and the *World In Figures*, by Victor Showers

6. Val Werier, *Winnipeg Free Press*, 25/08/90

7. *The Natural History of Manitoba: Legacy of the Ice Age*, James T. Teller, editor, p.14

8. Ibid., p. 15

9. Ibid., pp. 129–131

10. Ibid., p. 129

11. Manitoba Museum of Man and Nature exhibit

12. "Glacial Lake Agassiz", by Anthony P. Buchner, *Manitoba History*, Spring 1990, p. 27

13. James Teller interview, 27/01/00

14. Manitoba Model Forest Archaeological and Anishinabe Pimadaziwin Data Base Project 97–6–30, June 30, 1998, p. 10

15. Dr. Harvey Thorleifson, letter to Lorraine Sigvaldson, cc. Baldur Nelson, 21/08/98

16. Ibid.

17. Eric Nielsen interview, 24/11/99

18. Jens and Barbara Nielsen interview, 10/07/00

19. Roger Turenne interview, 10/01/00

20. *Narrative of The Canadian Red River Exploring Expedition of 1857 and of the Assiniboine and Saskatchewan Exploring Expedition of 1858*, by Henry Youle Hind, Vol. I, p. 474

21. Ibid., Vol. II, p. 18

22. Dr. Scott Norquay interview, 01/07/00

Chapter Two

1. Eric Robinson interview 1/4/00

2. Dennis Peristy, Land Use and Resource Analyst, Treaty and Aboriginal Rights Research Centre, interview 4/27/00

3. *The Ojibwa of Berens River, Manitoba, Ethnography into History*, by A. Irving Hallowell, Edited by Jennifer S.H. Brown, pp. 91–92

4. Ibid., p. 94

5. *Journal of American Folklore*, Vol.XIX, No.LXXII, 1906 pp. 337–340

6. *The Mishomis Book*, by Edward Benton-Benai, pp.2–3

7. *The Montana Cree*, by Verne Dusenberry, pp. 72–73

8. *Aboriginal Migrations: A History of Movements in Southern Manitoba*, by Leo Pettipas, p. 23

9. Pettipas, unpublished

10. Manitoba Geographical Names Program

11. *Alexander Henry, Travels and Adventures in Canada and the Indian Territories*, pp. 246–248

12. *Gold in Bissett*, by W.K. H.G. Clark and W.C. Hood,, Winnipeg, Energy Mines and Resources Canada, nd. p. 3 as quoted in Manitoba Model Forest Archaeolgoical and Anishinabae Pimadaziwin Data Base Project 97–6–30, p. 66

13. Pettipas, op. cit. pp. 134–138

14. *First Farmers in the Red River Valley*, by Historic Resources Branch, Manitoba Culture Heritage and Citizenship, p. 5

15. Benton-Benai, op.cit. pp. 94–102 as quoted in Pettipas, op. cit. p. 96

16. Manitoba Natural Resources Parks Branch Whiteshell Publication, by Katherine Pettipas

17. *American Anthropologist*, Vol 38, 1936, pp. 44–49

18. *Forty Years a Chief: George Barker*, by Judith Anne Rempel, Winnipeg, 1979, pp. 94–101

19. Jens and Barbara Nielsen interview 10/07/00

20. Manitoba Geographical Names Program

21. *By Canoe and Moccasin: Some Native Place Names of the Great Lakes*, by Basil H. Johnston. Lakefield, Ont.: Waapoose Publishing and Promotion, 1986, pp. 35–37

22. *Narrative of The Canadian Red River Exploring Expedition of 1857 and of the Assiniboine and Saskatchewan Exploring Expedition of 1858*, by Henry Youle Hind, Vol II, p. 133

23. Ibid., p.15

24. Hallowell, op. cit. p. 61

25. *The Orders of the Dreamed: George Nelson on Cree and Northern Ojibwa Religion and Myth, 1823*, by Jennifer S.H. Brown and Robert Brightman, pp. 108–110

26. *Great Leader of the Ojibway: Mis-quona-queb*, by James Redsky (Esquekesik), James R. Stevens, editor, pp. 110–111. Used by permission, McClelland & Stewart, Ltd., The Canadian Publishers.

27. E. Leigh Syms interview 1/27/00

28. Barker/Rempel, op. cit. p. 7

29. *Alexander Henry, Travels and Adventures* etc. op. cit., pp. 252–253

30. *The Sacred Forest: Oral History of the Hollow Water First Nation Elders*, by Gary Raven and Virginia P. Petch, p. 102 as quoted in Manitoba Model Forest, op. cit. p. 26

31. Animal Designs in Rock Paintings, by D. Elias and J. Steinbring. Winnipeg: *Zoolog*, Vol. 8, Issue 4, pp. 10–12

32. Me-wi-sha & Nou-qum Oo-ma-In-tish Ko-ni Gaming (Long Ago and Today on Our Reserve, Hollow Water, by George Barker, B. Contois, J. Bushie and A. Moneyas, nd. as quoted in Manitoba Model Forest, op. cit. p. 98

33. Raven and Petch, op. cit. p. 11, as quoted Manitoba Model Forest op. cit. p. 75

34. Barker et al., op. cit. as quoted in ibid., p. 100

35. Ibid., collected from John Cowley Sr. as quoted in ibid. p. 99

36. Barker/Rempel op. cit. p. 46 as quoted in ibid. p. 102

37. Ibid. p. 54 as quoted in ibid. pp. 105–106

38. *60 Years with Indians and Settlers on Lake Winnipeg*, by Brother Frederick Leach, O.M.I., pp. 38–39

39. Hind, op. cit. Vol. 1, p. 491

40. *Winnipeg Free Press* 1/8/66

41. *The Canadian Prairies, A History*, by Gerald Friesen, p. 23

42. PAM, 4571–4579 and PAM 4547–4552

43. *Lost Harvests*, by Sarah Carter, p. 210

Chapter Three

1. *Report of Progress Together with a Preliminary and General Report on the Assiniboine and Saskatchewan Exploring Expeditions*, London: George E. Eyre and William Spottiswoode, 1860, as quoted in *Grand Rapids, Manitoba*, by Martha McCarthy. Winnipeg: Manitoba Culture, Heritage and Recreation, Papers in Manitoba History. No. 1, 1988.

2. *Narrative of an Expedition to the Source of St. Peter's River, Lake Winnepeek, Lake of the Woods, etc. Performed in the Year 1823*, by William Keating. Vol. I. Minneapolis: Ross & Haines Inc., 1959 (First edition Boston, 1824) as quoted in *The Western Interior of Canada*, by John Warkentin, p. 141

3. Gerald Friesen interview, 07/02/00

4. *Danish Arctic Expeditions, 1605 to 1620*, Vol. II, C.C.A. Gosch, editor. London: Hakluyt Society, 1897, as quoted in Warkentin op. cit. 12

5. *The Voyages of Captain Luke Foxe of Hull, and Captain Thomas James of Bristol in Search of a North-West Passage in 1631–32*, Vol. II, Miller Christy, editor. London: Hakluyt Society, 1894, as quoted in ibid., p. 15

6. Manitoba Model Forest Archaeological and Anishinabae Pimadaziwin Data Base Project, p. 33

An endless deep blue edged with white caps, the north basin was sometimes called the "Sea Lake."

COURTESY OF ROGER TURENNE

7. *The Manuscript Journals of Alexander Henry and David Thompson*, edited by Elliott Coues, Vol I, p. 38. NOTE: "I should not omit to note the journal of Henry Kellsey of the H.B.Co., showing that he was on Lake Winnipeg in July and Aug., 1692: See Bell, 1.C."

8. *Twenty Years of York Factory 1694-1714, Jeremie's Account of Hudson Strait and Bay*, translated and edited by R. Douglas and J. N. Wallance. Ottawa: Thorburn and Abbott, 1926, as quoted in Warkentin, op. cit. 34

9. *Journals and Letters of Pierre Gaultier de Varennes de la Verendrye and His Sons, with Correspondence Between the Governors of Canada and the French Court, Touching the Search for the Western Sea*. Toronto: Champlain Society, 1927, as quoted in ibid., p. 44–45

10. *Journals and Letters*, p. 59–60

11. *La Verendrye, Fur Trader and Explorer*, by Nellis M. Crouse, p. 92

12. *An Account of the Countries Adjoining to Hudson's Bay, in the North-West Part of America*, by Arthur Dobbs. London: J. Robinson, 1744, as quoted in Warkentin, op. cit. p. 49

13. Henry's Memorandum to Joseph Banks on an Overland Route to the Pacific in *The Search for the Western Sea*, by L.J. Burpee. Toronto, 1908, as quoted in ibid., p. 62

14. *Voyages from Montreal, on the River St. Lawrence, through the Continent of North America to the Frozen and Pacific Oceans; in the Years 1789 amd 1793. With a Preliminary Account of the Rise, Progress and Present State of the Fur Trade of that Country*, by [Sir] Alexander Mackenzie. London: T. Cadell, as quoted in ibid., pp. 78–80

15. McCarthy, op. cit., pp. 8 and 136

16. *The Manuscript Journals of Alexander Henry and David Thompson*, edited by Elliott Coues. Vol I. *The Red River of the North*. Minneapolis: Ross & Haines Inc., 1897, reprinted 1965, p. 37–39

17. Ibid., Vol. II. *The Saskatchewan*. p. 450–461

18. *Narrative of a Journey to the Shores of the Polar Sea, In the Years 1819–20–21 and 22*, by [Sir] John Franklin. Appendix No. I, Geognostical Observations by John Richardson. London: 1823, as quoted in Warkentin, op. cit. p. 131–132

19. *The Papers of the Palliser Expedition 1857-1860*, edited by Irene Spry. Toronto, The Champlain Society, 1968, as quoted in ibid., p. 179

20. Hudson's Bay Company Archives B49/b/4 fo. 50d as quoted in McCarthy, op. cit. p. 59

21. "The Grand Rapids Tramway: A Centennial History", *The Beaver*, Autumn, 1977

22. Manitoba Geographical Names Program

Chapter Four

1. *The Gimli Saga*, Gimli Womens' Institute, p. 16

2. Ibid., p. 11

3. Ibid., p. 8

4. Ibid., p. 13

5. *As Their Natural Resources Fail: Native Peoples and the Economic History of Northern Manitoba, 1870 to 1930*, by Frank Tough, p. 81

6. Ibid., p. 86

7. *Chief Peguis and His Descendants*, by Chief Albert Edward Thompson, pp. 40–52

8. "Kristine Benson Kristofferson", *Icelandic Canadian Magazine*, 1984, Vol. 42, No. 3, reprinted in *Winnipeg Real Estate News*, July 24, 1998

9. David Arnason interview, 07/12/99

10. *Hecla*, by Dan McMillan. A FRED Project for Manitoba's Interlake. Winnipeg: Printed under authority of Hon. Renè Toupin, Minister of Recreation, Tourism and Cultural Affairs, Government of Manitoba, undated

11. Manitoba Geographical Names Program

12. Rick Hurst, Parks Branch Manitoba Conservation, interview 20/06/00

13. *Thor*, by W.D. Valgardson, c.1994, pictures by Ange Zange, unnumbered. First published in Canada by Groundwood Books / Douglas & McIntyre Ltd. Reprinted by permission of the publisher.

14. *The Icelanders*, by David Arnason and Michael Olito, p. 36. Reprinted by permission of the authors.

Chapter Five

1. *Winnipeg Free Press*, 16/07/66

2. "York Boat Brigade", by W. Cornwallis King as told to Mary Weekes. *The Beaver*, December, 1940, p. 26

3. "The Grand Rapids Tramway: a Centennial History", *The Beaver*, Autumn, 1977, p. 48

4. Letter to the Editor, *Winnipeg Free Press*, 01/02/00

5. *Winnipeg Free Press*, 13/04/74

6. *Winnipeg Tribune*, 23/07/66

7. Clifford Stevens interview, 18/02/00

8. *Steamboat Days Revisited*, by Clifford Stevens, p. 5

9. Roderick Campbell as quoted in *A History of Manitoba*, by W. L. Morton, p. 110

10. Select Standing Committee on Public Accounts, Minutes of Evidence, 1891, 1891, p. 26, Provincial Archives of Manitoba (PAM), MG12 E1, 5504

11. Ibid., p. 27, PAM MG12E1, 5505

12. PAM MG12E1, 5366A

13. PAM MG12E1, 5425

14. PAM MG12, 4820

15. Ibid.

16. PAM MG12E1, 5391 A

17. Ibid., 5392A

18. PAM MG12E1, 4829

19. PAM MG12E1, 4830

20. Ibid.

21. Charting Lake Winnipeg, 1901-04, International Cartographic Association Conference, Ottawa, 1999 Poster Session, Bob Lincoln, p. 3

22. PAM MG12E1, 4890

23. Lincoln, op. cit.

24. Anna Tillenius, *Winnipeg Free Press*, undated

25. Ed Nelson, *Winnipeg Free Press*, 23/11/63

26. Louise Smid, *Winnipeg Free Press*, 27/ 04/74

27. Ibid and Nelson, *Winnipeg Free Press*, 08/07/61

28. Nelson, *Winnipeg Free Press*, 08/11/58

29. Stevens, op. cit., pp. 6–7; Nelson, *Winnipeg Free Press*, 10/12/60

30. Stevens, ibid., pp. 17–19; Nelson, *Winnipeg Free Press*, undated

31. Nelson, *Winnipeg Free Press*, 13/0 8/60

32. *Winnipeg Tribune*, 29/07/65

33. Nelson, *Winnipeg Free Press*, 25/02/61

34. Stevens, op. cit., p. 25

35. *Forty Years a Chief: George Barker*, by Judith Anne Rempel, 1979, p. 29–30

36. Stevens, op. cit., pp. 8–9

37. Ibid., pp. 10–12 & 41

38. Nelson, *Winnipeg Free Press*, 11/0 8/62; Smid, *Winnipeg Free Press*, 04/0 5/74

39. Untitled, by Ted Kristjanson, p. 63

40. Stevens, op. cit., pp. 1–3; Kristjanson, ibid., pp. 18–19

41. Stevens, ibid., pp. 37–38

Chapter Six

1. Peter St. John, reminiscences, Summer 2000

2. Selkirk Enterprise, 24/09/75

3. PAM, Dance Hall Film Project, Vienna Badiuk, Winnipeg, Culture Heritage and Citizenship, Heritage Grants Program

4. *Wrinkled Arrows*, by Harold Dundas, pp. 95–96

5. *Winnipeg Free Press*, undated

6. *The Road Past Altamont*, by Gabrielle Roy, translated by Joyce Marshall, used by permission, McClelland & Stewart, Ltd. The Canadian Publishers, p. 58–69; 82–83

7. *The Corner Store*, by Bess Kaplan, pp. 196–207

8. *Wrinkled Arrows*, op. cit. pp. 93-94

9. Manitoba Geographical Names Program

10. *Town Talk* , 25/06/1898

11. *Ethnicity, Religion, and Class as Elements in the Evolution of Lake Winnipeg Resorts,* by John C. Lehr, H. John Selwood and Eileen Badiuk, Canadian Geographer. Toronto: University of Toronto Press, 1991, p. 51

12. Ibid, p. 51

13. Jean Loraine, as quoted in ibid., p.54

14. A Mini-History of Victoria Beach, by Allen Willoughby, editor, *The Victoria Beach Herald*, Summer 1998

15. Jim Brennan interview, 18/08/00

16. An Investment in Health: Children's Summer Camps in the Winnipeg Region, by John C. Lehr, Myron Schultz and H. John Selwood, Recreation Research Review, Vol. 10, No. 3, October 1983, p. 52

17. *Manitoba Free Press*, 10/05/29

18. *Winnipeg Tribune*, 08/07/43

19. *Winnipeg Tribune*, 20/08/55

20. *Winnipeg Tribune*, 19/09/55

21. *Winnipeg Tribune*, 22/08/55

Chapter Seven

1. The *National Geographic*, April 2000, p. 14

2. Phil Manaigre interview, 06/04/00

3. *Canoe Routes of the Voyageurs*, by Eric W. Morse, p. 29

4. Jens and Barbara Nielsen interview, 10/07/00

5. *Fur Trade Canoe Routes of Canada/Then and Now*, by Eric W. Morse, p. 90. Reproduced with the permission of the Minister of Public Works and Government Services Canada 2000.

6. *Canoe Routes* etc., op. cit. p. 29

7. PAM Leach Papers, quoted in *As Their Natural Resources Fail*, by Frank Tough, p. 50

8. NAC, RG 10, quoted in Tough, p. 51

9. United Church of Canada Archives, quoted in Tough, p. 52

10. *Narrative of the Canadian Red River Exploring Expedition*, etc., by Henry Youle Hind, Vol. 1, p. 471.

11. "Journey for Frances", with an introduction by Grace Lee Nute, *The Beaver*, June 1954

12. "York Factory to St. Boniface on Foot, 1836–37", by Pierre-Louis Morin d'Equilly, translated by Hubert G. Mayes, *The Beaver*, Winter 1979

13. "Crossing Lake Winnipeg by Dogs", *Manitoba History*, Autumn 1993

14. PAM MG1 B25

15. *Winnipeg Free Press*, 27/07/78 and 16/09/90

16. Margo Thomas interview, 21/12/00

17. *Canada's Forgotten Highway*, by Ralph Hunter Brine, pp. 152–153

18. "In the Spirit of the Voyageurs", by Ian and Sally Wilson, *The Beaver*, June/July 1999

19. *Where Rivers Run*, by Gary and Joanie McGuffin, p. 116

20. *Winnipeg Free Press*, 23/07/88

21. Roger Turenne interview, 10/01/00

22. Jerry Zaste interview, 18/01/00

Chapter Eight

1. Mia Rabson, *Winnipeg Free Press*, 4/21/04

2. David Schindler, *Maclean's*, 6/14/04

3. Author, *Winnipeg Free Press*, 1/29/04

4. Helen Fallding, *Winnipeg Free Press*, 4/21/03

5. Author, *Winnipeg Free Press*, 1/29/04

6. Tina Portman, *Winnipeg Free Press*, 4/18/04

7. Tina Portman, *Winnipeg Free Press*, 4/18/04

8. Author, *Winnipeg Free Press*, 1/29/04

9. Tina Portman, *Winnipeg Free Press*, 4/18/04

10. Mia Rabson, *Winnipeg Free Press*, 4/21/04

11. Author, Winnipeg Free Press, 3/19/04

12. Personal interview with author, 6/1/04

13. Personal interview with author, 6/1/04

14. Personal communication with author, 1/28/04

15. Helen Fallding, *Winnipeg Free Press*, 1/21/03

16. Personal interview with author, 6/1/04

17. Personal interview with author, 6/1/04

18. Tina Portman, *Winnipeg Free Press*, 4/18/04

19. Personal interview with author, 6/8/04

20. Personal communication with author, 5/20/04

Childhood and nature – two timeless subjects are featured in Walter J. Phillips' The Beach *(1926).*

WALTER J. PHILLIPS / COLLECTION OF THE PAVILION GALLERY /
GIFT OF JOHN P. CRABB

Index

With fluid lines, Sturgeon Clan *captures the interconnectedness of life on Lake Winnipeg.*

JACKSON BEARDY / BY PERMISSION OF PAULA BEARDY / COURTESY OF THE GOVERNMENT OF MANITOBA ART COLLECTION

Further Reading

Aboriginal Migrations: A History of Movements in Southern Manitoba, by Leo Pettipas. Winnipeg: Manitoba Museum of Man and Nature, 1996

Assiniboine Legends, Collected by Wil Nighttraveller and Gerald Desnomie, Saskatoon: Saskatchewan Indian Cultural College, Federation of Saskatchewan Indians, Curriculum Studies and Research Dept., 1973

As Their Natural Resources Fail: Native Peoples and the Economic History of Northern Manitoba, 1870 to 1930, by Frank Tough. Vancouver: UBC Press, 1996

Canada's Forgotten Highway: A Wilderness Canoe Route from Sea to Sea, by Ralph Hunter Brine. Galiano Island, B.C.: Whaler Bay Press, 1995

Canoe Routes of the Voyageurs: The Geography and Logistics of the Canadian Fur Trade, by Eric W. Morse. Ottawa: Queen's Printer, 1962

Chief Peguis and His Descendants, by Chief Albert Edward Thompson. Winnipeg: Peguis Publishers Ltd., 1973

Forty Years a Chief: George Barker, by Judith Anne Rempel. Winnipeg: Pequis Publishers, 1979

Fur Trade Canoe Routes of Canada / Then and Now, by Eric W. Morse. University of Toronto Press for Minister of Supply and Services Canada, Ottawa, Second edition, 1979

Grand Rapids, Manitoba, by Martha McCarthy. Winnipeg: Manitoba Culture, Heritage and Recreation, Papers in Manitoba History, No. 1, 1988

Great Leader of the Ojibway: Mis-Quona-queb, by James Redsky (Esquekesik), James R. Stevens, Editor. Toronto: McClelland & Stewart, 1972

Indians in the Fur Trade, by Arthur J. Ray. Toronto: University of Toronto Press, 1974

La Verendrye, Fur Trader and Explorer, by Nellis M. Crouse. Toronto: The Ryerson Press, 1956

La Verendrye, His Life and Times, by Martin Kavanagh. Brandon: M. Kavanagh, 1967

Lost Harvests, by Sarah Carter. Montreal and Kingston: McGill-Queen's University Press, 1990

Manitoba, A History, by W.L. Morton. Toronto: University of Toronto Press, 1957

Narrative of The Canadian Red River Exploring Expedition of 1857 and of the Assinniboine and Saskatchewan Exploring Expedition of 1858, by Henry Youle Hind. New York: Greenwood Press, 1969

Recollections of an Assiniboine Chief, by Dan Kennedy (Ochankugahe), Edited and introduction by James R. Stevens. Toronto: McClelland & Stewart Ltd., 1972

Tales of Early Manitoba from the Winnipeg Free Press, by Edith Paterson. Winnipeg, Winnipeg Free Press Centennial Collection, 1970

The Buffalo People, by Liz Bryan. Edmonton: University of Alberta Press, 1991

The Canadian Prairies, A History, by Gerald Friesen. Toronto, University of Toronto Press, 1987

The Geography of Manitoba, edited by John Welsted, John Everitt and Christoph Stadel. Winnipeg: The University of Manitoba Press, 1996

The Gimli Saga, by the Gimli Womens' Institute. Gimli: Gimli Womens' Institute, 1975

The Icelanders, by David Arnason and Michael Olito. Winnipeg, Turnstone Press, 1981

The Illustrated History of Canada, edited by Craig Brown. Toronto: Lester & Orpen Dennys. Ltd., 1987

The Mishomis Book: The Voice of The Ojibway, by Edward Benton-Banai. Hayward, Wisconsin: Indian Country Communications Inc., 1988

The Natural Heritage of Manitoba, James T. Teller, editor. Winnipeg: Manitoba Museum of Man and Nature and Manitoba Nature Magazine, 1984

The New Icelanders, by David Arnason. Winnipeg, Turnstone Press, 1994

The Northern Ojibwa & the Fur Trade, A History and Ecological Study, by Charles A. Bishop. Toronto: Holt, Rhinehart & Winston of Canada, 1974

The Ojibwa of Berens River, Manitoba, Ethnography into History, by A. Irving Hallowell, Edited by Jennifer S.H. Brown. Toronto: Harcourt, Brace College Publishers, 1992

The Orders of the Dreamed: George Nelson on Cree and Northern Ojibwa Religion and Myth, 1823, by Jennifer S.H. Brown and Robert Brightman. Winnipeg: University of Manitoba Press, 1988

The Plains Cree, by David G. Mandelbaum. Regina: Canadian Plains Research Centre, 1979

The Road Past Altamount, by Gabrielle Roy. Translated by Joyce Marshall. Toronto: McClelland & Stewart Ltd. New Canadian Library, 1989

The Western Interior of Canada: A Record of Geographic Discovery, edited and with an introduction by John Warkentin. Toronto: McCelland & Stewart Ltd., 1964

Thor, by W.D. Valgardson. Toronto: A Groundwood Book, Douglas & McIntyre, 1994

Where Rivers Run, A 6,000-Mile Exploration of Canada by Canoe, by Gary and Joanie McGuffin. Toronto: Stoddard Publishing, 1988

Wrinkled Arrows, by Howard Dundas. Winnipeg: Queenston House, 1980